# Using Data to Improve Student Achievement

A Handbook for Collecting, Organizing, Analyzing, and Using Data

DEBORAH*W*AHLSTROM

## Successline SMART Strategies Series

Successline Inc. • Virginia Beach, VA

# SUCCESSLINE INC.

Virginia Beach, Virginia
Telephone: 757-422-2802 • FAX: 757-422-5421
www.successlineinc.com

Deborah Wahlstrom, Ph.D., President
Mark G. Wahlstrom, Vice President

Cover and logo design: Elizabeth Dickason • Mousterpiece Designs • Chesapeake, VA
(mousedzine@aol.com)

Printed in the United States of America.
Successline Stock Number: SS-99-01  Price: $34.95
ISBN    0-9666662-6-7
For ordering information, please refer to the order form in the back of the book.

# Overview

## Using Data to Improve Student Achievement

The purpose of this book is to provide readers with a clear, easy-to-use way for using data to make decisions about student achievement. This is not a statistics book, but there are many excellent books available if this is a need of yours. (You'll find several of the references in the back of this book.) I've written this book so that the most novice user of school data can feel successful with its application and use. I've also kept in mind that not everyone is comfortable working with computers — you don't have to be a computer whiz to use this book. All you have to be is interested in the use of school and district data to improve student achievement.

You'll find the following strategies and tips can be used again and again.
- A model for collecting, organizing, analyzing, and using data.
- Three types of data — outcome, demographic, and process — and how you use the different types in your improvement efforts.
- A three-part model, *Pathway to Success*, that leads to high student achievement.
- A comprehensive list of data analysis questions to provide direction to your data collection and analysis. These questions are provided in a variety of important areas.
- A comprehensive list of factors to analyze for key areas. The questions provided here are the idea starters for thinking about why you're getting the results you're getting.
- Practical, relevant ways to analyze data including quick tips for designing a variety of charts and graphs.
- Customized, ready-to-use templates and data organizers to make setting up your data tables and analysis easy.
- Over 50 key definitions related to the use of data to improve student achievement.
- A comprehensive climate survey — ready for photocopying.
- A needs assessment for instructional strategies — ready to be photocopied.

# Contents

# About the Author

DEBORAH*W*AHLSTROM

Deborah Wahlstrom has served as an educational consultant to many schools and school divisions locally, nationally and internationally. She is an award-winning trainer and researcher — including two awards from the National School Boards Association. Her specialty areas include using data for improving student achievement, comprehensive classroom assessment, curriculum design, and instructional/learning strategies for student success.

Deborah has worked with thousands of school teams in their improvement efforts. She has developed customized curriculum databases and customized student achievement tracking software. She has also authored other books including *Practical Ideas for Teaching and Assessing the Virginia SOL* (1998, 1999) and *Assess for Success*: *Using Classroom Assessment Data to Improve Student Achievement*, (in press, Successline Publications). Deborah earned her doctorate in Urban Services from Old Dominion University in Norfolk, Virginia.

Deborah lives with her husband, Mark, and their dogs, Astro and Keesa, in Virginia Beach, Virginia. Together, they own Successline Inc. — a training, consulting, and publishing company which has provided services to schools and divisions since 1994. You may reach Deborah at the phone number and email address listed below.

## Successline Inc.
Telephone: (757) 422-2802
FAX: (757) 422-5421
Email: SuccessDeb@aol.com
www.successlineinc.com

# Special Thanks

## Using Data to Improve Student Achievement

I am indebted to the following people for their frank reviews of this book. I value and appreciate the breadth and depth of their knowledge and experiences in the school improvement processes.

- **Robert H. Bender**
  Owner, Northstar Development Services, Williamsburg, VA
  Bob is an avid writer, researcher, and thinker. As owner of Northstar Development Services, Bob uses his wealth of experiences as a researcher, school superintendent, and trainer to provide high quality services to schools, districts, businesses, and city governments in improvement processes. Bob is well-versed in the Malcolm Baldrige process and has served as a member of the Board of Examiners for the Malcolm Baldrige awards.

- **David Burgess**
  Principal, Henrico County Public Schools, Richmond, VA
  Dave is a school principal with one of the top school systems in America; adjunct professor, author of three published books and numerous journal articles on leadership and management; consultant and trainer; retired military officer, and a parent. He is a former teacher, guidance counselor, and state department of education program supervisor.

- **Elizabeth Dickason**
  Owner, Mouseterpiece Designs, Chesapeake, VA
  Elizabeth is currently a civil servant working for the United States Navy in Norfolk, VA. In addition to being a busy mom, Elizabeth spends her time designing book covers, editing, and designing products of creativity and imagination for others.

- **Diane Holland**
  Testing and Assessment, Portsmouth Public Schools, Portsmouth, VA
  Diane has worked in the Office of Research and Evaluation for many years. Her role has been to provide data support services to schools and the district. She has worked on key projects including the development of school and district data profiles and program evaluations.

- **Anne Meek**
  Vice President, Enterprise Assistance Inc., Norfolk, VA
  Anne is a gifted and thoughtful editor. Her business, Enterprise Assistance Inc., was established to help schools cultivate success. Her most recent book is *Communicating With the Public: A Guide for School Leaders*, published by ASCD. Anne designs and presents exciting workshops in areas such as creating effective communication programs and building support for schools.

- **Ron Nash**
  Organizational Development Specialist, Office of Organizational Development, Virginia Beach City Public Schools, Virginia Beach, VA
  Ron has worked for Virginia Beach City Public Schools for the past five years. He first served as the social studies coordinator for middle school and currently fills the role of organizational development specialist for the district. One of Ron's responsibilities is to help schools implement the tools and processes of Malcolm Baldrige.

- **Claude Parent**
  Director of Staff Development and Communications
  Portsmouth Public Schools, Portsmouth, VA

  Claude has been involved in education for thirty-two years. He has served the Portsmouth School System as director, principal, assistant principal, coordinator of federal programs and instructional technology. Mr. Parent co-published an article in AASA Quality Goes to School Journal entitled, *Portsmouth's Quality Initiative* and coordinated the United States Senate Productivity and Quality Award of Virginia process in which the division won the coveted medallion in 1994.

  Claude has been honored as Portsmouth's Teacher of the Year in 1970, Administrator of the Year in 1991, and in 1997, Elementary Principal of the Year by the PTA. He is listed in Who's Who in American Education and was selected in 1993 as a Virginia Urban Schools Fellow held at the College of William and Mary. Most recently, Mr. Parent received his appointment by the United States Department of Commerce and the National Institute of Standards and Technology to serve on the 1999 Board of Examiners of the Malcolm Baldrige National Quality Award.

- **Cathy Peyton**
  Elementary Science Coordinator, Virginia Beach City Public Schools, Virginia Beach, VA
  Cathy is an energetic thinker, trainer, and instructional coordinator. Cathy is a gifted facilitator and is often called on to facilitate meetings and work sessions for others. Recently, Cathy led an effort in redesigning the district's elementary science curriculum and included a piece called *TQ Science*. This part of the curriculum guide provides practical examples for integrating Total Quality tools in the classroom. Cathy has earned a quality award for this effort.

- **Fred Rovai, Ph.D.**
  Adjunct Assistant Professor, Old Dominion University, Norfolk, VA and On-Line Instructor for UCLA
  Fred has many experiences working with data. He enjoys working with data and spends much of his time helping graduate students prepare for the research portion of their candidacy exams. Fred has worked with Successline Inc. on a number of projects including the development of surveys and program evaluation.

- **Mark Wahlstrom**
  Vice-President, Successline Services, Virginia Beach, VA
  Mark owns Successline Services with his wife, Deborah. Mark's distinguished military career has provided him with a unique look at using data to make decisions in helping protect the security of our country. Mark's most recent tour was a NATO assignment with Second Fleet, in Norfolk, Virginia. His responsibilities included using data to measure the success of battlegroups in preparing for deployment. In addition to his work with the Navy, Mark works with Deborah in facilitating data workshops with school teams.

- **Bea Williams**
  Testing and Assessment, Portsmouth Public Schools, Portsmouth, VA
  Bea's responsibilities with the school district include the collection, analysis, and use of data. She coordinates the state testing program for the district and is responsible for many of the data-related reports required by the state. Bea has many years experience helping school teams develop, use, and monitor data-based school improvement plans.

# How To Use This Book

You'll find many ways to use this book. Sometimes you'll refer to it when you want a quick refresher of key ideas related to using data to improve student achievement. But sometimes you'll want to use the book to help you look more closely at your own school or district programs. The visual below shows an example of how you might use different parts of the book when you are studying an area for improvement.

## 1. Collect

Determine your data sources and types (Chapter 2). Go here first to get a quick glance at some of the data sources that are already available. Don't collect new data unless you have to. Think about the outcome, demographic, and process indicators you want to use.

## 4. Use

Begin to think about your school improvement plan (Chapter 10). Build everything you need to do in your school plan. Commit your decisions to paper. Use your plan to create and manage your improvement efforts.

## 2. Organize

Review the score reports and begin to visually organize your data (Chapters 3, 4, 5, 6). Where appropriate, make charts, graphs, and data tables. Disaggregate the demographic data and get everything ready to study more deeply.

## 3. Analyze

Ask questions about which factors have contributed to your success (Chapters 7, 8, 9). It's time to look at the process data — that data which leads to change.

# Chapter One
# Introduction to Data

Have you ever received a chain letter? Well there are chain letters for just about everything — even test scores! This is one that I received many years ago from an unknown source. Imagine opening an envelope and reading this:

> This chain letter is sent to bring you happiness. Unlike other chain letters, it does not cost money. This chain letter is meant for principals who are tired of their schools' test scores — in other words, principals who want a better set of scores.
>
> All you have to do is bundle up all of the test scores of your students and send them to the name at the bottom of the list below. (They just happen to be the names of principals who are also tired of their students' test scores.) You'll see that in just one week — you **will** receive 1,181 sets of student test scores . . . and one of them should be a dandy!
>
> P.S. One principal broke the chain and got her old test scores back.

## You Don't Need to Be Part of a Chain

You may sometimes wish you did have a place you could send your test scores — but, like the lottery, you'd have only a slim shot at getting a better set of scores. The good news is: when you use data effectively, you won't want to send your test scores off, you'll want to keep them. Analyzing, organizing, and using data can lead you to better test scores — better achievement results, and better learning.

## Why Use Data?

Using data is one way to help you make informed decisions that can lead to improved student achievement in a school. People who use data to make decisions will do so with more confidence that they are making the right decisions. While looking at performance or demographic data doesn't tell you *what* to do to improve an area, data will give you a wonderful picture of what needs to be improved. Studying data will help you focus on the right things.

As you read through this book, please remember that data will give you an idea of what's not working in your classroom, school, district, or program. But just as important — data will give you an idea of what *is* working! As you think about data and how to apply it in your own setting, please remember to use data to monitor and celebrate movement toward goals and objectives.

So, who needs to know how to use data? Classroom teachers. Administrators. Students. We all need to know the basics of data — and more importantly, how to use it to make improvements in our schools. Have you ever wondered how a teaching/learning strategy is working in the classroom? Data will tell you if it's working. Have you ever had to write or evaluate a grant? You'll need data for that! Have you ever had to design a school or district improvement plan? To evaluate your efforts, you'll be designing data-based improvement or strategic plans. Have you ever wondered what areas of the curriculum you need to focus on in order to see higher results in student achievement? Data will point you in the right direction!

## What Is Data?

Data is information that is organized for analysis and decision making. Achievement data is specifically related to student achievement, and achievement is the result of student effort on some sort of assessment. These assessments can be state, district, or classroom tests.

Data can be found in many different forms in a classroom, school, or district, and these are called data sources. Examples of classroom data sources include results from a unit test, portfolio, project, and overall course grades. Examples of sources for the school/district include standardized tests, attendance rates, enrollment projections, and more. There are literally hundreds of sources for data in a school and district, so if you're a bit overwhelmed by how to know which data piece to choose — you're normal! You'll learn which data pieces to use later in this book.

Learning to collect, organize, analyze, and use data can be one of the most rewarding professional skills you'll learn. You'll have a knowledge base that provides an important foundation in the entire teaching and learning process including curriculum, instruction, and assessment. If you're a classroom teacher, your skills will bring you and your students to new levels of performance. If you're a building-level administrator, you'll have skills that will help you make your school even better than it already is. If you're a central office administrator, your data skills will help you provide guidance, direction, support, and service to your colleagues in the schools.

Before you go any further, turn to the next page, *Data Skills Self-Assessment*. Then take a couple of minutes to complete the survey and tally your score.

# Data Skills Self-Assessment

There is much to learn about using data, but, chances are, you already have many of the data skills that will help you be a top-performing educator. Review this list of data skills, and circle the number (from 1-5) to show where you perceive yourself in using that skill. Give yourself a 1 if you're a novice in using the skill, a 3 if you have some comfort with the skill area, and a 5 if you have a level of the skill high enough to consider yourself an "expert."

|     |     | Novice | | | | Expert |
| --- | --- | --- | --- | --- | --- | --- |
| 1. | Interpret data from teacher-designed classroom assessments. | 1 | 2 | 3 | 4 | 5 |
| 2. | Interpret data from standardized norm-referenced tests. | 1 | 2 | 3 | 4 | 5 |
| 3. | Interpret data from standardized criterion-referenced tests. | 1 | 2 | 3 | 4 | 5 |
| 4. | Align school or district objectives with the content of state criterion-referenced tests. | 1 | 2 | 3 | 4 | 5 |
| 5. | Determine the adequacy and quality of a teacher-made test. | 1 | 2 | 3 | 4 | 5 |
| 6. | Analyze attendance patterns of students, teachers, and administrators. | 1 | 2 | 3 | 4 | 5 |
| 7. | Analyze enrollment patterns of students. | 1 | 2 | 3 | 4 | 5 |
| 8. | Interpret results of school and community surveys. | 1 | 2 | 3 | 4 | 5 |
| 9. | Analyze student performance on tests which accompany curriculum materials. | 1 | 2 | 3 | 4 | 5 |
| 10. | Determine student growth in content areas such as reading, writing, mathematics, science, and social studies. | 1 | 2 | 3 | 4 | 5 |
| 11. | Analyze patterns related to school data (e.g., percentage special education, percentage gifted & talented, attendance, enrollment). | 1 | 2 | 3 | 4 | 5 |
| 12. | Use computers to enter and retrieve student data. | 1 | 2 | 3 | 4 | 5 |
| 13. | Differentiate between different forms of student assessments (e.g., norm-referenced tests, criterion-referenced tests, portfolios, and a variety of classroom assessments). | 1 | 2 | 3 | 4 | 5 |
| 14. | Organize student achievement data for analysis. | 1 | 2 | 3 | 4 | 5 |

15. Prepare graphs and charts related to student outcome data.    1   2   3   4   5

16. Communicate student achievement data in writing (e.g., reports, newsletters, brochures).    1   2   3   4   5

17. Make inferences based upon student outcome data.    1   2   3   4   5

18. Formulate evaluation or focus questions.    1   2   3   4   5

19. Determine program merit based upon student outcome data.    1   2   3   4   5

20. Establish goals for student outcomes.    1   2   3   4   5

21. Use questionnaires to obtain student information.    1   2   3   4   5

22. Dissaggregate data by race, gender, and socioeconomic status.    1   2   3   4   5

23. Use dissaggregated data to monitor learning of all students.    1   2   3   4   5

24. Communicate student progress to others.    1   2   3   4   5

25. Review programs and practices shown to be effective in other school settings.    1   2   3   4   5

26. Communicate with data-processing personnel to retrieve data in a useful format.    1   2   3   4   5

27. Design data collection tools (e.g., questionnaires, focus group questions, alignment templates).    1   2   3   4   5

28. Design and use data organizers (e.g., disaggregation worksheets, data tables, graphic organizers)    1   2   3   4   5

29. Identify key performance indicators for the classroom, school, district, or program.    1   2   3   4   5

30. Determine whether an instructional strategy is effective.    1   2   3   4   5

**HOW TO COMPUTE YOUR MEAN SCORE**

Add numbers to get an overall total
Divide by 30

Name _____

Gender:   Male   Female

Level:   Elem   Middle   High

Mean Score _____ Date _____

So, how did you do? Compare your mean score on the *Data Skills Assessment* to the rating scale below to see where your personal data skills fall.

| | |
|---|---|
| 26-30 | Your data skills seem to be very strong. |
| 21-25 | Your data skills are good. |
| 15-20 | Your data skills are developing. |
| 0-14 | You're probably a real novice at using data. |

You now have an assessment of your own data skills. **As you use this book, please remember to think about how you can use data as one of your key leadership skills.** If you have areas on the *Data Skills Self-Assessment* where you indicated that you're not as strong — then pay special attention to those topics as you work through the book.


## Use Data Skills to LEAD With Data


You can use data as one of the many tools for leading others toward improvement. As a reminder of using data to lead, refer to the diagram on the next page, LEAD with Data. You can use data as a key tool for leading others toward school improvement — in other words, you can LEAD with data. **L**earn everything you can about your school or district. Ask questions. Collect, organize, and analyze data. Then look at all of the data and compare it to your **E**xpectations. Ask that difficult question, "Does the data reflect our expectations?" Are there gaps in what you have and what you want? If there is a gap, what are you going to do? What are your **A**lternatives? What else might you need to study to get clues about what to change? Continue to study and then **D**ecide, dream, and design what you're going to do. Commit this to paper — right in your school improvement plan. Use your school plan to focus your energies toward school improvement.

# LEAD With Data

**L** LEARN everything you can about your school or division. Ask questions. Collect, organize, and analyze data.

**E** EXPECTATIONS. Ask the hardest question of all: "Does your data reflect our expectations?" Are there gaps in what you have and what you want? If there are, what are you going to do?

**A** ALTERNATIVES. What else do you need to study to get clues about what to change? What resources might be available?

**D** DECIDE, DREAM, AND DESIGN what you're going to do. Commit this to paper — right in your school improvement plan. Use your school plan to focus your energies toward school improvement.

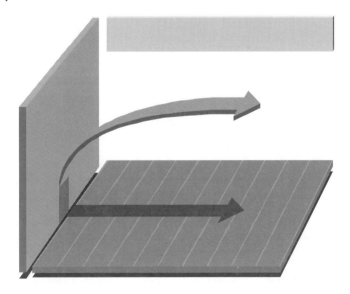

Okay, you're going to think about how you can use data as a tool to lead others — a faculty, a class of students, a school improvement team, a district staff. I want you to see a comprehensive list of specific examples of how an administrator might use data when leading.

The following two pages will give you examples of how you might apply your data skills. The page, *What An Administrator Can Do With Data*, highlights examples of skills for administrators. *What A Teacher Can Do With Data* highlights examples of skills for teachers.

# What An Administrator Can Do With Data

Learning to work with data will make you a more confident administrator. Whether you're leading a school team or just want to use data to make better decisions, you'll find that your repertoire of skills will increase as you learn to work with data. The *examples* of items listed below will give you an idea about how, as an administrator, you can use data in your leadership role.

**Decision-Making Skills**
- Make decisions about student placements (e.g., special education, gifted and talented, Title I).
- Use data to help figure out what is needed to improve student achievement.
- Make decisions about where to budget resources for the year.

**Classroom Assessment**
- Respond to inquiries by teachers about how to assess students.
- Suggest classroom assessments for the state standards.

**The External Testing Program**
- Explain scores from external tests (both norm-referenced and criterion-referenced) to faculty, school board, students, and parents.
- Determine the content and format alignment of practice tests to state tests.

**Communications/Media Relations**
- Conduct student and parent conferences which include test results.
- Talk with media regarding the results of standardized test scores, other state test scores, and student performance in general.
- Administer school/community surveys to assess the perceptions of student performance in individual schools or the school district.
- Design and prepare brochures explaining the state or district testing program.
- Prepare press packets for the media and general public when test scores are released.
- Create a school/district report card or scorecard.

**Use of Technology**
- Train staff to enter data into computers.
- Work with data-processing programmers to design reports, charts, and graphs.
- Make decisions about purchase of equipment and software needed to track data.
- Communicate needs about which technology is essential to support data collection and organization.

**Teacher Training**
- Design training programs for teachers related to using data to improve instruction.
- Evaluate effectiveness of teacher training programs.

**Curriculum**
- Determine if curriculum is aligned to state standards.
- Refine curriculum based upon alignment results.
- Establish priorities within the curriculum so that maximum student learning can be achieved.
- Establish minimum competency standards (or passing rates) for a school or school district.
- Use test results, grade reports, attendance records, and other methods to spot potential problems in curriculum and instruction.

**Collecting, Organizing, & Analyzing Data**
- Collect and organize student data.
- Prepare evaluation findings of student achievement.
- Develop criteria for using student achievement data to show improvement gains in individual schools.

**Policy**
- Develop policy statements regarding student achievement.
- Define standards of performance.

**Growth Plans**
- Develop school or district strategic plans based upon student outcome data.
- Develop a personalized professional growth plan.
- Design a professional development plan.

# What A Teacher Can Do With Data

Learning to work with data will make you a more confident teacher. When you use data appropriately, you'll have greater confidence in determining the achievement levels of your students. Whether you're serving as a member of a school team or just want to use data to help students do their best, you'll find that your repertoire of skills will increase as you learn to work with data. The *examples* of items listed below will give you an idea of the variety of ways you can apply data.

**Decision-Making Skills**
- Make decisions about student placements (e.g., special education, gifted and talented, Title I).
- Use data to help figure out what you need to do to improve student achievement.
- Make decisions about promotions and retentions.

**Classroom Assessment**
- Design and use classroom assessments appropriately.
- Use data from classroom assessments to inform instruction.
- Determine the content and context alignment of practice tests to other tests.
- Use data from comprehensive classroom assessments to help students achieve at higher levels.

**The External Testing Program**
- Use data from external tests as one indicator of student achievement.
- Explain scores from external tests (both norm-referenced and criterion-referenced) to students and parents.

**Communications with Parents**
- Conduct student and parent conferences which include test results.
- Administer school/community surveys and assess the perceptions of student performance in individual schools or the school district.

**Use of Technology**
- Enter data onto computers.
- Communicate needs about technology to support data.
- Use technology to organize and analyze data.

**Teacher Training**
- Participate in the design of training programs for teachers related to using data to improve instruction.

**Curriculum**
- Align the curriculum to state standards.
- Align classroom instruction to the curriculum and state standards.
- Refine curriculum based upon alignment results.
- Establish priorities within the curriculum so that maximum student learning can be achieved.
- Create a curriculum map.

**Instruction**
- Use data to make choices about research-based strategies to use in the classroom.
- Use data to determine acceleration and/or remediation strategies.

**Collecting, Organizing, & Analyzing Data**
- Collect and organize a variety of student data.
- Prepare analyses of student achievement data.
- Develop criteria for using student achievement data to show improvement gains in individual students.
- Identify achievement trends in my classroom.
- Diagnose my own teaching strengths and weaknesses.

**Growth Plans**
- Serve as a member of a team to develop school or district strategic plans based upon student outcome data.
- Develop a personalized professional growth plan.
- Design a professional development plan.

Okay, so you've thought a bit about using data as one of your key leadership skills, and you've seen some examples of using data in the educational setting. Now, let's begin the discussion about my general framework for using data — *Using Data to Improve Student Achievement: Collect, Organize, Analyze, and Use.*

## A Model For Using Data to Improve Student Achievement

Models help us organize our thoughts and actions. As I've used data over the years, I've found there are really four areas in which data tasks fall. These areas are **collecting**, **organizing**, **analyzing**, and **using data**. In just about anything you want to study with data, you'll have these four areas. The next page provides, in a graphic organizer, an overview and explanation of each part of the model. Use the model to guide you in the collection, organization, analysis, and use of your data.

# A Model For Using Data to Improve Student Achievement

## Collect • Organize • Analyze • Use

### Collect
- Determine what data is needed
- Select data sources
- Identify key performance indicators
- Develop data collection plan

### Organize
Topical Organization of Data
- By content area
- By correlate area
- By research questions
- By district goals

Physical Organization of Data
- Spreadsheets/Databases
- File folders
- Data boxes
- Notebooks

### Analyze
- Data tables
- Charts
- Graphs
- Triangulate
- Disaggregate
- Analysis questions
- Plenty of discussion
- Outcome data
- Demographic data
- Process data

### Use
- Make decisions about curriculum, instruction, and assessment
- Develop school improvement plans
- Set criteria for measurement
- Improve student achievement
- Communicate progress to others
- Determine needs

## Collect Data

The actual process for the physical collection of data is important. There's so much from which to choose. You'll want to determine what data is needed and then develop a data collection plan. This process will help you identify the required sources of data. In addition, you'll want to learn which data pieces to use as key performance indicators of achievement — those indicators that tell you whether or not achievement levels are where you'd like them. You'll gain ideas for knowing what data pieces to choose a bit later in the book.

## Organize Data

There are two parts to organizing data: topical organization and physical organization. You'll want to pay attention to both. One of the decisions you'll want to make is how, topically, you want to organize your data. Do you want to organize it by the key content areas of reading, writing, mathematics, science, and social studies? If you're using the Effective Schools model of school improvement, do you want to organize your data by correlate area? Examples of correlate areas are Monitoring, Achievement, Climate, High Expectations, and Parental Involvement (Lezotte, 1990). Perhaps you've got some research questions. Do you want to organize by these? Certainly, your district has some goals and objectives to which your plan should be aligned. Do you want to organize by district goals and objectives? There are many ways to topically organize your data, but choose what will work for you — it'll make your life a lot easier!

For most of the schools with whom I work, I recommend organizing data by content area. I recommend this since so many of our states have a standards-based test and this is where our performance is often judged. This certainly is not to say that you would organize your data only by content area — but it's a critical way to organize your data.

You'll also want to think about the physical organization of your data. How do you organize it now? Is it sitting in a box in the office somewhere just waiting for someone to sort through it? Is your data in a pile waiting to be filed?

If you enjoy working with computers, you may want to organize the data you're analyzing on a spreadsheet program, such as Microsoft Excel, a database program such as Microsoft Access, or a statistical analysis program such as SPSS. I use all of these software programs and have been pleased with the organization and output they provide. The key to success is organizing the data within these programs in a way which allows you to use the powerful tools they contain.

File folders always work — just make sure you label them correctly and have some sort of system for organizing the files. You may want to color code the files by content area to make the data from each area easier to find.

Data boxes are the portable plastic boxes that hold file folders. These boxes usually have some sort of handle on the lid, which makes them easy to carry. Data boxes are great if your job requires you to work on data with others. This is a nice way to organize it. You can store the boxes on a shelf, pull them off, and take them to your school improvement team meetings. When the meeting is over, the data goes back into the box and back on the shelf.

Some people like to use notebooks or three-ring binders to organize data. If you like to see the spine of a notebook on your shelves, this may very well be your style of data organization. Notebooks can be a good way to organize your data, but remember, testing companies usually don't send your school/district score reports already three-hole punched.

## Analyze Data

I've devoted much of this book to the analysis of data. In the analysis part of the model we'll put together data tables, charts, and graphs. You'll triangulate and disaggregate data. And you'll ask plenty of questions to help you understand the data. In this part of the model, I also recommend plenty of discussion — I want to encourage everyone to discuss data thoroughly before making decisions based on it.

## Use Data

There comes a time when you've got to do something with the information you've gleaned from the data. You'll make decisions about curriculum, instruction, and assessment. You use data to develop school improvement plans. You can use the data to set criteria for measurement. You'll use data to determine what you may want to do to improve student achievement. You'll communicate progress to others and of course, you'll use data to determine other needs of your school or division. Hey, you're using data!

## Summary

As you can tell, there is a lot to learn about collecting, organizing, analyzing, and using data. Taking time to learn skills related to the use of data will support you in whatever leadership role you have. You'll have the skills to LEAD with data toward higher student achievement. It's time to begin the journey, beginning with data sources and types, in the next chapter.

# 2 Chapter Two
# Data Sources/Types

It's time to collect some data — time to see what you already have on hand. One thing you'll want to become familiar with is all of the data that is readily available to you. There's so much out there! One of your challenges will be focusing on the important data for whatever it is you are trying to improve. But you've got to know what data is available to do this. There is much data collected at the school level, and there are also huge amounts of data collected at the district level — not all of it will pertain to your situation.

As I mentioned before, there are many sources and types of data. If you have the responsibility to collect and organize data, you'll want to know the sources and some of the types of data. To make it easy for you, I've designed an overall chart that lists examples of data sources and types. While I'm getting you started with the examples of data sources, remember to add your own items and customize this chart for your own classroom, school, or district.

The checklist, *Data Sources and Types for the Classroom, School, and District,* located on the next four pages should be useful to you in your school improvement efforts. On the left-hand side of the worksheet is an alphabetized listing of some of the data sources available to you — over a hundred examples of data sources, just to get you thinking. On the right side of the checklist you'll find areas where the data might be useful: reading, writing, mathematics, science, social studies, and your own school goals. Again, these are examples of areas and certainly not the only ones.

Please don't think that you should try to collect and organize every bit of this data — remember, one of the skills you'll want to have is determining which data sources to use. You'll want to pick and choose data sources based on your specific school and/or district needs.

# Examples of Data Sources and Types for the Classroom, School, and District

| | Directions: Use this worksheet to note the sources of data that are available to you. |
|---|---|

| | Areas Where Data Might Be Used | | | | |
|---|---|---|---|---|---|
| | English | Math | Science | Social Studies | School Goals |
| absentee rates, teachers' and students' | | | | | |
| accreditation ratings | | | | | |
| action research results | | | | | |
| acts of violence and substance abuse | | | | | |
| AP exam results | | | | | |
| attendance rates | | | | | |
| budget information | | | | | |
| California Achievement Test results | | | | | |
| census information | | | | | |
| checklist of instructional materials | | | | | |
| checklists for district/state standards | | | | | |
| class rankings | | | | | |
| classroom observation results | | | | | |
| college acceptance rates | | | | | |
| community partnerships | | | | | |
| community and staff surveys | | | | | |
| competition results | | | | | |
| computer literacy tests | | | | | |
| cooperative learning observations | | | | | |
| course enrollment information | | | | | |
| course failure rates | | | | | |
| curriculum audit findings | | | | | |
| curriculum guide analysis | | | | | |
| criterion-referenced test results | | | | | |
| degrees held by faculty | | | | | |
| detention rates | | | | | |
| diploma types (standard, advanced) | | | | | |
| district policies | | | | | |
| discipline records | | | | | |
| division report card (scorecard) | | | | | |
| dropout rates | | | | | |
| employment rates of graduates | | | | | |
| enrollment in Algebra (8th grade) | | | | | |

| Examples of Data Sources and Types (continued) | English | Math | Science | Social Studies | School Goals |
|---|---|---|---|---|---|
| enrollment in foreign languages | | | | | |
| enrollment in vocational courses | | | | | |
| enrollment rates in other courses | | | | | |
| essay contests | | | | | |
| expulsion rates | | | | | |
| extracurricular activities | | | | | |
| financial expenditures information | | | | | |
| focus group findings | | | | | |
| foreign languages proficiency tests | | | | | |
| gifted and talented information | | | | | |
| grades | | | | | |
| graduation rates | | | | | |
| grant evaluations | | | | | |
| International Baccalaureate diplomas | | | | | |
| Iowa Tests of Basic Skills results | | | | | |
| individual educational plans (IEPs) | | | | | |
| instructional practices surveys | | | | | |
| interview results | | | | | |
| inventory of supplies and equipment | | | | | |
| laboratory science grades | | | | | |
| lesson plans | | | | | |
| literacy test results | | | | | |
| Metropolitan Readiness Test results (K) | | | | | |
| minority enrollment in selected courses | | | | | |
| mobility rate/index | | | | | |
| National Merit Scholarship finalists and winners | | | | | |
| norm-referenced test results | | | | | |
| participation in community services projects | | | | | |
| participation rates (clubs, programs, sports, services) | | | | | |
| pass rates for core subjects | | | | | |
| performance assessment results | | | | | |
| physical fitness tests | | | | | |
| policies, school and district | | | | | |
| portfolios, professional development | | | | | |
| portfolios, student | | | | | |
| portfolios, school | | | | | |
| professional development plans | | | | | |

*Areas Where Data Might Be Used*

| Examples of Data Sources and Types (continued) | Areas Where Data Might Be Used | | | | |
|---|---|---|---|---|---|
| | English | Math | Science | Social Studies | School Goals |
| program evaluation findings | | | | | |
| projects | | | | | |
| promotion rates | | | | | |
| PSAT (Preliminary Scholastic Achievement Tests) results | | | | | |
| PTA, PTO, PTSA membership | | | | | |
| questionnaires | | | | | |
| quizzes | | | | | |
| reading information (e.g., running records, reading logs) | | | | | |
| reading levels | | | | | |
| referral rates | | | | | |
| report card grades (grade, teacher, gender, department) | | | | | |
| research papers | | | | | |
| retention rates | | | | | |
| Scholastic Achievement Test results | | | | | |
| satisfaction surveys | | | | | |
| scholarships | | | | | |
| school improvement data collected by school team | | | | | |
| school report card (scorecard) | | | | | |
| school-wide writing results | | | | | |
| September 30th count (or official membership count) | | | | | |
| special education information | | | | | |
| special honors (e.g., merit scholars) | | | | | |
| staff characteristics | | | | | |
| standardized achievement tests | | | | | |
| Stanford Achievement Test results | | | | | |
| state report card information | | | | | |
| state standards assessments | | | | | |
| student awards (e.g., honor roll, citizenship, poetry contests) | | | | | |
| student characteristics | | | | | |
| student interviews | | | | | |
| student performances on tests which accompany curriculum | | | | | |
| student work samples | | | | | |
| survey results | | | | | |
| suspension data | | | | | |
| teacher absences | | | | | |
| teacher certification | | | | | |
| teacher lesson plans | | | | | |

| Examples of Data Sources and Types (continued) | Areas Where Data Might Be Used | | | | |
|---|---|---|---|---|---|
| | English | Math | Science | Social Studies | School Goals |
| teachers with advanced degrees | | | | | |
| tests (classroom tests) | | | | | |
| verified credits for graduation | | | | | |
| vocational aptitude tests | | | | | |
| volunteers in school (reports) | | | | | |
| | | | | | |
| Use the spaces below to list additional data sources/types. | | | | | |
| | | | | | |
| | | | | | |
| | | | | | |
| | | | | | |
| | | | | | |
| | | | | | |
| | | | | | |
| | | | | | |
| | | | | | |
| | | | | | |
| | | | | | |
| | | | | | |
| | | | | | |
| | | | | | |
| | | | | | |
| | | | | | |
| | | | | | |
| | | | | | |
| | | | | | |
| | | | | | |
| | | | | | |
| | | | | | |
| | | | | | |
| | | | | | |
| | | | | | |

# Types of Data

Once you know what your data sources are, it's useful to know how to categorize the data by data type. Basically, there are three categories or types of data: Outcome/performance data, demographic data, and process data. All three are important, but we use them in different ways — and we get different types of information from each. Let's take a quick look at the three types of data.

## Outcome/Performance Data

This is the type of data that gives the outcome of all that's going on in a school or district. Outcome data tells us what the students learned, what they achieved. Outcome data paints the performance picture. These are the kinds of data that tell us what percentage of students passed the state writing test, and the percentage of students receiving E/F's in their classes, etc. These data pieces tell you how student achievement is going. This is the type of data that indicates whether or not there is quality in your classroom, school, or district.

## Demographic Data

This type of data describes the students who are included in the outcome data. This type of data gives us information such as minority student achievement, Limited English Proficiency (LEP) student achievement, attendance rates, mobility rates, and socioeconomic status of students. This is the type of data that tells you whether you have equity within the outcome measures.

## Process Data

Process data is power data. This is the type of data that gives you clues to why students achieved at the level they did. If student achievement in writing is low, you might look at data that tells you the types of writing that students do, or the percentage of time they spend writing, or the results of an alignment report of the school writing curriculum to that of the state's curriculum. You may even look at the percentage of your teachers who have had specialized training in teaching the processes of writing. You'll most likely choose to look at a variety of process data. This, by the way, is important data to review because this is the data that is at the heart of change in the classroom, school, or district. This is the data that impacts outcome/performance data.

Use the graphic organizer on the next page to review these three types of data.

# Three Types of Data

|  **1** |  **2** |  **3** |
|---|---|---|
| **Outcome** | **Demographic** | **Process** |
| **What they got** | **Who got it** | **How/why they got it** |
| Percentage of students passing the state writing test | Percentage of minority students passing the state writing test | Listing of types of writing students do in school |
| Percentage of students earning a D or E/F in English | Percentage of LEP students passing the state writing test | Percentage of time students spend writing |
| Percentage of students passing the school-wide writing prompt/test | Percentage of students who have been at school all year, passing writing test | Report of alignment results — writing objectives to state standards |
| **Key Performance Indicators** | **Disaggregation by race/ethnicity, gender and/or SES (Equity in Quality)** | **Change Agents (Let this data guide you toward change.)** |

You now realize that there are literally hundreds of sources of data. You also know that there are three types of data, and you still have some things to figure out. Once you have a data source, you'll want to know what to choose from that source to tell you how achievement is going in your classroom, school, or district. The data sources you choose to tell whether or not your program is effective are called key performance indicators – or KPIs. KPIs are the outcome indicators that tell you how you're doing. You'll bring your professional judgment into play here — and you'll choose indicators that you think will adequately reflect achievement for a given area.

Let's say you want to see how the writing program in your school is working. First, you'd take a look at the list of data sources and then determine what key performance indicators you'll need from those sources.

For example, let's say you're interested in determining how students are doing in the overall area of writing. Of course, you would look at your state's writing test, but there are a number of data sources to which you might go. For example, when I brainstorm the variety of KPIs I might use to get a handle on writing in a school, I might come up with this list of outcome, demographic, and process indicators.

## 1. Determine the Outcome/Performance Indicators

List several of the key performance indicators to find out whether there is indeed a need to focus time, energy, and resources in the area of improvement. One indicator of achievement doesn't necessarily mean you've got to stop everything and work on it. So I'll have to make a professional decision about which KPIs to pick and choose. First, I'll look at the writing objectives for my school/district; then I'll review the writing assessment my state has — and finally I'll select my KPIs using my professional judgment.

- Percentage of students passing the state writing test (source: state test results)
- Percentage of students failing the state writing test (source: state test results)
- Percentage of students earning a D or E/F in English/Language Arts (source: student report cards)

- Percentage of students passing the school-wide writing prompt (source: teacher grade sheets for writing prompt)

## 2. Determine Appropriate Demographic Indicators

I may be working in a school district where gaps in achievement between minority and white students are great and where attendance appears to be a problem. So I also choose indicators that give me a better handle on how different groups of students are performing.

- Percentage of students missing 11 or more days of school and percentages of these students passing or failing key tests (sources: school/district attendance report; state test results);
- Percentage of minority students passing the district writing test (source: state test results);
- Percentage of students who have been in school all year (compared with those who transferred in) passing the state tests (source: school/district enrollment report).

## 3. Determine Appropriate Process Indicators

In addition to the key performance indicators, I might also use a variety of process indicators — those data sources that help pinpoint why students are performing at the level which they are performing. Again, I'll use several of these data pieces to get as complete a picture as possible of what is contributing to performance results. And again, I'll use my professional judgment to pick and choose.

- Percentage of time students spend writing (source: teacher lesson plans);
- Percentage of students who indicate they enjoy writing (source: student writing survey);
- Percentage of teachers who have been trained in the writing process (source: faculty survey of training in writing process);
- Percentage of teachers trained in use of writing rubrics (source: faculty survey).

I recommend that you choose indicators where the data is already being collected — why do additional work if you don't need to? Also, choose some indicators that you can use during the school year. A number of indicators, like those from norm-referenced tests, are once-a-year indicators. I encourage you to use a variety of indicators so you get a handle on student achievement during the course of the year. You probably don't want to wait until the end of the year to find out that students are not performing at the level where they should be.

You may have noticed that I have asked you to list several outcome and process indicators. You may be wondering why I encourage you to use more than one indicator. Look at this piece of a picture below. (It represents one piece of data about your school or program.) What does the whole sheet of paper say? Can you tell? You might be able to tell part of the picture, but can you read the whole page with a high level of confidence?

Let me give you another part of the picture. (I've now given you two pieces of data.) What does the whole sheet of paper say? Can you now tell? You might be able to read more of the picture, but can you read the whole thing with a high level of confidence?

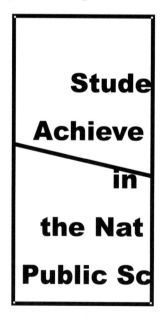

Now, let me give you a third piece of data. (Do you see a pattern starting to shape up?) Can you now read, with greater confidence, what the entire page says? Chances are, that with *three* pieces of data, you are able to read the page with great confidence. It's the same with schools. **The more indicators you choose to paint a picture of achievement, the more confidence you'll have — and the more accurate a picture you'll paint**. Data helps you paint an accurate picture of student achievement in your school. But you have to look at enough data to really get the big picture.

What happens when a single test score is reported by the media? Does it really reflect all of the great things that are going on in your classrooms, schools, and districts? Does one score show the whole picture of your school? Of course not. But reports don't necessarily triangulate data when providing the public testing results. They're presenting just one piece of the overall picture. And, as Herman says, "One piece of data just doesn't represent the complexity of our students, classrooms, schools, or districts" (Herman, 1992).

So when you're looking at achievement, you'll want to use multiple indicators — or multiple measures — at least three. Using three or more indicators (ideally from different sources) to paint a picture about whatever you are studying is called triangulation. Triangulation will help make the picture clear and will give you confidence in your decisions. While I encourage you to use at least three pieces of data, you don't have to stop there.

You may be wondering which three (or more) pieces of data you should use. I recommend that you start by using whatever data for which your school or district holds you accountable. If you have a state norm-referenced test, use the results from it. If you have to give a state criterion-referenced test, use the results from it. If there are meaningful pieces of data that your school collects, use them also. Then pick and choose other indicators that help paint that complete and accurate picture for your school.

The following pages provide you with a starter set of possible data indicators for reading, writing, mathematics, science, and social studies. Here are a few suggestions for using these lists:

1. Use these lists as idea sheets when your school improvement team determines what measurement pieces it may need for the team's goals.

2. Use the lists when writing a grant application for your school.

3. Use the lists as a reference when conducting action research in your school or district.

4. Use the list to determine the evidences of need and evidences of success for your school or district improvement plans.

Please note that I have probably not thought of everything, so you'll want to add your own indicators to these lists.

# Examples of Data Indicators for Analysis of Writing

Directions: Place a check mark next to those data types that will be useful to you in analyzing student achievement in writing.

| | Disaggregation | | | |
|---|---|---|---|---|
| | Race | Gender | SES | Other |
| **EXAMPLES OF OUTCOME/PERFORMANCE INDICATORS** | | | | |
| percentage of students passing the state writing test | | | | |
| percentage of students failing the state writing test | | | | |
| percentage of students earning a D or E/F in English/Lang. Arts | | | | |
| percentage of students scoring at minimum level on state test | | | | |
| percentage of students scoring at advanced level on state test | | | | |
| percentage of students passing school-wide writing prompt | | | | |
| percentage of students failing school-wide writing prompt | | | | |
| percentage of students scoring in each domain on state writing test | | | | |
| percentage of students receiving satisfactory grade on portfolios | | | | |
| percentage of students writing on grade level | | | | |
| **EXAMPLES OF DEMOGRAPHIC DATA** | | | | |
| percentage of students missing 11 or more days of school | | | | |
| percentage of minority students passing state writing test | | | | |
| percentage of Limited English Proficiency students passing writing test | | | | |
| **EXAMPLES OF PROCESS DATA** | | | | |
| percentage of time teachers have students write in class | | | | |
| listing of types of writing assignments given by teachers | | | | |
| percentage of teachers trained in using scoring rubrics | | | | |
| percentage of teachers trained in the processes of writing | | | | |
| percentage of students who indicate they enjoy writing | | | | |
| percentage of staff development offerings related to writing | | | | |
| report of alignment results — writing objectives to state standards | | | | |
| percentage of objectives pertaining to writing at each grade level | | | | |
| percentage of teachers who indicate they like to teach writing | | | | |
| number of resources available to support writing (e.g., materials, supplies) | | | | |
| percentage of time students use computers for writing | | | | |
| percentage of students mastering each writing objective/standard | | | | |
| percentage of time students spend writing | | | | |
| percentage of writing homework assigned/completed | | | | |
| percentage of students entering essay contests | | | | |
| | | | | |

# Examples of Data Indicators for Analysis of Reading

Directions: Place a check mark next to those data types that will be useful to you in analyzing student achievement in reading.

| | Disaggregation | | | |
|---|---|---|---|---|
| | Race | Gender | SES | Other |
| **EXAMPLES OF OUTCOME/PERFORMANCE INDICATORS** | | | | |
| percentage of students passing the state reading test | | | | |
| percentage of students failing the state reading test | | | | |
| percentage of students earning a D or E/F in reading | | | | |
| percentage of students scoring at minimum level on state test | | | | |
| percentage of students scoring at advanced level on state test | | | | |
| percentage of students receiving satisfactory grade on reading portfolios | | | | |
| percentage of students reading on grade level | | | | |
| percentage of students mastering each reading objective/standard | | | | |
| percentage of students with a percentile score of 50 or higher on state test | | | | |
| **EXAMPLES OF DEMOGRAPHIC DATA** | | | | |
| percentage of students missing 11 or more days of school | | | | |
| percentage of minority students passing state reading test | | | | |
| percentage of Limited English Proficiency students passing reading test | | | | |
| **EXAMPLES OF PROCESS DATA** | | | | |
| percentage of time teachers assign reading | | | | |
| listing of types of reading given by teachers | | | | |
| percentage of teachers trained in using scoring rubrics for reading | | | | |
| percentage of teachers trained in teaching reading | | | | |
| percentage of students who indicate they enjoy reading | | | | |
| percentage of staff development offerings related to reading | | | | |
| report of alignment results — reading objectives to state standards | | | | |
| percentage of reading objectives at each grade level | | | | |
| percentage of teachers who indicate they like to teach reading | | | | |
| number of resources available to support reading (e.g., library books, tutors) | | | | |
| percentage of time students use computers for reading | | | | |
| percentage of students mastering each reading objective/standard | | | | |
| percentage of time students spend on reading | | | | |
| percentage of reading homework assigned/completed | | | | |
| percentage of students entering reading contests | | | | |
| percentage of time students are read to | | | | |
| percentage of teachers trained in assessing reading skills of students | | | | |

# Examples of Data Indicators for Analysis of Science

Directions: Place a check mark next to those data types that will be useful to you in analyzing student achievement in science.

| | Disaggregation | | | |
|---|---|---|---|---|
| | Race | Gender | SES | Other |
| **EXAMPLES OF OUTCOME/PERFORMANCE INDICATORS** | | | | |
| percentage of students passing the state science test | | | | |
| percentage of students failing the state science test | | | | |
| percentage of students earning a D or E/F in science | | | | |
| percentage of students scoring at minimum level on state test | | | | |
| percentage of students scoring at advanced level on state test | | | | |
| percentage of students scoring in each domain on state science test | | | | |
| percentage of students mastering each science objective/standard | | | | |
| percentage of students scoring 3 or higher on science AP exams | | | | |
| percentage of students receiving satisfactory grade on science portfolios | | | | |
| percentage of students with percentile score of 50 or higher on science test | | | | |
| **EXAMPLES OF DEMOGRAPHIC DATA** | | | | |
| percentage of students missing 11 or more days of school | | | | |
| percentage of minority students passing state science test | | | | |
| percentage of males and females passing state science test | | | | |
| **EXAMPLES OF PROCESS DATA** | | | | |
| percentage of time teachers assign science | | | | |
| listing of types of science assignments given by teachers | | | | |
| percentage of teachers trained in scientific investigation | | | | |
| percentage of teachers trained in science content | | | | |
| percentage of students who indicate they enjoy science | | | | |
| percentage of staff development offerings related to science | | | | |
| report of alignment results — science objectives to state standards | | | | |
| percentage of science objectives at each grade level | | | | |
| percentage of teachers who indicate they like to teach science | | | | |
| number of resources available to support science (e.g., equipment) | | | | |
| percentage of time students use computers for science | | | | |
| percentage of time students spend on science | | | | |
| percentage of students reading on grade level | | | | |
| percentage of science homework assigned/completed | | | | |
| percentage of students entering science contests | | | | |
| percentage of teachers certified to teach higher-level science courses | | | | |

# Examples of Data Indicators for Analysis of Math

Directions: Place a check mark next to those data types that will be useful to you in analyzing student achievement in math.

| | Disaggregation | | | |
|---|---|---|---|---|
| | Race | Gender | SES | Other |
| **EXAMPLES OF OUTCOME/PERFORMANCE INDICATORS** | | | | |
| percentage of students passing the state math test | | | | |
| percentage of students failing the state math test | | | | |
| percentage of students earning a D or E/F in math | | | | |
| percentage of students scoring at minimum level on state test | | | | |
| percentage of students scoring at advanced level on state test | | | | |
| percentage of students scoring in each domain on state math test | | | | |
| percentage of students mastering each math objective/standard | | | | |
| percentage of students scoring 3 or higher on math AP exams | | | | |
| percentage of students receiving satisfactory grade on math portfolios | | | | |
| percentage of students with percentile score of 50 or higher on math NRT | | | | |
| **EXAMPLES OF DEMOGRAPHIC DATA** | | | | |
| percentage of students missing 11 or more days of school | | | | |
| percentage of minority students passing state math test | | | | |
| percentage of Limited English Proficiency students passing math test | | | | |
| **EXAMPLES OF PROCESS DATA** | | | | |
| percentage of time teachers assign math | | | | |
| listing of types of math assignments given by teachers | | | | |
| percentage of teachers trained in problem-solving strategies | | | | |
| percentage of teachers trained in math content | | | | |
| percentage of students who indicate they enjoy math | | | | |
| percentage of staff development offerings related to math | | | | |
| report of alignment results — math objectives to state standards | | | | |
| percentage of math objectives at each grade level | | | | |
| percentage of teachers who indicate they like to teach math | | | | |
| number of resources available to support math (e.g., manipulatives) | | | | |
| percentage of time students use technology, including computers, for math | | | | |
| percentage of time students spend on math | | | | |
| percentage of math homework assigned/completed | | | | |
| percentage of students entering math contests | | | | |
| percentage of teachers certified to teach higher-level math courses | | | | |
| | | | | |

# Examples of Data Indicators
# for Analysis of Social Studies

Directions: Place a check mark next to those data types that will be useful to you in analyzing student achievement in social studies.

| | Disaggregation | | | |
|---|---|---|---|---|
| | Race | Gender | SES | Other |
| **EXAMPLES OF OUTCOME/PERFORMANCE INDICATORS** | | | | |
| percentage of students passing the state social studies test | | | | |
| percentage of students failing the state social studies test | | | | |
| percentage of students earning a D or E/F in social studies | | | | |
| percentage of students scoring at minimum level on state test | | | | |
| percentage of students scoring at advanced level on state test | | | | |
| percentage of students scoring in each domain on state social studies test | | | | |
| percentage of students mastering each social studies objective/standard | | | | |
| percentage of students scoring 3 or higher on social studies AP exams | | | | |
| percentage of students with %ile score of 50 or higher on soc. studies test | | | | |
| **EXAMPLES OF DEMOGRAPHIC DATA** | | | | |
| percentage of students missing 11 or more days of school | | | | |
| percentage of minority students passing state social studies test | | | | |
| percentage of Limited English Proficiency students passing social studies test | | | | |
| **EXAMPLES OF PROCESS DATA** | | | | |
| percentage of time teachers assign social studies | | | | |
| listing of types of social studies assignments given by teachers | | | | |
| percentage of teachers trained in questioning strategies | | | | |
| percentage of teachers trained in social studies content | | | | |
| percentage of students who indicate they enjoy social studies | | | | |
| percentage of staff development offerings related to social studies | | | | |
| report of alignment results — social studies objectives to state standards | | | | |
| percentage of social studies objectives at each grade level | | | | |
| percentage of teachers who indicate they like to teach social studies | | | | |
| number of resources available to support social studies | | | | |
| percentage of time students use computers for social studies | | | | |
| percentage of social studies homework assigned/completed | | | | |
| percentage of students entering social studies contests | | | | |
| percentage of teachers certified to teach higher-level social studies courses | | | | |
| | | | | |
| | | | | |
| | | | | |

# Data Collection Tools

If you are the type of person who likes to think ahead about all of the data you've got to collect, you'll find data collection tools useful. On the next page, you'll find a completed example of how you might think about data collection for example outcome data for writing. Then, I've included three templates — one each for outcome/performance data, demographic data, and process data. (If you're using more than three outcome indicators, just use extra copies of the forms.)

When using this form, the Program Goal Area refers to your overall goal area. Many school teams I've worked with use the correlates of Effective Schools (Lezotte, 1990) as organizers for the goal area. Examples of goal areas include such things as achievement, high expectations, parental involvement, safety, leadership, climate, and community involvement.

The Program Objective refers to what, within the goal area, you're trying to specifically improve. Examples of program objectives for the goal area of achievement are listed below.

- Improve writing skills;
- Improve math problem-solving skills;
- Improve scientific investigation skills.

You may have several program objectives for key goal areas and each program objective may required different data sources and types.

## Program
## Goal Area: Achievement

## Program
## Objective(s): Improve Writing Skills
Specific statements describing what will be accomplished, by when, for whom, and how success will generally be measured.

## Outcome/Performance Indicators

Key Performance Indicators are used to determine the Evidences of Success (as well as Evidences of Need) in school, district, or program objectives. These indicators are noted in **BOLD** type in the Evidences of Success column.

| | Evidences of Success | Data Source | Who will collect the data? Is the data collected at the school level? District level? | When will the data be collected? You may want to include the dates that the reports will be available as well as monitoring dates. |
|---|---|---|---|---|
| 1 | Increase in the **percent of students scoring a 3.0 or higher on the composition domain of the state writing test** from 32% to 50% | Standards of Learning Tests — Writing Results | Office of Research gets the district reports. Our school gets a school report. School Committee will collect information from both places. | Writing tests are given in March. Results are expected in May. |
| 2 | Increase in the **percent of students scoring a 3.0 or higher on the sentence formation domain of the state writing test** from 38% to 55% | Standards of Learning Tests — Writing Results | Office of Research gets the district reports. Our school gets a school report. School Committee will collect information from both places. | Writing tests are given in March. Results are expected in May. |
| 3 | Increase in the **percent of students scoring a 400 or higher on the writing portion of the state writing test** from 48% to 65% | Standards of Learning Tests — Writing Results | Office of Research gets the district reports. Our school gets a school report. School Committee will collect information from both places. | Writing tests are given in March. Results are expected in May. |

# Program
# Goal Area

# Program
# Objective(s)

Specific statements describing what will be accomplished, by when, for whom, and how success will generally be measured.

# Outcome/Performance Indicators

Key Performance Indicators are used to determine the Evidences of Success (as well as Evidences of Need) in school, district, or program objectives.

| Evidences of Success | Data Source | Who will collect the data? Is the data collected at the school level? District level? | When will the data be collected? You may want to include the dates that the reports will be available as well as monitoring dates. |
|---|---|---|---|
| **1** | | | |
| **2** | | | |
| **3** | | | |

# Program Goal Area

# Program Objective(s)

Specific statements describing what will be accomplished, by when, for whom, and how success will generally be measured.

# Demographic Data

Key Performance Indicators (KPIs) are the data used to determine the Evidences of Success (as well as Evidences of Need) in school, district, or program objectives. Usually, outcome/performance data and demographic data serve as KPIs.

| Evidences of Success | Data Source | Who will collect the data? Is the data collected at the school level? District level? | When will the data be collected? You may want to include the dates that the reports will be available as well as monitoring dates. |
| --- | --- | --- | --- |
| 1 | | | |
| 2 | | | |
| 3 | | | |

## Program Goal Area

Achievement
Climate
Leadership
Safety

## Program Objective(s)

Specific statements describing what will be accomplished, by when, for whom, and how success will generally be measured.

# Process Data

Process Data Indicators are the data used to determine what might bring about change in the improvement area. These include indicators from curriculum, instruction, assessment, and more.

| | Process Indicators | Data Source | Who will collect the data? Is the data collected at the school level? District level? | When will the data be collected? You may want to include the dates that the reports will be available as well as monitoring dates. |
|---|---|---|---|---|
| 1 | | | | |
| 2 | | | | |
| 3 | | | | |

# 3 Chapter Three Interpreting Test Scores

## It's Really Not That Hard!

Learning to collect, organize, analyze, and use data means that you'll need to know how to do such complicated things as reading and interpreting test scores. And, yes, you'll want to know what some of the basic terms mean. It's really not that hard — in fact, much of this material will probably be a review of your basic tests and measurement course.

## It All Starts With Raw Scores

Just about everything we do with testing data is based on raw scores. The raw score is simply the number of questions that a student gets right on a test. There are raw scores for classroom tests, there are raw scores for norm-referenced tests, there are raw scores for criterion-referenced tests, and there are raw scores for standardized tests. Raw scores are the basis for all other scores.

## Transforming Raw Scores Into Other Scores

Once you have a raw score, you can transform or convert this score into other score systems. If you've ever made up a chart that says, "If a student misses one question, he or she gets a 95; if he or she misses two questions, it's a 90" — then you've transformed and converted a raw score into another score system: percent correct. But in the world of assessment, the percent correct score is not the only one we use. You'll want to know some of the other score systems that you are likely to see when reviewing results from various achievement tests.

You've seen some of those score systems — percentile scores, scale scores, and the like. Let's take a quick review of a few of the common score systems you're likely to run into when looking at scores from tests. Review the graphic organizer on the next page, and then read the more detailed description that follows. (Please remember that these are select score systems and not the only ones you may be using.) The key idea for the graphic organizer is that one raw score can be transformed to a variety of other score systems. So a raw score of 26 (out of 40 questions) could be converted into score systems such as percentile scores, percent correct scores, scaled scores, and grade equivalent scores.

# Raw Scores Can Be Converted to a Variety of Score Systems

A 5th-grade student takes a test with 40 questions. The student gets 26 questions right.

**Raw Score**
**26**

**Percentile Score**

If we want to know how the student did in relation to other students.

**72**

With a raw score of 26, this student scored as well as or better than 72% of the students, from the norming group, who took the test.

**Percent Correct**

If we want to know what percent of the questions the student got right.

**65%**

The student got 65% of the test items right. The formula is: 26 items correct/ 40 items possible x 100.

**Scaled Score**

If we want to know student achievement in relation to an established scale.

**400**

With a scale of 0-600, where scores from 400-600 are passing, this student would pass.

**Grade Equivalent Score**

If we want to know if a student is performing at an expected grade level.

**6.1**

This student performed as well as a student who, in the 6th grade/1st month, might have scored on the same test.

Are there other scoring systems? Of course! But these will be a great start as you analyze school/district data.

# Percentile Scores

If you've ever worked with a norm-referenced test like the *Iowa Tests of Basic Skills*, the *California Achievement Tests*, or the *Stanford Achievement Tests*, you've had a chance to work with percentile scores. A percentile score gives you the student's relative standing in the norm group in terms of the percentage of students who scored below him or her. For example, if a student achieves at the 60th percentile, that means that the student scored as well as or higher than 60 percent of those students in the norming group who took the test, and lower than 40 percent of the students who took the test.

In other words, one student's score is respective of other students who took the test. Percentile scores don't tell you how well a student did in relation to specific learning targets or standards, they only tell you what percentage of students were outperformed. Percentile scores range from 1-99, and these scores are not equal interval scores — which means the distance from 1-10 is not the same as the distance between 40 and 50. (Therefore, you don't average percentile scores.) A student's percentile rank or score can change from test to test depending on which norming group is used to determine the ranking.

National Percentile Rank (NPR) is a score that shows how a student performed in relation to a group of students who were tested under the same conditions at the same time of the year during national standardization. A Local Percentile Rank (LPR) is a score given to a student upon comparison with a local group — the students in the school district at the tested grade level, for example.

## Percentage or Percentile?

Let's make a quick distinction between percentiles and percentages — two score systems that are often confused. Remember, a percentile score tells how a student did in relation to other students in a norming group. A percentage score tells you what percent of the questions a student answered correctly on the test. (You can actually have both scores for the same test.) Every now and then I'll hear someone say, "Joey scored at the 68th percentile," when what the person was meaning to say was, "Joey got 68 percent correct on this test."

# Scaled Scores

A participant in one of my workshops defined scaled scores as "the scores fishermen use when they cite the weight of fish they just caught." That's not exactly right, even though his definition was a lot more fun. Testing companies will often use scaled scores in addition to percentile scores when representing student achievement on a test. So you'll also want to know what these scores mean. Scaled scores may also be called growth scale values, developmental standard scores, and standard scores — and may have different units to report the scores (Rudner 1989). You should not compare the scaled scores from one achievement test to another since different achievement tests measure different things and have different scaled score systems. So if you have a state test that reports student achievement in a variety of areas, and the scores are scaled, you wouldn't compare the results to one another.

A scaled score usually refers to the scores that are assigned by the test-makers on the basis of a student's achievement on the tests. The better the student performs on the test, the higher the scaled score the student will receive. Scaled scores are arbitrary scales to represent levels of achievement or ability (Popham 1993). Don't worry if you don't understand the conversion — remember that the scales are quite arbitrary — yes, somebody makes up what the range of scores in the scale will be.

For example, one state has assigned a scaled-score range of 0-600 for each of the 27 tests it requires students to take. So no matter which test the students take, the range of scores will always be the same. The Board of Education has approved cut scores — the score that tells us if a student has passed the tests — and these cut scores, while actually different for each test, are called the same thing when scaled. For example, the approved cut score on an Earth Science test is 30 questions correct. The pass score for any test is a 400 on the 0-600 range, so if a student gets 30 questions right on the Earth Science test — he or she will get a score of 400. Let's say that on the Biology test a student must get 34 questions right. That student's score will be also be called a 400, the number that represents the pass score on any of the tests. The cut scores are converted to the scaled-score range.

# Percent Correct Scores

Here's a scoring system that is familiar to just about everyone. This is simply the percentage of the test items a student gets right. To get percent correct, you simply divide the number of questions a student answered correctly by the number of questions he or she could have answered correctly and then multiply by 100.

Some state tests give information in relation to the percentage of items a student answered correctly. We use percent correct in many classrooms when we convert the number of questions a student answers correctly into a percent correct score.

## Percent Correct Conversions

| Number of Questions Correct | Percent of Questions Correct | Number of Questions Wrong | Number of Questions Correct | Percent of Questions Correct | Number of Questions Wrong |
|---|---|---|---|---|---|
| 25 | 100% | 0 | 12 | 48% | 13 |
| 24 | 96% | 1 | 11 | 44% | 14 |
| 23 | 92% | 2 | 10 | 40% | 15 |
| 22 | 88% | 3 | 9 | 36% | 16 |
| 21 | 84% | 4 | 8 | 32% | 17 |
| 20 | 80% | 5 | 7 | 28% | 18 |
| 19 | 76% | 6 | 6 | 24% | 19 |
| 18 | 72% | 7 | 5 | 20% | 20 |
| 17 | 68% | 8 | 4 | 16% | 21 |
| 16 | 64% | 9 | 3 | 12% | 22 |
| 15 | 60% | 10 | 2 | 8% | 23 |
| 14 | 56% | 11 | 1 | 4% | 24 |
| 13 | 52% | 12 | 0 | 0% | 25 |

## HOW TO COMPUTE PERCENT CORRECT SCORES

$$\frac{\text{Number of Test Questions Answered Correctly}}{\text{Total Number of Test Questions}} \times 100 = \% \text{ Correct}$$

# Mean Scores

Hooray, a score that's really easy to understand. The mean score is the arithmetic average of all the scores of students who took the test.

Many state tests use mean scores in the reporting of student achievement results. They might use the mean number correct, the mean percent correct, the mean scaled score, the mean grade equivalent score — you get the idea. So how do you compute the mean? Just add all of the scores together and divide by the total number of scores.

| Classroom Set of Scaled Scores (400 Is a Passing Score) | | | | | |
|---|---|---|---|---|---|
| 386 | 588 | 444 | 522 | 450 | 322 |
| 489 | 388 | 452 | 421 | 379 | 375 |
| 322 | 357 | 390 | 365 | 385 | 400 |
| 407 | 398 | 533 | 378 | 333 | 404 |

**Mean Scaled Score = 412**
(add all of the scores and divide by 24)

### HOW TO COMPUTE THE MEAN

$$\frac{\text{Sum of All of the Scores}}{\text{Number of Scores}}$$

# Median and Mode Scores

Median and mode scores are used to help describe a set of scores. The median is the score that falls in the exact middle of a range of scores. If you want to find the median, the first thing you'll need to do is to sort the scores. You can sort them in ascending (low to high) or descending (high to low) order. Then count how many scores there are. If the number of scores is odd, the median will be the score that is the middle. If the number of scores is even, you'll take the two middle scores and calculate an average for them. The calculated score is then your median score. What the median score does is to divide your set of scores into two equal parts. Half of the scores fall below the median score and the other half of the scores are above.

When you look at a set of scores, there may be a score that occurs more than any other. The score that occurs with the greatest frequency in a set of scores is called the mode. It is the most common score. Sometimes, a set of scores can have two sets of scores that are most common. So the set of scores would have more than one mode.

Here's the median and mode of a small set of classroom test scores.

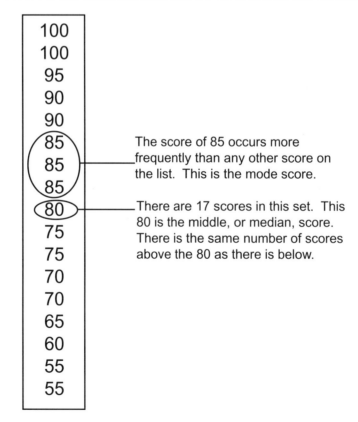

The score of 85 occurs more frequently than any other score on the list. This is the mode score.

There are 17 scores in this set. This 80 is the middle, or median, score. There is the same number of scores above the 80 as there is below.

# Percent Passing Scores

The percent passing score is simply the percentage of students who passed a particular test. If the individual pass, or cut score, on a test is a 400, then the percent passing score would be the percentage of students who achieved a 400 or better on the test. In the classroom set of scores below, 11 of the 24 students who took the test passed — a 48 percent pass rate. (The shaded cells in the table represent students who passed the test.)

| Classroom Set of Scaled Scores (400 Is a Passing Score) | | | | | |
|---|---|---|---|---|---|
| 386 | 588 | 444 | 522 | 450 | 322 |
| 489 | 388 | 452 | 421 | 379 | 375 |
| 322 | 357 | 390 | 365 | 385 | 400 |
| 407 | 398 | 533 | 378 | 333 | 404 |

---

**HOW TO COMPUTE PERCENT PASSING SCORES**

$$\frac{\text{Number of Students in the Group Who Passed the Test}}{\text{Number of Students Who Took the Test}} \times 100 = \% \text{ Correct}$$

# Relationship Between School/District Mean and Percent Passing Scores

Many states use the mean and percent passing scores as part of their score systems. You'll want to think about the relationship between these two types of score systems and be cautious when interpreting the mean. You'll most likely want compare the mean with other data, such as the percent passing score for your school or district.

Let's say that a school received its test results for the state test, and here are the scores in the chart below. (It's a school with only 24 students at this grade level.) This state has an individual pass rate of 400, and a school pass rate of 70% — which means that 70% of the students have to achieve 400 or better on the test. You look at the mean scaled score and think, "uhm, this is pretty good." The mean scaled score is better than 400 for our school. But remember, the real significance for the 400 is for students; a school can have a mean scaled score of 400 or greater but not have enough students individually attaining 400, which is the pass score for this test. (In the example below, the mean scaled score is 412, but only 48 percent of the students passed the test.)

| Classroom Set of Scaled Scores (400 Is a Passing Score) | | | | | |
|---|---|---|---|---|---|
| 386 | 588 | 444 | 522 | 450 | 322 |
| 489 | 388 | 452 | 421 | 379 | 375 |
| 322 | 357 | 390 | 365 | 385 | 400 |
| 407 | 398 | 533 | 378 | 333 | 404 |

# Range of Scores

Scores from the lowest to the highest, and all of the scores in between represent the range of scores for your classroom, school, or district. The range of scores can provide useful information because it tells how high and how low the scores go.

You've given the state assessment, and you've gotten your tests back. The scaled score range is from 0 to 600, with 0 being a pretty pitiful score and 600 being a perfect score. You take a look at the range of scaled scores for the students in your school and find that the lowest score any student got was 322 and the highest score was 588. The range on this test is 266 scaled score points.

The range also adds balance to your mean scaled score. (Remember, extremely low and high scores can move the overall mean up or down.)

| Classroom Set of Scaled Scores (400 Is a Passing Score) | | | | | |
|---|---|---|---|---|---|
| 386 | 588 | 444 | 522 | 450 | 322 |
| 489 | 388 | 452 | 421 | 379 | 375 |
| 322 | 357 | 390 | 365 | 385 | 400 |
| 407 | 398 | 533 | 378 | 333 | 404 |

### HOW TO COMPUTE RANGE OF SCORES

Highest Score - Lowest Score = Range of Scores

# Stanines

Some testing companies break down the scores into a scoring system called standard nines, or stanines, in which there are nine intervals into which scores can fall. The stanines represent groupings of the percentile ranks.

Like percentile ranks, a student's stanine depends on the group being referenced. And, also like percentile ranks, a student's national stanine score may be different from the student's local stanine score because these two scores represent different reference, or norming groups. The chart below shows the relationship between percentile ranks and stanines.

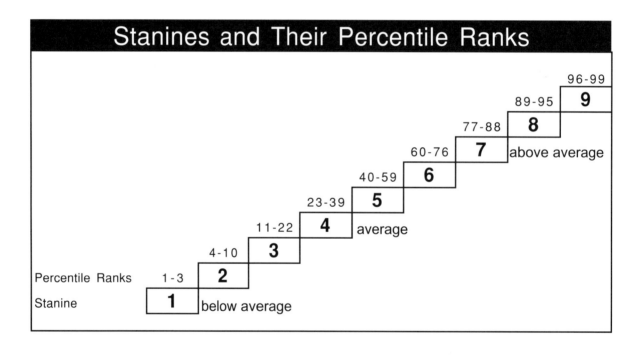

## Stanines and Their Percentile Ranks

# Grade-Equivalent Scores

Grade-equivalent scores are used to relate a given student's test score to the average score of other students who took the test based on grade and month. For example, a score of 10.2 indicates performance equal to that of a typical tenth grade student who may have taken the same test in the second month (November) of the school year. Such scores are often provided for nationally standardized tests and can be easily converted to raw scores by simply looking up the raw score in the test publisher's report.

However, grade-equivalent scores must be interpreted with caution. For example, take a fifth grader who takes a standardized test in December. We would expect a grade-equivalent score of 5.3 for this student. Suppose that, contrary to our expectations, this student achieves a grade-equivalent score of 8.0. This score does not mean that the student is ready for the eighth grade! It simply means that this fifth-grade student scored as well as an eighth grader who may have taken this fifth-grade test. Obviously the eighth grader is expected to possess other knowledge and skills that are not yet understood by our fifth grader and which were not included on the fifth grade test.

## Grade-Equivalent Scores

|  | Sep | Oct | Nov | Dec | Jan | Feb | Mar | Apr | May | June |
|---|---|---|---|---|---|---|---|---|---|---|
| Kindergarten* | K.0 | K.1 | K.2 | K.3 | K.4 | K.5 | K.6 | K.7 | K.8 | K.9 |
| First Grade | 1.0 | 1.1 | 1.2 | 1.3 | 1.4 | 1.5 | 1.6 | 1.7 | 1.8 | 1.9 |
| Second Grade | 2.0 | 2.1 | 2.2 | 2.3 | 2.4 | 2.5 | 2.6 | 2.7 | 2.8 | 2.9 |
| Third Grade | 3.0 | 3.1 | 3.2 | 3.3 | 3.4 | 3.5 | 3.6 | 3.7 | 3.8 | 3.9 |
| Fourth Grade | 4.0 | 4.1 | 4.2 | 4.3 | 4.4 | 4.5 | 4.6 | 4.7 | 4.8 | 4.9 |
| Fifth Grade | 5.0 | 5.1 | 5.2 | 5.3 | 5.4 | 5.5 | 5.6 | 5.7 | 5.8 | 5.9 |
| Sixth Grade | 6.0 | 6.1 | 6.2 | 6.3 | 6.4 | 6.5 | 6.6 | 6.7 | 6.8 | 6.9 |
| Seventh Grade | 7.0 | 7.1 | 7.2 | 7.3 | 7.4 | 7.5 | 7.6 | 7.7 | 7.8 | 7.9 |
| Eighth Grade | 8.0 | 8.1 | 8.2 | 8.3 | 8.4 | 8.5 | 8.6 | 8.7 | 8.8 | 8.9 |
| Ninth Grade | 9.0 | 9.1 | 9.2 | 9.3 | 9.4 | 9.5 | 9.6 | 9.7 | 9.8 | 9.9 |
| Tenth Grade | 10.0 | 10.1 | 10.2 | 10.3 | 10.4 | 10.5 | 10.6 | 10.7 | 10.8 | 10.9 |
| Eleventh Grade | 11.0 | 11.1 | 11.2 | 11.3 | 11.4 | 11.5 | 11.6 | 11.7 | 11.8 | 11.9 |
| Twelfth Grade | 12.0 | 12.1 | 12.2 | 12.3 | 12.4 | 12.5 | 12.6 | 12.7 | 12.8 | 12.9 |

*Kindergarten grade-equivalent scores are sometimes reported as 0.0, 0.1, etc.

# Normal Curve Equivalents

Normal curve equivalent (NCE) scores are yet another standardized scoring system that is based on the normal curve and a standard deviation of approximately 21 so that the range of probable scores is 1-99. Yes, that's the same as percentile scores, but they're not the same thing. The NCE scores are derived from percentile ranks, but provide an equal-interval scale which makes them okay to average.

Since it is okay to average NCEs, they are often used to describe group performance or check growth over time. NCEs are commonly used with the measurement of performance in federal programs such as Title I. The chart below shows the conversion table for normal curve equivalents and percentile ranks.

## Percentile Ranks And Corresponding Normal Curve Equivalents

| PR | NCE | PR | NCE | PR | NCE | PR | NCE |
|----|-----|----|-----|----|-----|----|-----|
| 1 | 1.0 | 26 | 36.5 | 51 | 50.5 | 76 | 64.9 |
| 2 | 6.7 | 27 | 37.1 | 52 | 51.1 | 77 | 65.6 |
| 3 | 10.4 | 28 | 37.7 | 53 | 51.6 | 78 | 66.3 |
| 4 | 13.1 | 29 | 38.3 | 54 | 52.1 | 79 | 67.0 |
| 5 | 15.4 | 30 | 39.0 | 55 | 52.6 | 80 | 67.7 |
| 6 | 17.3 | 31 | 39.6 | 56 | 53.2 | 81 | 68.5 |
| 7 | 18.9 | 32 | 40.2 | 57 | 53.7 | 82 | 69.3 |
| 8 | 20.4 | 33 | 40.7 | 58 | 54.3 | 83 | 70.1 |
| 9 | 21.8 | 34 | 41.3 | 59 | 54.8 | 84 | 70.9 |
| 10 | 23.0 | 35 | 41.9 | 60 | 55.3 | 85 | 71.8 |
| 11 | 24.2 | 36 | 42.5 | 61 | 55.9 | 86 | 72.8 |
| 12 | 25.3 | 37 | 43.0 | 62 | 56.4 | 87 | 73.7 |
| 13 | 26.3 | 38 | 43.6 | 63 | 57.0 | 88 | 74.7 |
| 14 | 27.2 | 39 | 44.1 | 64 | 57.5 | 89 | 75.8 |
| 15 | 28.2 | 40 | 44.7 | 65 | 58.1 | 90 | 77.0 |
| 16 | 29.1 | 41 | 45.2 | 66 | 58.7 | 91 | 78.2 |
| 17 | 29.9 | 42 | 45.7 | 67 | 59.3 | 92 | 79.6 |
| 18 | 30.7 | 43 | 46.3 | 68 | 59.8 | 93 | 81.1 |
| 19 | 31.5 | 44 | 46.8 | 69 | 60.4 | 94 | 82.7 |
| 20 | 32.3 | 45 | 47.4 | 70 | 61.0 | 95 | 84.6 |
| 21 | 33.0 | 46 | 47.9 | 71 | 61.7 | 96 | 86.9 |
| 22 | 33.7 | 47 | 48.4 | 72 | 62.3 | 97 | 89.6 |
| 23 | 34.4 | 48 | 48.9 | 73 | 62.9 | 98 | 93.3 |
| 24 | 35.1 | 49 | 49.5 | 74 | 63.5 | 99 | 99.0 |
| 25 | 35.8 | 50 | 50.0 | 75 | 64.2 | | |

# Gain Scores

Remember that when monitoring achievement, there are really only three ways the results can go: they can go up, they can go down, or they can stay the same. Gain scores are simply the change or difference between two repetitions of the same test administered to the same students. For example, if students took an achievement pretest at the beginning of the year and a post-test at the end of the year, the difference between the two test scores would be the gain score. Obviously, gain scores let you determine whether a student (or group) has shown improvement. The chart below shows how you might set up a data table to look at gain scores.

## Chart of Gain Scores

| Student | Pretest Score | Posttest Score | Gain Score |
|---------|---------------|----------------|------------|
| 1 | 53 | 89 | 36 |
| 2 | 77 | 97 | 20 |
| 3 | 65 | 76 | 11 |
| 4 | 59 | 92 | 33 |
| 5 | 68 | 89 | 21 |
| 6 | 32 | 89 | 57 |
| 7 | 48 | 78 | 30 |
| 8 | 57 | 95 | 38 |
| 9 | 48 | 92 | 44 |
| 10 | 56 | 89 | 33 |
| Group Averages | 56.3 | 88.6 | 32.3 |

# Test Score Reports

Testing companies provide many useful pieces of information to help you understand test scores. They provide interpretive reports for students, teachers, administrators, and parents. When you get the score reports from the testing/scoring companies you'll usually find information presented to you in three ways: numbers, charts/graphs, and a written narrative.

A variety of score reports will generally be provided, depending on the options a school division has purchased. Typical score reports include Individual Score Reports, School Summary Reports, and District Summary Reports. Many testing companies will also disaggregate the achievement data for you. Most testing and scoring companies will even provide your school/district data on a computer disk for a fee. Often, this price reflects a certain cost per student in the district. It can be well worth the money to have the data ready to download into your own computer system. (Naturally, that means you'll have to have someone on hand who can work with the data in the system — otherwise the money may not be so well spent — you could be better off with just the hard copy of your scores.)

Most testing companies also publish interpretive guides for their tests. These are well worth the cost because they contain much information that is useful to you in interpreting test information. The interpretive guides will explain each of the score systems used in the publisher's test and how to use this information.

# Two Types of Tests

There are two basic types of tests that you'll use when looking at student achievement data. The two types are norm-referenced and criterion-referenced tests. External tests (those that the state or district mandates) may be either. If you give a test like the *Stanford Achievement Tests*, the *Iowa Tests of Basic Skills*, or the *California Achievement Tests* — you're giving a norm-referenced test. Norm-referenced tests let you see how students are doing in relation to other students. If you're giving a test designed to measure achievement toward your state standards, you're giving a criterion-referenced test.

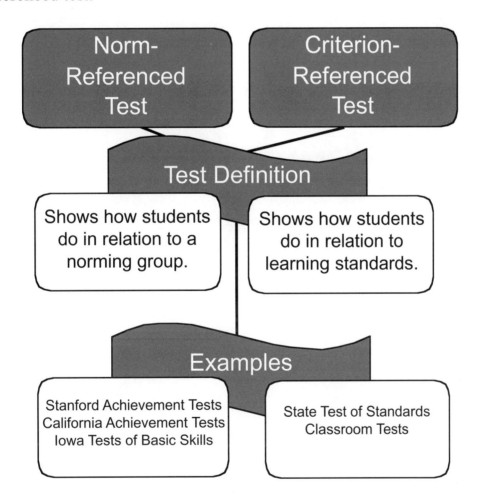

For those of you who want to see the score systems in relation to the bell curve, you'll find that on the next page. The following graphic shows the normal distribution curve and some of the various score systems. This should be a nice reference for you. A normal distribution of scores, when graphed, produces a normal curve — the bell-shaped curve. In a perfect bell-shaped curve, the mean, median and mode are the middle of the distribution with half the scores on one side and half the scores on the other. This is represented by the 0 at the center of the curve. Many scoring systems are based on standard deviation units. Standard deviation is a measure of variability in a set of scores and the units represent how far away individual or group scores are from the mean. A small standard deviation means there is not much variance in the scores. A large standard deviation means there is variance in the scores.

# The Normal Curve

## The Normal Curve & Various Score Systems

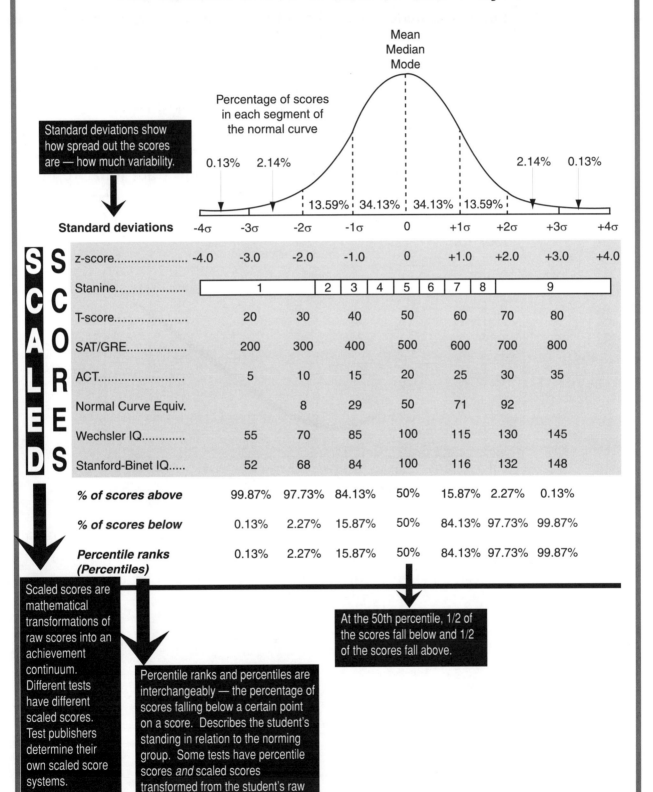

Standard deviations show how spread out the scores are — how much variability.

Percentage of scores in each segment of the normal curve

Mean
Median
Mode

0.13%   2.14%        13.59%  34.13%  34.13%  13.59%        2.14%   0.13%

**Standard deviations**

| | -4σ | -3σ | -2σ | -1σ | 0 | +1σ | +2σ | +3σ | +4σ |
|---|---|---|---|---|---|---|---|---|---|
| z-score | -4.0 | -3.0 | -2.0 | -1.0 | 0 | +1.0 | +2.0 | +3.0 | +4.0 |
| Stanine | | 1 | | 2 | 3 | 4 | 5 | 6 | 7 | 8 | 9 |
| T-score | | 20 | 30 | 40 | 50 | 60 | 70 | 80 | |
| SAT/GRE | | 200 | 300 | 400 | 500 | 600 | 700 | 800 | |
| ACT | | 5 | 10 | 15 | 20 | 25 | 30 | 35 | |
| Normal Curve Equiv. | | | 8 | 29 | 50 | 71 | 92 | | |
| Wechsler IQ | | 55 | 70 | 85 | 100 | 115 | 130 | 145 | |
| Stanford-Binet IQ | | 52 | 68 | 84 | 100 | 116 | 132 | 148 | |
| **% of scores above** | | 99.87% | 97.73% | 84.13% | 50% | 15.87% | 2.27% | 0.13% | |
| **% of scores below** | | 0.13% | 2.27% | 15.87% | 50% | 84.13% | 97.73% | 99.87% | |
| **Percentile ranks (Percentiles)** | | 0.13% | 2.27% | 15.87% | 50% | 84.13% | 97.73% | 99.87% | |

**SCALED SCORES**

Scaled scores are mathematical transformations of raw scores into an achievement continuum. Different tests have different scaled scores. Test publishers determine their own scaled score systems.

Percentile ranks and percentiles are interchangeably — the percentage of scores falling below a certain point on a score. Describes the student's standing in relation to the norming group. Some tests have percentile scores *and* scaled scores transformed from the student's raw score.

At the 50th percentile, 1/2 of the scores fall below and 1/2 of the scores fall above.

# The J Curve

You've heard a lot about normal curves, but what we're looking for in improving student achievement are results that, when charted, look like a "J" curve (Lezotte, 1990). On a J curve, all students can progress toward the highest level on the curve — when given enough time, resources, and support. (Remember, not everyone learns at the same rate, the same time, or in the same way.) The J curve describes the student's standing in relation to learning designated standards, as measured with the tools of comprehensive assessment. (Comprehensive assessment tools include traditional forms of assessment, such as paper-and-pencil tests, as well as alternative types of assessment.) Review the graph below to see what a J curve might look like.

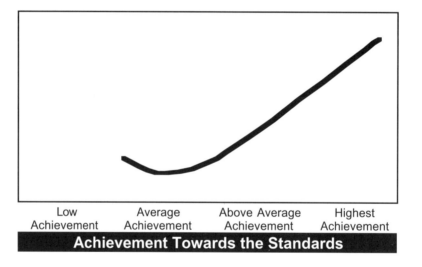

| Low Achievement | Average Achievement | Above Average Achievement | Highest Achievement |

**Achievement Towards the Standards**

The idea here is that 50 percent of the students aren't expected to fall below the 50th percentile, as with a normal curve. If you're really interested in improving student achievement, this is your curve!

# 4 Chapter Four
# Data Disaggregation

Larry Lezotte (1990), in his Effective Schools work, has highlighted the importance of disaggregating data to determine whether there is equity in serving various populations or subgroups of students (e.g., by race, gender, and socioeconomic status). Most school teams I work with have the phrase, "learning for all," somewhere in their mission statements. Disaggregation is one of those things you do with data to determine whether there is indeed learning for all.

## What Is Disaggregation?

Disaggregation is the breaking apart of data by subgroups in order to see how different groups performed on a test or how they compare in other areas, such as attendance. Let's look at an analogy for disaggregation. Think about a great big jar of M&M candies (my personal favorites). I've placed it on your desk and have asked you to report on what is inside. You could just tell me that there are 346 pieces of candy. Or you could sort the candies by color and type (e.g., peanut, almond, plain) to give me a richer picture of what's in the jar. If you sort the candies by color and type when you're taking them out of the jar and recording the results, you're actually disaggregating the information about what kinds of M&M candies are inside the jar. We disaggregate numbers related to student achievement to get a richer picture of how students perform.

# Why Disaggregate Student Achievement Data?

In practice, I use the definition of an improving school from the Effective Schools literature. According to the Effective Schools literature, an improving school/program/district is one that meets the concept of equity *in* quality (Lezotte, 1990, 1992). **Quality** is "how good" a school is. Is student achievement high? Does achievement improve from year to year? **Equity** represents how close together groups of students are performing in that school. Equity tells us if there is learning for all. A school that has 95% of its students passing a key test has quality (at least on that test). A school that has 45% of its students passing that same key test does not have quality on that assessment. A school in which males perform similarly to the females has gender equity. A school in which minority students perform at a similar level as whites has race equity. A school in which the poorest students perform at levels comparable to students from wealthier homes has SES (socioeconomic status) equity. We can disaggregate data to monitor whether or not there is equity in the achievement levels of the students we are serving. Remember, disaggregate to find out whether you have "learning for all" on your assessments. Let me show you what I mean.

Take a look at the chart below. This chart lists five schools with their outcome data on a writing test. These schools are part of a school district that has "learning for all" in its mission statement. Which of these five schools would you say is doing the *best* job of helping all of its students achieve on this particular writing assessment? (As you are reviewing the data, keep in mind that the school pass rate required for writing is 70 percent of the students passing the test — which is the quality indicator for the test.)

## Which School Is Most Effective On This Writing Assessment?

School A:     92% of the students passed the writing test

School B:     70% of the students passed the writing test

School C:     32% of the students passed the writing test

School D:     85% of the students passed the writing test

School E:     88% of the students passed the writing test

Are you having trouble determining which of the five is most effective? One way to determine the effectiveness of a school — and to determine whether a school is improving — is to look more closely at your data in order to get more information. You see, I didn't give you quite enough information to make a professional judgment about which school is most effective on this particular assessment. So let me give you more data.

In the chart below, I've added demographic data to the outcome data. Look at those five schools with the additional data and again answer the question: *Which school do you think is most effective on this particular writing test?*

---

### Which School Is Most Effective On This Writing Assessment?

School A:  92% of the students passed the writing test

   minority:  60% passed

   white:   95% passed

School B:  70% of the students passed the writing test

   minority:  60% passed

   white:   85% passed

School C:  32% of the students passed the writing test

   minority:  30% passed

   white:   30% passed

School D:  85% of the students passed the writing test

   minority:  85% passed

   white:   70% passed

School E:  88% of the students passed the writing test

   minority:  88% passed

   white:   90% passed

---

Well, let's see how you did.

In **School A**, 92 percent of the students passed (quality), but there is a gap of 35 in the achievement levels of minority and white students (no equity here).

In **School B**, 70 percent of the students passed (borderline quality), and there was an achievement gap of 25 between the two groups of students.

**School C** had 32 percent of the students passing (definitely not quality) and no gap in the performance level of the two groups of students. (This is "no learning for all.")

In **School D**, 85 percent of the students passed (quality) and a gap of 15 (approaching equity).

In **School E**, 88 percent of the students passed the writing test (quality) and the gap in achievement between the two groups of students is only 2 percentage points (equity). So school E is the strongest example of *equity in quality* on this particular writing assessment.

The difference between the achievement levels of subgroups of students is called an achievement gap. A difference (gap) of 0 percentage points is a good thing. A gap that's greater than 10 percentage points may give you cause for concern — and may be something you do indeed want to monitor.

## Disaggregation Basics

There are a few things that are helpful to know in order to disaggregate data. I want to walk you through the steps of a simple manual disaggregation (that's one you do by hand), but remember that what I'm showing here can also be completed using a software program such as Microsoft Excel, a popular spreadsheet program. You can even build in the formulas to do the calculations for you. Start with this simple process, and you'll be on your way to disaggregating just about anything you want.

So how do you disaggregate? First of all, put together your disaggregation template, and add the raw data. In this case, the raw data are the numbers of students, by gender, passing and failing each test. Be sure to be accurate on this part of the disaggregation process — if the numbers are wrong here, they're going to be wrong throughout the chart.

### Disaggregation of Data by Pass/Fail and Gender

| | Males | | Females | | Gap |
|---|---|---|---|---|---|
| | # | % | # | % | |
| Pass | 121 | | 89 | | |
| Fail | 36 | | 58 | | |

| | | |
|---|---|---|
| Column Totals | 157 | 147 |

| Total (Males + Females) | 304 |
|---|---|

| Total Students Passing | |
|---|---|

| % of Students Passing | |
|---|---|

Now get out your calculator and figure up all of the percentages. If you follow the format of the disaggregation template, you shouldn't go wrong here. We're trying to find out what percentage of students passed within each subgroup, so we divide the number of students in both of the Pass/Fail blocks for males by 157, and for females by 147. You can also go ahead and fill in the total number and percentage of students passing.

### Disaggregation of Data by Pass/Fail and Gender

| | Males | | Females | | Gap |
|---|---|---|---|---|---|
| | # | % | # | % | |
| Pass | 121 | 77% | 89 | 61% | 16 |
| Fail | 36 | 23% | 58 | 39% | |

| | | | | |
|---|---|---|---|---|
| Column Totals | 157 | 100% | 147 | 100% |

| Total (Males + Females) | 304 |
|---|---|

| Total Students Passing | 210 | (# of males and females passing test) |
|---|---|---|

| % of Students Passing | 69% | (# of males and females passing test/Total males and females X 100) |
|---|---|---|

See the next page for the annotated completed chart.

# Disaggregation of Data by Pass/Fail and Gender

| | Males | | Females | | Gap |
|---|---|---|---|---|---|
| | # | % | # | % | |
| **Pass** | 121 | 77% | 89 | 61% | 16 |
| **Fail** | 36 | 23% | 58 | 39% | ⬆ |

| | | | | |
|---|---|---|---|---|
| **Column Totals** | 157 | 100% | 147 | 100% |

| | |
|---|---|
| **Total (Males + Females)** | 304 |

| | | |
|---|---|---|
| **Total Students Passing** | 210 | (# of males and females passing test) |

| | | |
|---|---|---|
| **% of Students Passing** | 69% | (# of males and females passing test/Total males and females X 100) |

Look for an acceptable gap between 0-10. (You'd want to monitor this gap of 16.) Remember, this is your **equity** indicator.

The overall percentage of students who passed an assessment gives you the **quality** indicator. If the achievement bar here was 75% of the students passing the test, the school wouldn't quite be at the quality measurement on this assessment.

Once it's all together, you can determine whether you have equity in quality on an assessment. To determine equity, look at the gap in achievement between the performance of the males and the females. If the gap is greater than 10, you'd probably want to monitor it. To determine quality, look at the overall percentage of students who passed the test. Of course, the higher the percentage of students passing the test, the better.

After you disaggregate this information, then you may want to display it using a chart or a graph. The disaggregated data would then look like this.

**Disaggregation of Pass/Fail Rates of Students on State Writing Tests by Gender • Spring 2000**

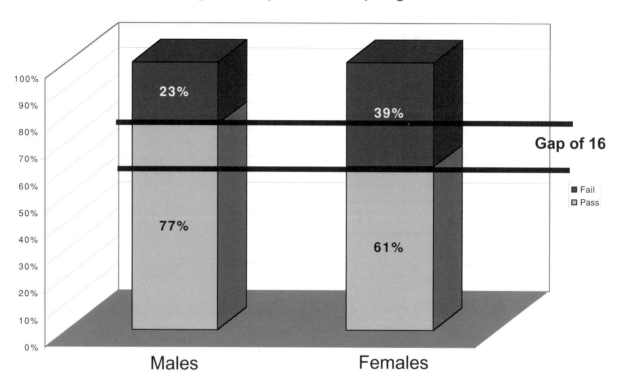

- A total of 304 students took the Spring 2000 version of the state writing test. Of these, 157 were males and 147 were females.
- A greater percentage of males (77%) passed the writing test than the females (61%). This represents a gap of 16 between the two groups.
- Since the gap is greater than 10, we should monitor achievement in terms of gender during the next couple of years.

## More About Disaggregation

According to the Effective Schools research (Lezotte, 1990), disaggregation answers the important question of, "For whom are we effective?" Disaggregation is another piece of data, another piece of evidence, about how students are performing. Remember that list of data sources from Chapter Two? You can disaggregate just about everything on that list. (That's why you'll see the disaggregation columns on the right of the chart.) You can disaggregate things like attendance, grades, test scores, discipline referrals, and more, by race/ethnicity, gender, and SES. You can get a handle on who is/is not attending school, who is/is not achieving well, who is/is not getting in trouble in school. Through disaggregation, you truly can determine if you're attaining "learning for all."

Data Tip: When you disaggregate a variable, monitor it over time. Ask yourself: What is the trend from past to present? Which groups have changed over time? Which groups have stayed the same?

## Disaggregation Templates

I like to design disaggregation templates that are ready to use when I sit down to analyze data. I've included a number of these disaggregation templates in the next chapter where I also introduce a variety of data organizers. I hope you'll refer to these for ideas of how to set up your own disaggregation templates.

## Disaggregation Tips

Now, don't sit down and begin disaggregating everything in sight. Before you begin, ask yourself these two questions:

1.  Will the results of the disaggregation provide me with useful information? If not, don't waste your time.

2.  Does it pass the 15 percent test? Does each subgroup contain at least 15 percent of the population? For example, let's say you want to disaggregate data by gender. You check your overall

percentages for males and females and note that the school population is made of 48 percent males and 52 percent females. Each subgroup makes up at least 15 percent of the total population. It's okay to disaggregate.

Now, let's do the 15 percent test for another example — race/ ethnicity. Here's the percentages of each of the race/ethnic categories in a school division. Use the 15 percent test to guide you in identifying the categories you should or should not disaggregate.

1%    American Indian (not 15 percent — don't disaggregate)
2%    Asian (not 15 percent — don't disaggregate)
1%    Hispanic (not 15 percent — don't disaggregate)
21%   Black (15 percent — okay to disaggregate)
75%   White (15 percent — okay to disaggregate)

By the way, sometimes when a school population has few numbers of students in a race/ethnicity category, it may combine the groups into one "minority" category. For example, one of the data points the National Science Foundation (NSF) tracks in its Comprehensive Partnerships for Mathematics and Science Achievement is that of race/ ethnicity. Overall, the NSF looks at the following race/ethnicity categories: American Indian, Asian, Pacific Islander, Black, Hispanic, White, and Other.

When determining whether minority achievement is improving, data collectors at NSF combine American Indian, Blacks, and Hispanics, in a category called underrepresented minority students. So you can certainly group populations of people together — just do it the same way every year so you can monitor changes in equity over time.

Use the 15 percent disaggregation rule as a safeguard to ensure you disaggregate only those populations for which you'll get statistically appropriate results.

# Disaggregation at the Classroom Level

You might be thinking that disaggregating data may be a good idea for a school division or even the NSF, but is it something that serves a purpose in the classroom? The answer is a definite "yes." You can disaggregate at the school, district, or classroom level. Disaggregated data will help you see if there is *learning for all*. Disaggregated data at the classroom level can let a teacher know if all of his or her students are learning equally by subgroups.

Here's how one teacher used disaggregation to check gender equity in her classes. A math teacher designed a special unit around the theme of basketball. She wanted to integrate skills of math with other basic skills (e.g., reading, writing, listening, speaking, technology). Her unit had the students follow basketball scores during the Big 10. She had approximately 120 students in her five classes. This teacher wanted to find out if there was a difference in interest between the males and females in her class. She gave the students an interest survey, looked at the test results (disaggregated by male and female), and looked at achievement differences between males and females on her other classroom tests.

Here's what she learned from disaggregating her classroom data. When looking at the interest survey, she learned that the males loved the unit, and the females thought it was okay. When she looked at the unit test results, she found that the males scored 15 percentage points higher than the females. She looked at the results of the tests from other units and found the difference in how males and females performed to be only five percentage points.

This teacher learned that the females did like the unit, but they weren't as excited about it as the males. And she was concerned about the difference in achievement. She wants to use this information to improve and wondered what she should do. Should she replace this unit with another next year? Absolutely not. The males loved the unit. She can use the data to make changes in the students' learning experiences. She could design a unit with a theme for females that would have a high interest level. She could then give students a choice.

She could also try a couple of other things with her basketball unit to make it more interesting for females. She might ask the females: What would make this unit more interesting for you? She may bring in more of the personal side of the basketball players — who they are, how old they are, and other interesting facts. She could even show clips from ESPN so the females can view female sportscasters providing game information. She may even include women's basketball statistics in her unit. The main thing is that the teacher used data to reflect on student learning in her classroom.

The next page, *Disaggregation Overview*, provides a quick look at the disaggregation process. You may want to use it as a brief summary of the information in this chapter.

# Disaggregation Overview

Take a minute to review the process of getting data from a score — combining it with the scores of other students — and then disaggregating the scores (based on SES or socioeconomic status in this example).

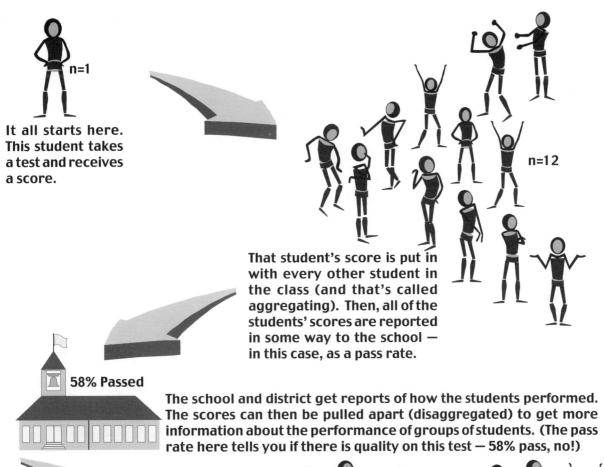

**n=1**

It all starts here. This student takes a test and receives a score.

**n=12**

That student's score is put in with every other student in the class (and that's called aggregating). Then, all of the students' scores are reported in some way to the school — in this case, as a pass rate.

**58% Passed**

The school and district get reports of how the students performed. The scores can then be pulled apart (disaggregated) to get more information about the performance of groups of students. (The pass rate here tells you if there is quality on this test — 58% pass, no!)

Disaggregation will let you answer a host of questions: Who performed well on this test? Boys or girls? Low SES or High SES? Minority or White students? Students in special programs or not? The diagram on the right shows the results of disaggregating this very small group of students on a test by socioeconomic status (SES).

Special Note: The small numbers here are for illustrative purposes only — you normally wouldn't disaggregate when the numbers are this small.

83% (5/6) of the middle/ high SES students passed the test.

33% (2/6) of the low SES students passed the test.

This disaggregation tells you whether there is equity on the test. (No, there's a gap of 50 between the performance level of the two groups.)

So there you have it. Disaggregation is breaking down of data to find out if you can claim your school provides " learning for all." In addition to race, gender, and socioeconomic status, you can disaggregate by other factors. For example, you might disaggregate data by:

- **attendance** (students with good attendance compared with students with poor attendance)
- **mobility** (students you've had in the school all year compared with students who transferred in)
- **special education** (special education students compared with regular education students)
- **LEP** (limited English proficiency students compared with English-speaking students)
- **discipline** (students with good discipline compared with students with poor discipline)
- **special programs** (students who participated in a special program compared with those who did not)

# 5 Chapter Five
# Data Tables

It's a matter of fact when working with data: In order to analyze and use data, you'll need to organize it. So if you want to organize and analyze data efficiently, you'll want to use data organizers. These are not friendly people who organize your data for you. Rather, data organizers are templates, visual tools, and think sheets that let you organize data in various ways so you can better analyze it. Examples of data organizers include disaggregation templates, graphic organizers, and other tools that guide your thinking, but the key organizer is the data table. The data tables included here can be used to guide you in how to set up some of your own data in a database and/or spreadsheet. Of course, the information in the data tables can then be graphed for even easier analysis of the data.

The templates included in this chapter will guide you in understanding how you manually disaggregate data. (I talked about disaggregation in the last chapter.) If you're using a spreadsheet program such as Microsoft Excel, Microsoft Works, Clarisworks — these templates will save you huge amounts of time in the design and set up of your data tables.

## Jump-start Analyses/Helpful Hints for the Data Tables

A few of the data organizers included in this chapter have what I call a jump-start analysis. A jump-start analysis provides descriptive statements about the chart or graph and gives you an idea of what to say or write once you've completed a data table. What you write should always be the same as what you see. In addition, the organizers in this chapter have helpful hints — just to ensure your success in setting up and thinking about information.

This chapter, because it provides many ideas for setting up data tables, will be one you'll want to earmark to use again and again.

## Visual Displays of Data Usually Begin With Data Tables

There are many ways to visually display data — and a starting point for data display is the data table. Data tables contain your numbers, and can be used as stand-alone tools for data analysis. A frequency chart/table is one example of a data table that can be used as a stand-alone tool. You'll turn many of the data tables you make into charts and graphs.

# Designing a Data Table

Constructing data tables is an important skill when learning to work with data. Many of the charts and graphs you construct will begin with a data table. Designing good data tables is really quite easy. Simply think about the factors you want to explore. In this example, the variables are the number of curriculum objectives by core content area and grade levels. This example provides information about the key parts of an easy-to-read data table.

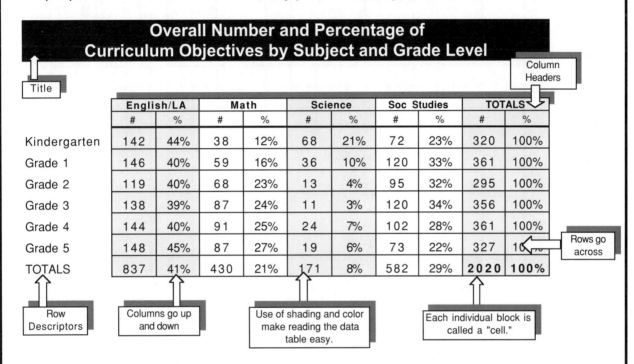

**Overall Number and Percentage of Curriculum Objectives by Subject and Grade Level**

| | English/LA | | Math | | Science | | Soc Studies | | TOTALS | |
|---|---|---|---|---|---|---|---|---|---|---|
| | # | % | # | % | # | % | # | % | # | % |
| Kindergarten | 142 | 44% | 38 | 12% | 68 | 21% | 72 | 23% | 320 | 100% |
| Grade 1 | 146 | 40% | 59 | 16% | 36 | 10% | 120 | 33% | 361 | 100% |
| Grade 2 | 119 | 40% | 68 | 23% | 13 | 4% | 95 | 32% | 295 | 100% |
| Grade 3 | 138 | 39% | 87 | 24% | 11 | 3% | 120 | 34% | 356 | 100% |
| Grade 4 | 144 | 40% | 91 | 25% | 24 | 7% | 102 | 28% | 361 | 100% |
| Grade 5 | 148 | 45% | 87 | 27% | 19 | 6% | 73 | 22% | 327 | 100% |
| TOTALS | 837 | 41% | 430 | 21% | 171 | 8% | 582 | 29% | 2020 | 100% |

Title · Column Headers · Rows go across · Row Descriptors · Columns go up and down · Use of shading and color make reading the data table easy. · Each individual block is called a "cell."

When you are working with data, you'll generally begin with the raw data and organize the information into a data table. (You'll see lots of examples of data tables in this book.) Once you've designed your table, you can then painlessly create a chart or graph to show the data graphically. The data table above is a very simple data table — sometimes you'll need to create one that is a bit more comprehensive. For example, suppose you wanted to look at more than gender when reviewing enrollment. Perhaps you want to look at race/ethnicity and gender. And you want to look at this by grade level. You'll see how to set up a data table that shows more factors on the next page.

# Disaggregation of Enrollment by Gender and Race

**Males** | **Females** | **Total Students**

| Grade | American Indian # | % | Asian # | % | Pacific Islander # | % | Black # | % | Hispanic # | % | White # | % | MALE TOTALS # | % | American Indian # | % | Asian # | % | Pacific Islander # | % | Black # | % | Hispanic # | % | White # | % | FEMALE TOTALS # | % | American Indian # | % | Asian # | % | Pacific Islander # | % | Black # | % | Hispanic # | % | White # | % | ALL TOTALS # | % |
|---|---|---|---|---|---|---|---|---|---|---|---|---|---|---|---|---|---|---|---|---|---|---|---|---|---|---|---|---|---|---|---|---|---|---|---|---|---|---|---|---|---|---|---|---|
| 1 | | | | | | | | | | | | | | | | | | | | | | | | | | | | | | | | | | | | | | | | | | |
| 2 | | | | | | | | | | | | | | | | | | | | | | | | | | | | | | | | | | | | | | | | | | |
| 3 | | | | | | | | | | | | | | | | | | | | | | | | | | | | | | | | | | | | | | | | | | |
| 4 | | | | | | | | | | | | | | | | | | | | | | | | | | | | | | | | | | | | | | | | | | |
| 5 | | | | | | | | | | | | | | | | | | | | | | | | | | | | | | | | | | | | | | | | | | |
| 6 | | | | | | | | | | | | | | | | | | | | | | | | | | | | | | | | | | | | | | | | | | |
| 7 | | | | | | | | | | | | | | | | | | | | | | | | | | | | | | | | | | | | | | | | | | |
| 8 | | | | | | | | | | | | | | | | | | | | | | | | | | | | | | | | | | | | | | | | | | |
| 9 | | | | | | | | | | | | | | | | | | | | | | | | | | | | | | | | | | | | | | | | | | |
| 10 | | | | | | | | | | | | | | | | | | | | | | | | | | | | | | | | | | | | | | | | | | |
| 11 | | | | | | | | | | | | | | | | | | | | | | | | | | | | | | | | | | | | | | | | | | |
| 12 | | | | | | | | | | | | | | | | | | | | | | | | | | | | | | | | | | | | | | | | | | |
| Sp Ed | | | | | | | | | | | | | | | | | | | | | | | | | | | | | | | | | | | | | | | | | | |
| Ungrd | | | | | | | | | | | | | | | | | | | | | | | | | | | | | | | | | | | | | | | | | | |
| TOTAL | | | | | | | | | | | | | | | | | | | | | | | | | | | | | | | | | | | | | | | | | | |

> This data table helps you organize your data by gender and race/ethnicity. Use the same ethnic codes required by your state or district. List these in the same order that you'll find them on school and district reports and you'll save a lot of time.

> Use numbers and percentages, especially if you're going to track this data from year to year.

> Of course, the overall total should be 100 percent.

# Overall Number and Percentage of Curriculum Objectives by Subject and Grade Level

| | English/LA | | Math | | Science | | Soc Studies | | TOTALS | |
|---|---|---|---|---|---|---|---|---|---|---|
| | # | % | # | % | # | % | # | % | # | % |
| Kindergarten | | | | | | | | | | 100% |
| Grade 1 | | | | | | | | | | 100% |
| Grade 2 | | | | | | | | | | 100% |
| Grade 3 | | | | | | | | | | 100% |
| Grade 4 | | | | | | | | | | 100% |
| Grade 5 | | | | | | | | | | 100% |
| Grade 6 | | | | | | | | | | 100% |
| Grade 7 | | | | | | | | | | 100% |
| Grade 8 | | | | | | | | | | 100% |
| Grade 9 | | | | | | | | | | 100% |
| Grade 10 | | | | | | | | | | 100% |
| Grade 11 | | | | | | | | | | 100% |
| Grade 12 | | | | | | | | | | 100% |
| TOTALS | | | | | | | | | | |

This chart provides useful information related to the curriculum. When you complete the information on this chart, you'll be able to tell whether or not the curricular areas are balanced.

## Jump-start Data Analysis

- The chart above provides an overview of the total objectives, by subject area, for the school/district.
- There are a total of ____ objectives that students are expected to learn in grades K-12. Of these, _____ (___%) are from English, _____ (____%) are from math, _____ (____%) are from science, and _____ (____%) are from social studies.
- The largest number of objectives is taught and learned in grade _____, while the least number of objectives is taught in grade _____.
- Overall, there is/is not a balance of objectives among the grade levels.
- Overall, there is/is not a balance of objectives among the core subject areas of English/Language Arts, Math, Science, and Social Studies.

# Number and Percentage of Students
# At or Above Grade Level Reading

| | Total Students | On Grade Level Spring 1999 | | On Grade Level Spring 2000 | | On Grade Level Spring 2001 | |
|---|---|---|---|---|---|---|---|
| | | # | % | # | % | # | % |
| **K** Pre-Emergent | | | | | | | |
| **1** Beginner | | | | | | | |
| **2** Advanced Beginner | | | | | | | |
| **3** Transitional | | | | | | | |
| **4** Intermediate | | | | | | | |
| **5** Intermediate Plus | | | | | | | |

| | | | | | | | |
|---|---|---|---|---|---|---|---|
| **T** School Totals | | | | | | | |

## Jump-start Data Analysis

- Each student in our school was given the ____ reading test to determine whether or not he or she is on grade level for reading.
- The chart above provides trend data for the number and percentage of students at or above grade level over a three-year period.
- The highest percentage of students at or above grade level reading was at ___ grade.

## Factors to Analyze

- Are there too many students who are not reading on grade level?
- Can you identify the specific weaknesses of students reading below grade level?
- Are you teaching the district's curriculum?
- Do students spend a lot of time reading?

# Student Enrollment by Grade Level

|  | 1998-99 | 1999-00 | 2000-01 | 2001-02 | 2002-03 | 2003-04 |
|---|---|---|---|---|---|---|
| Pre-Kindergarten |  |  |  |  |  |  |
| Kindergarten |  |  |  |  |  |  |
| Grade 1 |  |  |  |  |  |  |
| Grade 2 |  |  |  |  |  |  |
| Grade 3 |  |  |  |  |  |  |
| Grade 4 |  |  |  |  |  |  |
| Grade 5 |  |  |  |  |  |  |
| Grade 6 |  |  |  |  |  |  |
| Grade 7 |  |  |  |  |  |  |
| Grade 8 |  |  |  |  |  |  |
| Grade 9 |  |  |  |  |  |  |
| Grade 10 |  |  |  |  |  |  |
| Grade 11 |  |  |  |  |  |  |
| Grade 12 |  |  |  |  |  |  |
| Special Education |  |  |  |  |  |  |
| Ungraded |  |  |  |  |  |  |
| Totals |  |  |  |  |  |  |

> This data table provides just the enrollment numbers, but you could also add percents.
>
> You could easily adapt this chart to show enrollment for an entire district by putting the names of schools across the top (instead of the years).
>
> Hint: When you're tracking enrollment from one year to the next, use whatever official enrollment count is used by your State Department of Education (e.g., September 30th membership count).

# Jump-start Data Analysis

- The chart above provides enrollment information, by grade level, for the years 1998-99 through 2003-04.
- During the 1998-99 school year, a total of _____ students were enrolled in our division.
- Grade _____ had the largest number of students, while grade _____ had the fewest.
- Approximately _____ special education students were enrolled in our district during the _____ school year. This represents an increase or a decrease of _____ from the previous school year.

> **Want a graph? A bar graph is a good choice for enrollment.**

# Student Enrollment by Level (Elementary, Middle, High) 1998-99 to 2002-03

|  | 1998-99 | | 1999-00 | | 2000-01 | | 2001-02 | | 2002-03 | |
|---|---|---|---|---|---|---|---|---|---|---|
|  | # | % | # | % | # | % | # | % | # | % |
| Elementary |  |  |  |  |  |  |  |  |  |  |
| Middle |  |  |  |  |  |  |  |  |  |  |
| High |  |  |  |  |  |  |  |  |  |  |
|  |  |  |  |  |  |  |  |  |  |  |
| Special Education |  |  |  |  |  |  |  |  |  |  |
| Ungraded |  |  |  |  |  |  |  |  |  |  |
| TOTALS |  |  |  |  |  |  |  |  |  |  |

> Sometimes you may want to give a simpler picture of enrollment, by just breaking it into elementary, middle, and high school categories. This is an example of how you might do this.

## Jump-start Data Analysis

- A total of _____ students were enrolled in the school division during the 1998-99 school year.
- Of these, _____% were elementary, _____% were middle, and _____% were high.
- The overall total also includes two other groups of students. Special education students account for _____% of the overall population and ungraded students account for _____%.

# Students Scoring a D or E/F
# in Two or More Classes/Subject Areas

| | Males | | Females | | Totals | | Gap |
|---|---|---|---|---|---|---|---|
| | # | % | # | % | # | % | |
| Grade 3 | | | | | | | |
| Grade 4 | | | | | | | |
| Grade 5 | | | | | | | |
| Grade 6 | | | | | | | |
| Grade 7 | | | | | | | |
| Grade 8 | | | | | | | |
| Grade 9 | | | | | | | |
| Grade 10 | | | | | | | |
| Grade 11 | | | | | | | |
| Grade 12 | | | | | | | |
| TOTALS | | | | | | | |

So why might you track these students? These are students who may need special assistance and support to be more successful in school.

This disaggregation worksheet helps you look at students by gender who are at risk for failing two or more courses. Remember, you can also disaggregate student data by race/ethnicity or other variables of your choice.

# Number and Percent of Students With a Grade of D or E/F in the Core Content Areas

| | English/LA | | Math | | Science | | Social Studies | |
|---|---|---|---|---|---|---|---|---|
| | # | % | # | % | # | % | # | % |
| Grade 3 | | | | | | | | |
| Grade 4 | | | | | | | | |
| Grade 5 | | | | | | | | |
| Grade 6 | | | | | | | | |
| Grade 7 | | | | | | | | |
| Grade 8 | | | | | | | | |
| Grade 9 | | | | | | | | |
| Grade 10 | | | | | | | | |
| Grade 11 | | | | | | | | |
| Grade 12 | | | | | | | | |
| TOTALS | | | | | | | | |

At the school or district level, you may want to study the percentages of students who are at risk for failing classes by each of the four content areas. You may find there is a content area that has a greater percentage of at-risk learners than others — and you'll want to ask why.

# Disaggregation of Percentile Scores by Race/Ethnicity and Stanford 9 Subtests

| SAT 9 Subtests | Minority<br>Percentile Score | White<br>Percentile Score | Gap |
|---|---|---|---|
| Vocabulary | | | |
| Reading Comprehension | | | |
| Total Reading | | | |
| Pre-Writing | | | |
| Composing | | | |
| Editing | | | |
| Total Language | | | |
| Problem Solving | | | |
| Procedures | | | |
| Total Math | | | |
| Basic Battery | | | |
| Science | | | |
| Social Studies | | | |
| Total Battery | | | |

This is an example of disaggregation of norm-referenced test results by race/ethnicity. This is how you might set up a data table for the Stanford 9 subtests. (If you use a different norm-referenced test in your school or district, of course you would use the subtest information from those tests.

Consider shading the key tested areas as shown (i.e., total reading, total language, total math, basic battery, and total battery) to make the chart even easier to read.

# Disaggregation of Test Scores • 4-Year Trend by Race/Ethnicity and Stanford 9 Subtests

| SAT 9 Subtests | School Year | | | | | | | | | | | |
|---|---|---|---|---|---|---|---|---|---|---|---|---|
| | 1998-1999 | | | 1999-2000 | | | 2000-2001 | | | 2001-2002 | | |
| | M | W | Gap | M | W | Gap | M | W | Gap | M | W | Gap |
| Vocabulary | | | | | | | | | | | | |
| Reading Comprehension | | | | | | | | | | | | |
| Total Reading | | | | | | | | | | | | |
| Pre-Writing | | | | | | | | | | | | |
| Composing | | | | | | | | | | | | |
| Editing | | | | | | | | | | | | |
| Total Language | | | | | | | | | | | | |
| Problem Solving | | | | | | | | | | | | |
| Procedures | | | | | | | | | | | | |
| Total Math | | | | | | | | | | | | |
| Basic Battery | | | | | | | | | | | | |
| Science | | | | | | | | | | | | |
| Social Studies | | | | | | | | | | | | |
| Total Battery | | | | | | | | | | | | |

Trend data can be very useful — and while it's best to track the same group of students from one year to the next, your local school board will probably want to see your progress on a year-by-year basis. You'll most likely track norm-referenced test results for certain grade levels each year. If you are going to look at growth in student achievement from one year to the next, use the norm-referenced test's scaled scores and not the percentile scores.

# Percentages of Students in the Four Quartiles

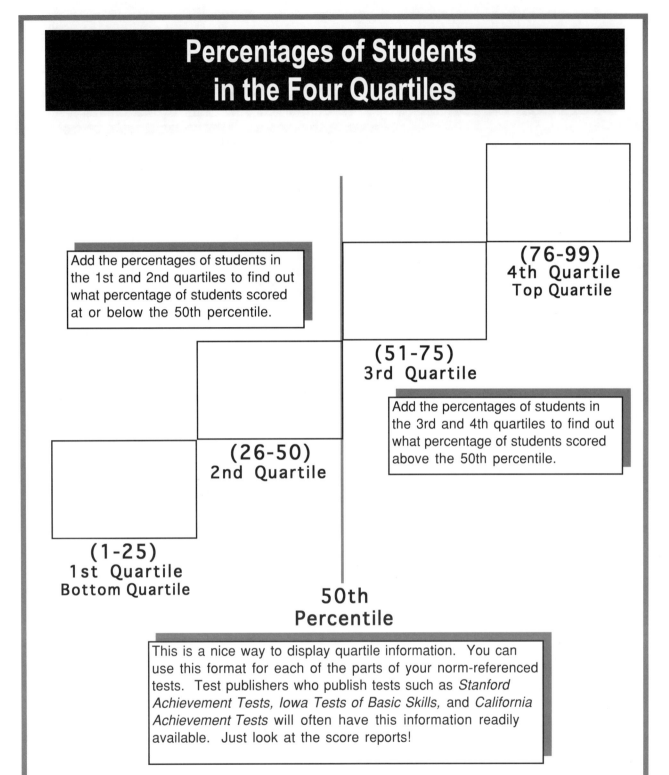

Add the percentages of students in the 1st and 2nd quartiles to find out what percentage of students scored at or below the 50th percentile.

(76-99)
4th Quartile
Top Quartile

(51-75)
3rd Quartile

Add the percentages of students in the 3rd and 4th quartiles to find out what percentage of students scored above the 50th percentile.

(26-50)
2nd Quartile

(1-25)
1st Quartile
Bottom Quartile

50th
Percentile

This is a nice way to display quartile information.  You can use this format for each of the parts of your norm-referenced tests.  Test publishers who publish tests such as *Stanford Achievement Tests, Iowa Tests of Basic Skills,* and *California Achievement Tests* will often have this information readily available.  Just look at the score reports!

# Stanford 9 Test Scores Disaggregated by Percentage of Students in Each Quartile and Race/Ethnicity

| | Minority | | White | | Gap |
|---|---|---|---|---|---|
| | # | % | # | % | |
| 4th Quartile (76-99) | | | | | |
| 3rd Quartile (51-75) | | | | | |
| 2nd Quartile (26-50) | | | | | |
| 1st Quartile (1-25) | | | | | |

The top half of this data organizer is shaded to let you quickly see what percentage of students scored above the 50th percentile.

| | | | | | |
|---|---|---|---|---|---|
| Totals | | | | | |

# Number and Percent of Students Who Passed/Failed Key State Tests by Test Area

| | Pass | | Fail | | Totals | |
|---|---|---|---|---|---|---|
| | # | % | # | % | # | % |
| 9-11 English Reading | | | | | | |
| 9-11 English Writing | | | | | | |
| Algebra I | | | | | | |
| Geometry | | | | | | |
| Algebra II | | | | | | |
| World History to 1000/Geog | | | | | | |
| World History From 1000/Geog | | | | | | |
| U.S. History | | | | | | |
| World Geography | | | | | | |
| Earth Science | | | | | | |
| Biology | | | | | | |
| Chemistry | | | | | | |

> You'll want to know what tests are given in your state. Put those tests in the left-hand column. You wouldn't put the norm-referenced tests such as the *Stanford Achievement Tests, Iowa Tests of Basic Skills,* or *California Achievement Tests* here since students don't pass or fail those tests.

# Content Area Analysis
## Standards Passed/Mastered
## by Varying Percentages of Students

| Percent of Students Passing | Standards/Objectives |
|---|---|
| **76-100%** | Place the standard numbers in this column. For example: Language Arts 2.01, 2.02, 2.03. Yyou don't need to write out the entire standard, although you certainly can. When you put a standard in this block you're saying that 76-100 percent of the students met the standard. |
| **51-75%** | You can do this school-level analysis by subject area (e.g., reading, writing, mathematics, science, social studies) or by grade levels — or both. How will you know if students have mastered the standards? Good classroom assessment comes into play here! |
| **26-50%** | |
| **0-25%** | |

# Classroom Analysis
## Standards Passed/Mastered
## by Varying Percentages of Students

| Percent of Students Passing | Standards/Objectives |
|---|---|
| **76-100%** | |
| **51-75%** | |
| **26-50%** | |
| **0-25%** | A classroom teacher can use this chart to determine what percentage of his or her students are mastering the learning targets or standards. (Do you already have some sort of monitoring system in place? If not, it's not too late to think about this.) |

# Listing of Students and State Tests Failed

| Student Names | Tested Area | | | | | | | | | | Total Tests Failed |
|---|---|---|---|---|---|---|---|---|---|---|---|
| 01. | | | | | | | | | | | |
| 02. | | | | | | | | | | | |
| 03. | | | | | | | | | | | |
| 04. | | | | | | | | | | | |
| 05. | | | | | | | | | | | |
| 06. | | | | | | | | | | | |
| 07. | | | | | | | | | | | |
| 08. | | | | | | | | | | | |
| 09. | | | | | | | | | | | |
| 10. | | | | | | | | | | | |
| 11. | | | | | | | | | | | |
| 12. | | | | | | | | | | | |
| 13. | | | | | | | | | | | |
| 14. | | | | | | | | | | | |
| 15. | | | | | | | | | | | |
| 16. | | | | | | | | | | | |
| 17. | | | | | | | | | | | |
| 18. | | | | | | | | | | | |
| 19. | | | | | | | | | | | |
| 20. | | | | | | | | | | | |

Many states have high-stakes tests — tests that have consequences for students, teachers, and/or schools. It's our professional responsibility to help every student be successful in school. Hence, we need to know who is not achieving — and help them.

# Percentage of Students Passing SOL Tests
## School, District, and State Comparison
## Grade 5

|  | Spring 98 | | | Spring 99 | | | Spring 00 | | |
|---|---|---|---|---|---|---|---|---|---|
|  | School | District | State | School | District | State | School | District | State |
| 5 English Reading |  |  |  |  |  |  |  |  |  |
| 5 English Writing |  |  |  |  |  |  |  |  |  |
| 5 Mathematics |  |  |  |  |  |  |  |  |  |
| 5 Science |  |  |  |  |  |  |  |  |  |
| 5 History/Social Science |  |  |  |  |  |  |  |  |  |
| 5 Computer Technology |  |  |  |  |  |  |  |  |  |

You'll probably want to track your school data and how it compares to the district and the state.

# Count of Students With Two or More Discipline Referrals

|  | Males | | Females | | TOTALS | |
|---|---|---|---|---|---|---|
|  | # | % | # | % | # | % |
| American Indian |  |  |  |  |  |  |
| Asian |  |  |  |  |  |  |
| Pacific Islander |  |  |  |  |  |  |
| Black |  |  |  |  |  |  |
| Hispanic |  |  |  |  |  |  |
| White |  |  |  |  |  |  |
| Total |  |  |  |  |  |  |

Student discipline is something many schools track. This disaggregated chart provides an overview of discipline referrals by race/ethnicity and gender. You can also design these by grade level and race/ethnicity — and you can track the type of discipline problem the students displayed (e.g., talking back, fighting).

# Designing a Frequency Chart or Table

A frequency chart is a data table that provides important information about the number of students who obtained each score or fall within each of the test's score intervals on a test. You put together a frequency chart to display where all of the students scored on the test. You'll get a picture of how many students scored high, low, and in between. And, you'll know how many students obtained each score on the test. You can construct a frequency chart for the scores on a classroom test, results of a state criterion-referenced test, and even a norm-referenced test, among other things.

To set up a frequency chart, you start with a set of scores.

## Set of Scores

| | | | | | |
|---|---|---|---|---|---|
| 98 | 100 | 90 | 99 | 91 | 90 |
| 76 | 89 | 87 | 91 | 88 | 92 |
| 100 | 96 | 82 | 93 | 90 | 86 |
| 81 | 82 | 94 | 84 | 78 | 80 |
| 82 | 86 | 91 | 80 | 81 | 97 |
| 95 | 90 | 81 | 91 | 84 | 88 |
| 71 | 91 | 85 | 89 | 92 | |
| 88 | 97 | 94 | 83 | 95 | |
| 90 | 93 | 90 | 92 | 89 | |
| 99 | 87 | 89 | 90 | 84 | |

Not much organization to this, is there? You can make this a more useful tool by setting up a frequency chart, which includes the following columns: Score, frequency, percent, cumulative percent. Look at the next page to see how a frequency chart would look for this set of data.

# Designing a Frequency Chart
# or Table, no. 2

Number of students who received the score

Percent of students who received the score

| Score | Frequency | Percent | Cumulative % |
|-------|-----------|---------|--------------|
| 100 | 2 | 3.57% | 3.57% |
| 99 | 2 | 3.57% | 7.14% |
| 98 | 1 | 1.79% | 8.93% |
| 97 | 2 | 3.57% | 12.50% |
| 96 | 1 | 1.79% | 14.29% |
| 95 | 2 | 3.57% | 17.86% |
| 94 | 2 | 3.57% | 21.43% |
| 93 | 2 | 3.57% | 25.00% |
| 92 | 3 | 5.36% | 30.36% |
| 91 | 5 | 8.93% | 39.29% |
| 90 | 7 | 12.50% | 51.79% |
| 89 | 4 | 7.14% | 58.93% |
| 88 | 3 | 5.36% | 64.29% |
| 87 | 2 | 3.57% | 67.86% |
| 86 | 2 | 3.57% | 71.43% |
| 85 | 1 | 1.79% | 73.21% |
| 84 | 3 | 5.36% | 78.57% |
| 83 | 1 | 1.79% | 80.36% |
| 82 | 3 | 5.36% | 85.71% |
| 81 | 3 | 5.36% | 91.07% |
| 80 | 2 | 3.57% | 94.64% |
| 78 | 1 | 1.79% | 96.43% |
| 76 | 1 | 1.79% | 98.21% |
| 71 | 1 | 1.79% | 100.00% |
| Totals | 56 | 100.00% | |

Approximately 52% of the students scored a 90 or above on this test.

Total number of students who took this test

So that's how you put together a frequency chart. Use these charts to look at how often something happens, how many students get a certain score, how many days students attended school, numbers of students suspended from school, and numbers of students scoring in different levels of domains of writing.

## Summary

Working with data tables will make the task of dealing with data much easier. Data tables help you organize your data for further manipulation and analysis. Even the visual display of data begins with a data table. Data tables help you look at overall achievement scores, provide you with a structure to disaggregate scores, and even help you look at process data that may be useful to you in improving student achievement.

# 6 Chapter Six
# Visual Tools for Data

Many states have criterion-referenced tests for their standards. When the scores from these tests are reported, often just in numbers — there may not be charts or graphs to go along with the score reports. One thing you can do with the data in order to help you analyze it is to create visual tools, such as charts and graphs, to get the best picture you can. Your brain loves shapes, patterns, and connections — and by creating visuals, you support your brain in its search for meaning. There are many types of visual tools you can use: statistical graphs, graphic organizers, charts and tables, time displays, flowcharts, and representational renderings of information. (Please refer to the one page overview of select visual tools on the next page.) Remember that while you use the visual tools to help you understand data, you'll also use many of these visual tools to communicate data to others — in such ways as reports and presentations.

The basic steps to creating any visual are easy. Just collect your data. Then organize your data into an appropriate visual tool. Of course, you'll need to know what types of data tables to organize and which charts and graphs are appropriate for analyzing and presenting data. I've included a quick overview of graphing formats, what the formats show, and examples of when you might use these graphing formats.

This chapter will provide you with some of the basics of designing high-impact visual tools — with an emphasis on a variety of graphs. This chapter is designed to be a resource chapter for designing visuals for your data.

# S•I•X

# Visual Tools

## Organizing, Analyzing, and Communicating Data

Visual tools can help you organize, analyze, and communicate data. According to *Business Presentations and Public Speaking,* (Engel, 1996), examples of visual tool categories include: statistical graphs, graphic organizers, charts and tables, time displays, process diagrams (flowcharts) and representations. The following chart provides examples in each of the visual tool categories.

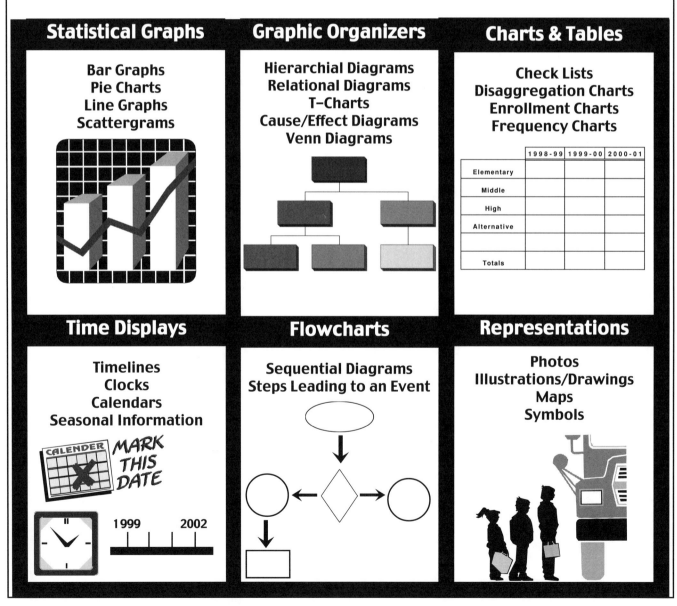

**Statistical Graphs**

Bar Graphs
Pie Charts
Line Graphs
Scattergrams

**Graphic Organizers**

Hierarchial Diagrams
Relational Diagrams
T–Charts
Cause/Effect Diagrams
Venn Diagrams

**Charts & Tables**

Check Lists
Disaggregation Charts
Enrollment Charts
Frequency Charts

|  | 1998-99 | 1999-00 | 2000-01 |
|---|---|---|---|
| Elementary |  |  |  |
| Middle |  |  |  |
| High |  |  |  |
| Alternative |  |  |  |
|  |  |  |  |
| Totals |  |  |  |

**Time Displays**

Timelines
Clocks
Calendars
Seasonal Information

CALENDER MARK THIS DATE

1999    2002

**Flowcharts**

Sequential Diagrams
Steps Leading to an Event

**Representations**

Photos
Illustrations/Drawings
Maps
Symbols

# Graphing Formats for Organizing and Analyzing Data

In this chapter, my examples focus on statistical charts, graphs, and tables. I've chosen eight different graphing formats: line graphs, pie charts, scatter diagrams, horizontal bar graphs, deviation bar graphs, stacked bar graph, pictographs, and box-and-whisker plots. On the following two pages, you'll find a quick overview of each of these graphing formats — what they show and example uses for each.

After that, you'll also find design ideas for a variety of graphs including bar graphs, stacked bar graphs, pie charts, line graphs, Pareto charts, paired scatter plots, and box-and-whisker plots.

# Graphing Formats for Organizing and Analyzing Data

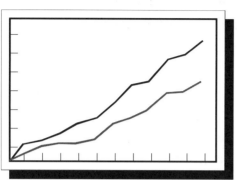

## Line Graph

- Shows series of numbers or change over time. A sloping segment represents the change. The steeper the slope, the greater the change. An upward slope is a positive change. A downward slope is a negative change.
- Examples: responses to questionnaires, attendance rates , school improvement plan target vs. actual achievement, enrollment.

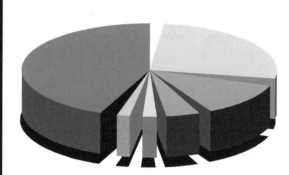

## Pie Chart

- Shows parts of the whole. Shows the size of each part as a percentage of the total.
- Examples: race/ethnicity percentages, gender percentages, budget percentages, quartile percentages, enrollment patterns, promotion and retention rates.

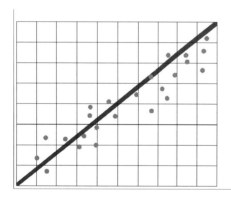

## Scatter Diagram

- Shows correlations and relationships.
- Examples: attendance and achievement, parent attitudes and student attitudes, minutes spent studying and grades in school, reading readiness tests and reading abilities, mobility index and test scores, school rubric and state rubric comparison.

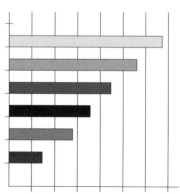

## Horizontal Bar Graph

- Shows ranking of items. Shows change over time. (Similar to a regular bar graph, except that the bars are horizontal rather than vertical.)
- Examples: enrollment patterns, discipline referrals, achievement test scores, mean scores from inservice evaluation, mean percentile scores from a norm-referenced test.

# Graphing Formats for Organizing and Analyzing Data

(continued)

## Deviation Bar Graph

- Shows the pluses and minuses; above and below.
- Examples: percentage of students passing/failing key tests, budget expenditures.

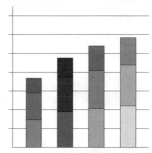

## Stacked Bar Graph

- Shows components that make up the total.
- Examples: quartile percentages, percentage of students passing/failing key tests, proficiency levels, ethnicity of students at various grade levels.

## Pictographs

- Shows data using representative pictures. A nice variance from the usual bar charts. (Audiences will appreciate the extra effort for creativity and imagination!)
- Examples: Use pictographs to show the same types of data you would with other graphs: enrollment patterns, transportation facts, favorite after-school sport, results of a science survey – and more.

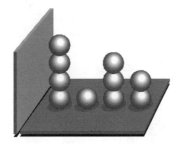

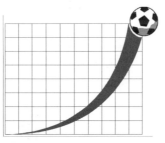

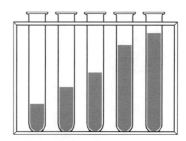

## Box-and-Whisker Plot

- Shows the distribution of scores in a data set – including the range of scores.
- Examples: classroom test results, norm-referenced test results, criterion-referenced test results.

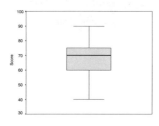

# Designing a Bar Graph

Constructing a good bar graph is easy. Just remember to include the important parts and your graphs will be professional and easy-to-use. The key parts of the graph include: a title, some sort of scale (based on the numbers or percents you're working with), labels for the vertical axis, and labels for the horizontal axis. The graph below is a vertical bar graph (the bars go up and down), but you could show the same information on a horizontal bar graph (the bars go across).

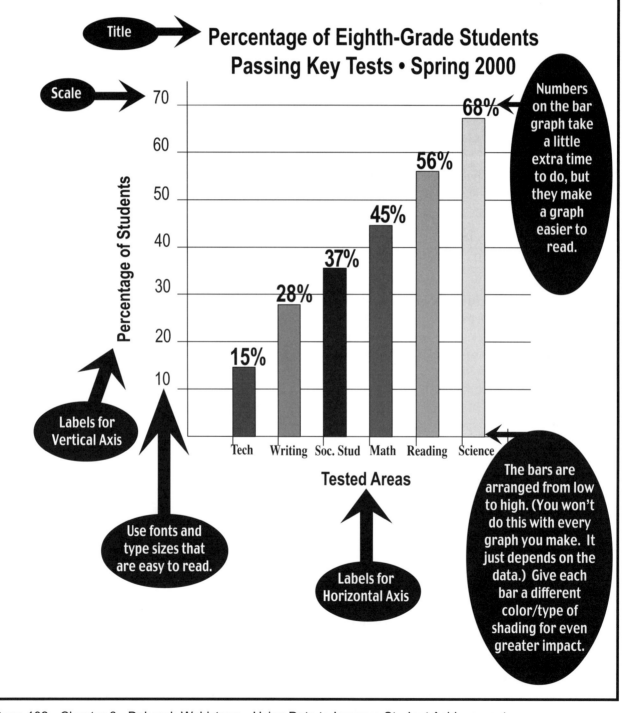

**Title** → Percentage of Eighth-Grade Students Passing Key Tests • Spring 2000

**Scale** →

Numbers on the bar graph take a little extra time to do, but they make a graph easier to read.

68%

56%

45%

37%

28%

15%

Percentage of Students

Labels for Vertical Axis

Use fonts and type sizes that are easy to read.

Tech   Writing   Soc. Stud   Math   Reading   Science

Tested Areas

Labels for Horizontal Axis

The bars are arranged from low to high. (You won't do this with every graph you make. It just depends on the data.) Give each bar a different color/type of shading for even greater impact.

# Designing a Stacked Bar Graph

A stacked bar graph is one that shows the percent of cases in a set of data so you can see how the percentages "stack up." A stacked bar graph may be horizontal, like the one below, or it may be vertical. The example below shows a stacked bar graph for the control levels for a state writing test. It's a good choice for this type of data because you can see the domains of writing (represented by the bars) and you can easily compare the percentages of students in each domain control level.

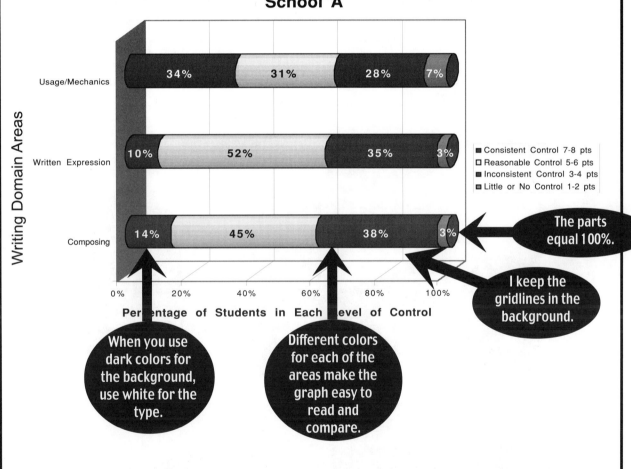

**Percent of Students Earning Each Domain Score**
**SOL Direct Writing Test • Spring 1998**
**School A**

The parts equal 100%.

I keep the gridlines in the background.

When you use dark colors for the background, use white for the type.

Different colors for each of the areas make the graph easy to read and compare.

# Designing a Pie Chart

A pie chart is a type of graph used to show the percentage of cases in a set of data. The circular shape gives the pie chart its name. It's easy to construct a good pie chart. Include the key components (e.g., title, wedge categories, percentages) and your pie charts will be professional and easy-to-use. In this example, an administrator had to respond to a school board request for class sizes in the school. The school board was studying the effects of class size on student achievement. The administrator was asked to divide the data into three class size ranges: 1-20 students, 21-26 students, and 27 or more students. The administrator created the following data table and corresponding pie chart.

| Elementary Class Size Characteristics | | |
|---|---|---|
| Class Size Range | Number | Percent |
| 1 - 2 0 | 1 9 6 | 2 7 % |
| 2 1 - 2 6 | 3 8 0 | 5 3 % |
| 27 or more | 1 4 4 | 2 0 % |
| TOTALS | 7 2 0 | 1 0 0 % |

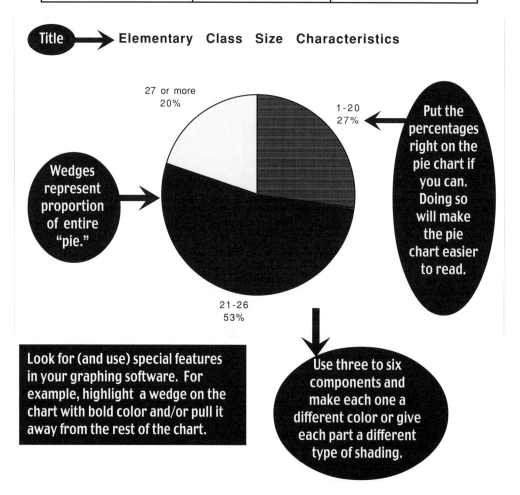

Title ➡ Elementary Class Size Characteristics

27 or more
20%

1-20
27%

Put the percentages right on the pie chart if you can. Doing so will make the pie chart easier to read.

Wedges represent proportion of entire "pie."

21-26
53%

Look for (and use) special features in your graphing software. For example, highlight a wedge on the chart with bold color and/or pull it away from the rest of the chart.

Use three to six components and make each one a different color or give each part a different type of shading.

# Designing a Line Chart

A line chart is a type of graph that lets you easily see trends in data over time. A principal wanted to compare the results of a literacy test over a four-year period. The test had three parts: reading, writing, and math. Since the state tracked the pass rates of students as part of the accountability process, the principal wanted to begin to track results very closely. She reviewed the passing rates for each of the tests over a four-year period and made the following data table.

### State Literacy Tests • 4-Year Trend

| Test Area | Percent Pass Rate By Year | | | |
|---|---|---|---|---|
| | 1998-1999 | 1999-2000 | 2000-2001 | 2001-2002 |
| Reading | 78 | 75 | 65 | 63 |
| Writing | 65 | 70 | 73 | 75 |
| Math | 87 | 92 | 87 | 90 |

The principal then constructed a line chart to make it easier to compare the data. The line chart is presented below. (Special note: Don't put too many lines on one graph — you'll drive everyone crazy!)

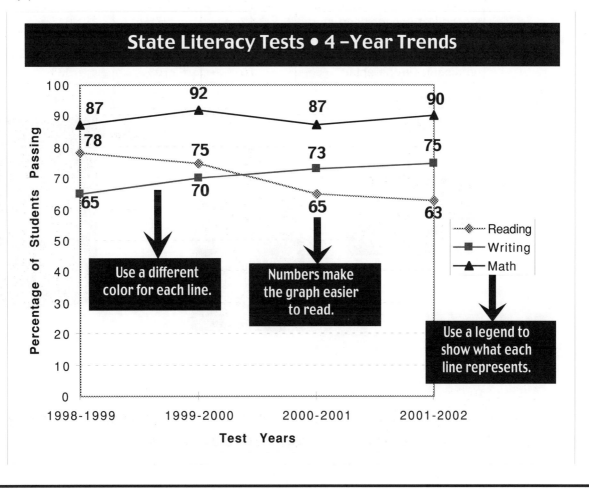

# Designing a Pareto Chart

A Pareto chart is a type of bar graph that makes it easy to analyze the frequency of a category or identify the relative importance of a number of different problems or solutions. Have you heard of the 80/20 rule? That's Mr. Pareto's rule — and he says that 80 percent of our problems come from 20 percent of the items. So if we can get a handle on what's creating the bulk of the problems, we can go after them first in our improvement efforts.

Let's say that you wanted to identify the reasons that students are late to school. You'd collect data during the semester to keep track of the reasons. There have been a total of 156 tardies at your school during the semester and the students give the reason for being late in one of five categories. You've tracked the information and are now ready to put your data into a data table, like the one shown below.

## Reasons Students Are Late to School

**Column Titles** ➔

| Category | Frequency | % of Total | Cumulative % |
|----------|-----------|------------|--------------|
| overslept | 58 | 37% | 37% |
| stopped at convenience store | 42 | 27% | 64% |
| late breakfast | 30 | 19% | 83% |
| argument with parents | 15 | 10% | 93% |
| finished homework | 11 | 7% | 100% |
| **TOTALS** | 156 | 100% | |

List categories in descending order, from highest frequency to lowest.

Count the number of times each reason was reported and list the number with the category.

Determine the percentage for each category. Just divide the number in the frequency column by 156 (total number of reasons) to get the percent.

The next step is to design a Pareto chart from the information in the data table. An example of how you might design your Pareto chart is presented on the next page.

# Designing a Pareto Chart, no. 2

You've collected your data, organized it into a data table, and now you'll construct a Pareto chart as a tool to help you analyze the data. Here's how to construct a Pareto chart. Notice that these types of bar graphs have both a left and right vertical axis. The left vertical axis shows the frequency counts and the right vertical axis shows what percentage of the totals those frequency counts represent.

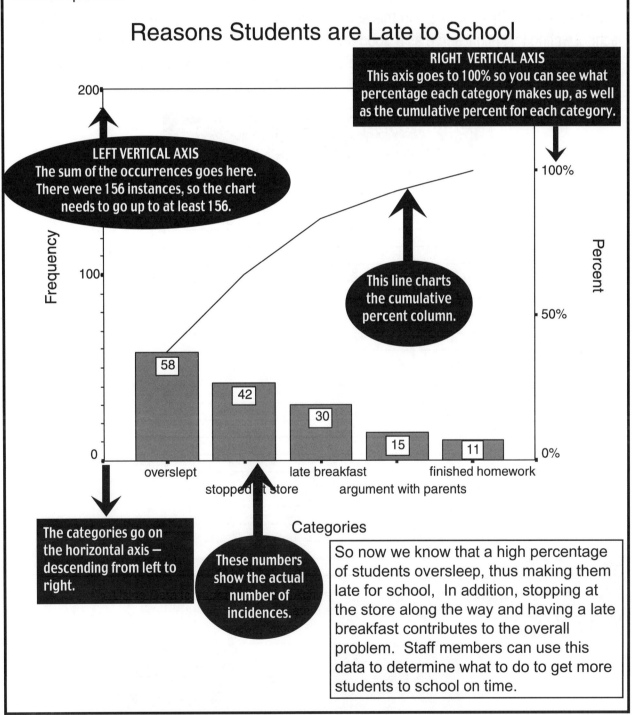

Reasons Students are Late to School

**RIGHT VERTICAL AXIS**
This axis goes to 100% so you can see what percentage each category makes up, as well as the cumulative percent for each category.

**LEFT VERTICAL AXIS**
The sum of the occurrences goes here. There were 156 instances, so the chart needs to go up to at least 156.

This line charts the cumulative percent column.

The categories go on the horizontal axis — descending from left to right.

These numbers show the actual number of incidences.

So now we know that a high percentage of students oversleep, thus making them late for school, In addition, stopping at the store along the way and having a late breakfast contributes to the overall problem. Staff members can use this data to determine what to do to get more students to school on time.

# Paired Scatter Plot

A Paired Scatter Plot lets you see whether there is a relationship between two variables. You could even call this an alignment grid, because it lets you see if there is indeed alignment between the two variables. The two variables in this example are the student scores for a school writing test and the student scores for a state writing test. Both of these tests were scored using rubrics. The school writing test and rubric were locally designed. The state writing test is scored using a commercially-designed rubric. In this scenario, a classroom teacher wanted to find out if the school writing test might serve as a good predictor for how students would do on a state writing test. Once she had the results for the school writing test and the state writing test, she constructed a data table. (Please note that the rubric scoring systems for the school and state rubrics are different.)

## Data Table for State and School Rubric Scores • Set 1

| Student | State Rubric | School Rubric 1 |
|---------|--------------|-----------------|
| 1 | 4 | 3 |
| 2 | 5 | 3 |
| 3 | 6 | 4 |
| 4 | 4 | 3 |
| 5 | 8 | 4 |
| 6 | 5 | 3 |
| 7 | 6 | 3 |
| 8 | 4 | 3 |
| 9 | 8 | 4 |
| 10 | 6 | 3 |
| 11 | 7 | 4 |
| 12 | 6 | 4 |
| 13 | 5 | 2 |
| 14 | 4 | 3 |
| 15 | 6 | 3 |
| 16 | 6 | 4 |
| 17 | 6 | 4 |
| 18 | 7 | 3 |
| 19 | 7 | 4 |
| 20 | 7 | 4 |
| 21 | 4 | 3 |
| 22 | 6 | 4 |
| 23 | 6 | 4 |
| 24 | 8 | 4 |

A total of 24 students took both of the writing tests.

The student scores for the state writing test.

The student scores for the school writing test.

# Paired Scatter Plot, no. 2

Because the teacher wanted to know whether there might be a relationship between the two tests, she plotted the scores on a scatter diagram (or scatter plot). Here are the visual results:

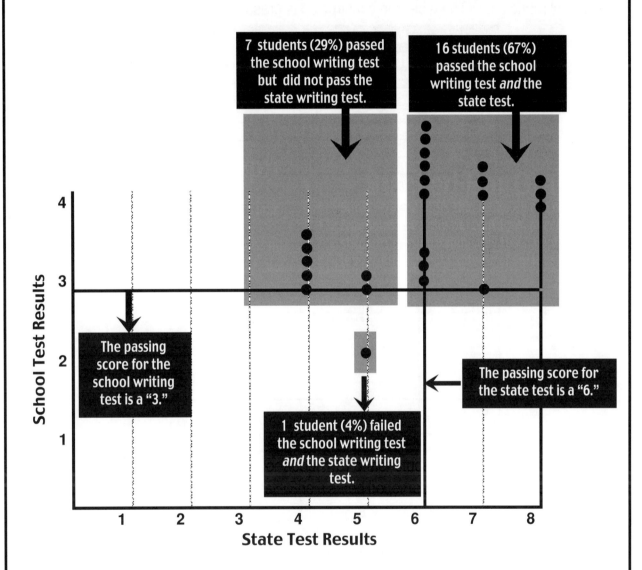

This teacher concluded that the school writing test was not a good predictor for success on the state test. She noted that 29 percent (or about 1/3) of her students passed the school writing test but did not pass the state writing test. She wanted better results than that. She decided to review information for the state test, including the state curriculum standards for writing, the state's test blueprint for writing, and the state's scoring rubric. In addition, this teacher decided to refine the local rubric to give it tighter alignment (stronger match) to the state rubric. After the students papers were scored with the refined rubric, the teacher constructed an updated data table and then made another scatter plot.

# Paired Scatter Plot, no. 3

Since a different set of scores was taken for the school rubric, this teacher had to create another simple data table. The teacher was still able to use the state rubric data, she just had to update the school rubric data. The table she constructed is presented below.

## Data Table for State and School Rubric Scores • Set 2

| Student | State Rubric | School Rubric 2 |
|---------|--------------|-----------------|
| 1 | 4 | 2 |
| 2 | 5 | 2 |
| 3 | 6 | 3 |
| 4 | 4 | 2 |
| 5 | 8 | 4 |
| 6 | 5 | 2 |
| 7 | 6 | 3 |
| 8 | 4 | 2 |
| 9 | 8 | 4 |
| 10 | 6 | 3 |
| 11 | 7 | 3 |
| 12 | 6 | 3 |
| 13 | 5 | 2 |
| 14 | 4 | 2 |
| 15 | 6 | 3 |
| 16 | 6 | 3 |
| 17 | 6 | 3 |
| 18 | 7 | 3 |
| 19 | 7 | 3 |
| 20 | 7 | 3 |
| 21 | 4 | 2 |
| 22 | 6 | 3 |
| 23 | 6 | 3 |
| 24 | 8 | 4 |

The results of the plotting on the scatter diagram are presented on the next page.

# Paired Scatter Plot, no. 4

Once again, the test scores for each of the 24 students were plotted to see if there was a relationship between the achievement results on the two tests. As soon as the teacher constructed this scatter plot, she knew she was on the right track with her scoring rubric. In every case in the scatter plot below, if a student failed the school test, that student also failed the state test. In addition, if a student passed the school test, he or she also passed the state test. This teacher knew that she could begin to rely on her own classroom writing assessments to determine how students might do on the state writing test.

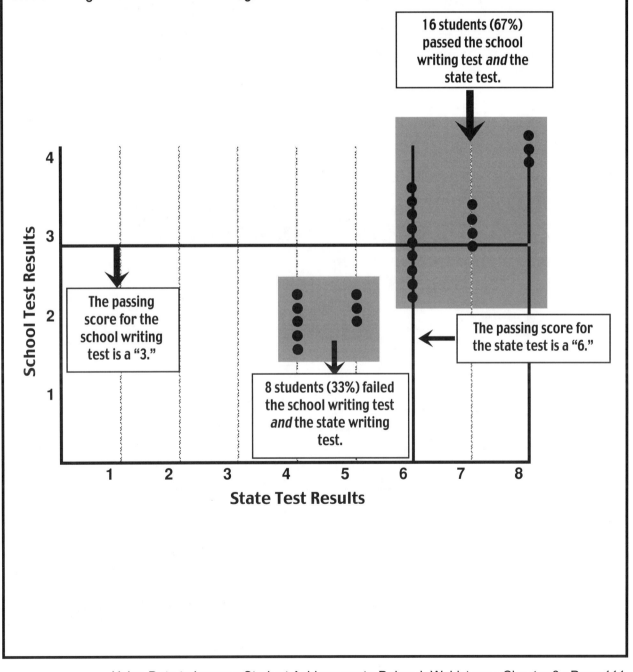

16 students (67%) passed the school writing test *and* the state test.

The passing score for the school writing test is a "3."

The passing score for the state test is a "6."

8 students (33%) failed the school writing test *and* the state writing test.

School Test Results

State Test Results

# Designing a Box-and-Whisker Plot

A box-and-whisker plot is another visual tool used to summarize and display a distribution of scores (Jaeger 1993). Box-and-whisker plots show the shape of the score distribution. But, before you can make a box-and-whisker plot, you must have your raw data. Here are the results of a test that one teacher gave in his classroom. The teacher made a quick data table to show the scores his students received.

## Student Scores on Classroom Test

| | | | |
|---|---|---|---|
| 40 | 60 | 50 | 40 |
| 70 | 75 | 80 | 70 |
| 60 | 40 | 65 | 55 |
| 70 | 85 | 75 | 70 |
| 65 | 75 | 90 | 75 |
| 75 | 70 | 75 | 80 |

He then constructed a frequency chart, a chart that includes the following categories: raw score, frequency, percent, and cumulative percent.

## Frequency Chart of Scores on Classroom Test

| Raw Score | Frequency | Percent | Cumulative % |
|---|---|---|---|
| 90 | 1 | 4.17% | 100.00% |
| 85 | 1 | 4.17% | 95.83% |
| 80 | 2 | 8.33% | 91.67% |
| 75 | 6 | 25.00% | 83.33% |
| 70 | 5 | 20.83% | 58.33% |
| 65 | 2 | 8.33% | 37.50% |
| 60 | 2 | 8.33% | 29.17% |
| 55 | 1 | 4.17% | 20.83% |
| 50 | 1 | 4.17% | 16.67% |
| 40 | 3 | 12.50% | 12.50% |
| TOTAL | 24 | 100.00% | |

We used 2 decimal places to the right, but you could just round off to the nearest percent.

# Designing a Box-and-Whisker Plot

From the data table, the teacher constructed a box-and-whisker plot to visually show how students performed on the assessment.

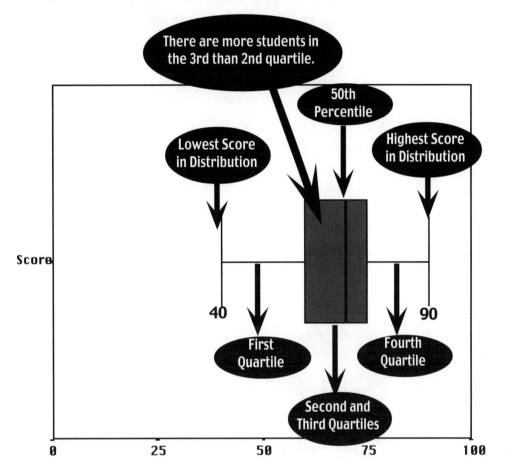

The lowest score obtained in this distribution (on this test) was 40. The highest score obtained was 90. The median score, where half the scores are above and half are below the 50th percentile, is at about 68. Half of the students in this class scored 68 or above. Half the students scored below 68. (As a teacher, I probably wouldn't be thrilled that one-half of my students scored below 68.)

Let's review a couple of features of the box-and-whisker plot. The horizontal lines that extend out from the box are called the whiskers. The length of the whiskers may be different depending on the scores. The whisker on the left shows the score range of 25 percent of the scores — in this case, 40 to about 60. This whisker is the first quartile. The whisker on the right shows that the students who earned the top 25 percent of the scores were in the score range of 76-90. This is the fourth quartile. The box in the middle shows the score range of half of the students in the class — in this case, the scores range from about 61 to 75.

# Using a Box-and-Whisker Plot to Compare Results of Test Scores for Four Classes

The vertical line through the center of the box shows the score value that divides the score distribution exactly in half. In other words, half the scores fall below this value and half the scores fall above. The box holds the scores for the second and third quartiles.

Now, take this one step further and use the box-and-whisker plot to visually show and compare results for several classes.

The box-and-whisker plot can provide a nice visual display of data, making it easy to analyze. The box-and-whisker plot below shows the results of four classes of students on a test. Notice how quickly you can compare the ranges of the test as well as the 50th percentile score for the test. (Also note, that box-and-whisker plots can be designed so the information is displayed horizontally or vertically.)

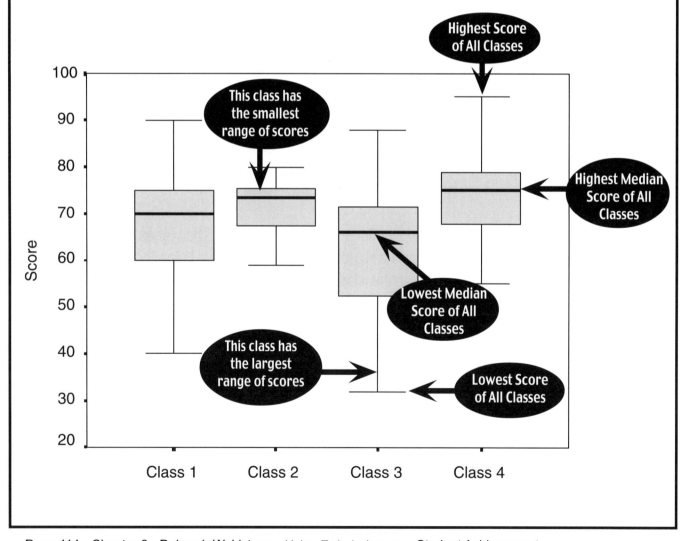

Now, are these all of the charts and graphs you'll ever need to use in your life? Certainly not, but I hope I've provided some of the key visual tools for analyzing data. Do remember that whether you're making data tables, charts, or graphs, there are some basic principles to constructing high-impact visuals.

1.  Include a title for each chart and graph. Work with the title until it describes exactly what is on the chart or graph.

2.  On a chart or table, include row descriptors and column headers. Use shading to highlight important parts of the chart or table.

3.  For graphs, include the numerical scale. Add data labels (the numbers) to graphs to make analysis quicker and easier. Label the horizontal and vertical axis and use font types and sizes that are easy to read.

4.  Provide basic information such as school name, district name, location, grade level(s), test(s) given, date(s) given, etc.

After you've designed your high-impact visuals, you'll want to spend time thinking about their meanings. The next chapter provides quick lists of key analysis questions to help you think about and understand your data.

# 7 Chapter Seven
# Analysis Questions

Before I begin this chapter, I want you to know that this is one of my favorite parts of the book. I think it begins to get at the essence of using data to improve student achievement. In working with hundreds of school improvement teams, I often hear the question, "How do we begin to analyze our data?" Assuming you will have that same question, I've included some questions that will help you focus on the analysis of your data. If you've ever looked at a chart or graph and then wondered what you're supposed to learn from it, you'll love this chapter, too!

I've designed analysis questions to help you with the important process of analyzing and asking the hard questions about your data. I like to organize most of the data I work with by content area — since in reality, that's where the accountability emphasis usually falls. Academic achievement is usually a strong focus for school improvement teams — and if it's not, it should be.

In this chapter, you'll find a variety of areas for which I have included data and factors to analyze. When you're looking at the questions under *Data to Analyze*, you'll see questions that give you an idea of what kinds of data to collect and what types of charts and graphs might be helpful for analysis. You'll get ideas for the types of outcome and demographic data you may want to collect. When looking at the questions under *Factors to Analyze*, you'll find questions that can serve as a springboard for discussion and reflection — questions that will lead you to figuring out what needs to be improved. Remember, the numbers don't tell you what to work on, they just indicate a need for improvement. The factors give you an idea of what to think about to bring improvement. The factors also remind you what process data you might want to think about.

The graphic organizer on the next page provides an overview of using the *Data Analysis Questions* and *Factors to Analyze* to get focused and think deep. You may want to quickly review the graphic organizer to get the big picture of how this chapter is organized.

You now have the big picture of the *Data Analysis Questions* and *Factors to Analyze.* But to what do you apply these? Actually, you can apply them to just about anything you're studying in your school or district. You can use these with state, district, and classroom assessments, special demographics (e.g., attendance, student dropouts, mobility), special programs (e.g., special education, gifted and talented, Title I), and curriculum (e.g., writing, science). I've included a number of areas, just to get you started:

> State Criterion-Referenced Tests (CRT)
> State Norm-Referenced Tests (NRT)
> Student Dropouts
> Attendance
> Student Mobility
> Paper/Pencil Tests
> Performance Tests
> Curriculum
> Writing
> Science
> Title I
> Special Education (does not include Factors to Analyze)
> Gifted and Talented (does not include Factors to Analyze)

I've designed this so that the *Data Analysis Questions* and the *Factors to Analyze* both have their own page for each study area. I hope you'll use these to guide your data collection and your thoughtful analysis of areas you are studying. Don't forget to add your own analysis questions to the lists.

# Getting Focused and Thinking Deep

↓

## Area of Analysis

**(e.g., writing, reading, state norm-referenced tests, state criterion-referenced tests, Title I, dropouts, gifted and talented)**

### Data Analysis Questions

What data might we want to study?

Provides guidance in what kinds of data to collect, organize, analyze, and use. (Includes outcome and demographic data.)

### Factors to Analyze

What questions might we like to ask?

Provides guidance in talking about factors that can lead to change. (Includes process data.)

# Data Analysis Questions
## State CRT

1.   What is the school score for each test (e.g., reading, writing, math, science, social studies) and each subtest (e.g., computation, problem solving) on the state test? Is there **quality** in student achievement?

2.   How do our scores compare to the scores for the school district? The state? How do the scores compare to where we want to be?

3.   In which subtests within each content area did students perform worst? Best? Can we even tell?

4.   How did our students do on each domain of the writing test? (Examples of domains are composing, written expression, and mechanics.) In which part of the direct writing test did we do best? Worst?

5.   What is the pass rate of the students in our school for each of the content areas? How does this compare from year to year? How does our pass rate compare to our district? The state? How does our pass rate compare to where we want to be?

6.   How well do our students do on the state tests? Are we barely making it? Strong results? Stellar results? How do the percentages of students in each range compare from year to year? Does a greater percentage of students achieve in the advanced range each year? Is a greater percentage of students in the upper part of the proficient range?

7.   Are subgroups of students (e.g., race/ethnicity, gender, SES) performing at similar levels on the state tests? Are there differences in achievement between groups of students? Is there **equity** in student achievement on the state tests?

8.   What percentage of students obtained verified credits in key courses such as Algebra I, Algebra II, Geometry, Biology, Chemistry, Earth Science, U.S. History, World History, and English? How does this compare from year to year? (Some states, like Virginia, use the state test to verify achievement in a course.)

# Factors to Analyze
# State CRT

1. Do we have the materials needed to teach concepts measured by the state tests (especially for the subtests or reporting categories where we may not have done well)? Are these materials tightly aligned with the state's standards? If not, are we reviewing materials and making recommendations for the upcoming budget? What is the quality and currency of the textbooks and other instructional materials?

2. Did we have (or make) enough time to teach concepts in the standards? Did students have enough time to learn the standards? How was our time allocated across subject areas? Was the time allocated to each concept proportional to the weighted value?

3. Were the assessment blueprints/test specifications readily available to all teachers? Did teachers have time to become familiar with the information in the blueprints?

4. Were all the standards taught before the state tests were given? Are we teaching all  the standards?

5. Were students familiar with the format of the state assessments (as noted in the assessment blueprints)? Were teachers familiar with the testing format?

6. How was class time used? How much time is spent in lecture, laboratory settings, problem solving, critical thinking, research, writing, groupwork, projects, or other learning strategies? What kinds of tasks were students asked to do? Did students complete the type of work that leads to learning the different standards?

7. Was there a need for training in strategies that are useful in teaching and learning the standards? Did we know what teaching strategies to use to help students learn different standards? Did we know how to teach students effective learning strategies?

8. Is there a need for training in ways to assess the standards in the classroom? Is the picture of what a standard looks like when a student is achieving it clear? Did we know when a student has achieved the standards?

9. Did we do everything possible to make the testing experience good for our students? Did we let them take the test in a comfortable environment? Did we allow them to stay in one place during the entire testing period? Did we let students take the test with teachers they are familiar with? Did we keep the testing groups small — such as in a regular class size?

10. Did we (and do we all year long for other tests) talk with students about test anxiety, test motivation, and test wiseness? If not, what can we do for the upcoming school year to address these three factors that can make a difference in student scores?

11. Did we know which specific students are not meeting the standards? What assistance do we provide to these individual students?

# Data Analysis Questions
## State NRT

1. How do our students perform on the state's norm-referenced achievement test? How does this compare to how we've achieved in previous years? Is there **quality** in student achievement on this assessment?

2. How do students perform at various grade levels? Do students perform better at some grade levels than at others?

3. In a cohort (group) of students over time, does achievement increase? Decrease? Remain the same?

4. Are there any differences in achievement between different groups of students (i.e., differences between race/ethnicity, gender, SES)? Is there **equity** in student achievement on this assessment?

5. In which subtests did students perform best?

6. In which subtests did students perform worst?

7. What percentage of students scored in each quartile? How does this compare to previous years?

# Factors to Analyze
# State NRT

1.  Were students familiar with the testing format? Were teachers familiar with the testing format?
2.  Have students been taught the basics of taking a test including the basic strategies that will help them with any test given during their lives.
3.  Did we do everything possible to make the testing experience good for our students? Did we let them take the test in a comfortable environment? Did we let students take the test with teachers they know? Did we keep the testing groups small — such as a regular class size?
4.  Did we (and do we all year long) talk with students about test anxiety, test motivation, and test wiseness? If not, what can we be doing for the upcoming school year to address these three factors that can affect student scores?
5.  Have we reviewed the materials that are published with the norm-referenced tests — materials that help us become more comfortable with the test?
6.  Have we reviewed the alignment between our state standards and the norm-referenced test?
7.  Have we verified the alignment between the curriculum and the skills measured by the state's norm-referenced test? (If your state uses your norm-referenced test as part of your school and/or district accountability, this verification is critical.)

# Data Analysis Questions
# Student Dropouts

1. What is the dropout pattern in our school/district?
2. What is the trend of dropouts over the past 3-5 years at the middle and high school levels? Has the dropout rate decreased? Increased? Stayed the same?
3. What do these patterns look like when disaggregated by race/ethnicity, gender, and SES?
4. What is the dropout pattern of different schools in the division?
5. How does the dropout pattern of our school compare to that of the district? The state?
6. Is there a grade level that has a higher percentage of students dropping out?
7. What are the achievement levels of students who drop out of school? What are their grades? How do they perform on norm-referenced tests? How do they perform on criterion-referenced tests?
8. What are the attendance patterns of students who drop out of school?
9. What are the discipline patterns of students who drop out of school?
10. What are the legal patterns (i.e., arrests) of students who drop out of school?
11. What percentage of students are 2 or more years over-age in the fourth grade? What percentage of students are 2 or more years over-age in the eighth grade?
12. What is the self-concept of students in our school?
13. What characteristics (Hale, 1992) are held by our dropouts? Frequent academic failure? Reading difficulty? Little or no interest in school? No participation in extra-curricular activities? Excessive absenteeism? Disruptive school behavior? Two or more years behind grade level? Low socioeconomic status? Teenage pregnancies? Race/ethnicity, social, or language minority status?

# Factors to Analyze
# Student Dropouts

1. What are the primary goals of our dropout prevention programs?
2. What activities do we include in our dropout prevention program? Have we included activities that will lead to increased student achievement? How do we know?
3. What are our intervention programs? Are they effective?
4. What counseling services are provided to students who are at risk for dropping out of school? Do we have an effective system to provide ongoing, rather than one time, services to these students?
5. What attitudes do our high school students have toward school?
6. Do we have mentor relationships (such as relationships between counselors and students) for students at-risk for dropping out of school?
7. Are there any partnerships between the community and programs that serve students who are at-risk for dropping out of school?
8. Do we have an effective system/method for identifying potential dropouts?
9. Do we have a system for involving parents of potential dropout students in providing assistance to students?
10. Do we have a plan for promoting attendance? How effective is our plan?

# Data Analysis Questions
## Attendance

1. What is the attendance rate for the school? How have attendance patterns changed over the years?

2. What are the differences in student attendance when disaggregated, if appropriate, by race/ethnicity, gender, and SES?

3. What days of the week are students most often absent? What days does the attendance rate go up or down? What are the trends by year, quarter, month, week, or fractions of a day? Are there any cyclical or seasonal variations?

4. At what times during the year does the attendance rate go up or down?

5. What percentage of students miss 11 or more days of school? Who are these students?

6. How does the school's attendance rate compare to the district's? The state's? The nation's?

7. Are there grade level differences in attendance patterns? Are there school differences in attendance patterns?

8. What is the school's promotion rate?

9. How do promotion rates and attendance rates compare? Which students are promoted? Those students with better attendance rates?

10. What percent of absences are excused? What are the reasons for student absences?

11. What is the tardy rate? Are the trends for tardiness and absences similar?

12. What is the dropout rate (if a high school)? What have been the attendance patterns for students who choose to drop out of school?

13. What percent of the absences are due to chronic truants? How does the attendance rate of the student population look when comparing chronic truants to the other students in the school?

$$\text{Attendance Rate} = \frac{\text{Actual Student Attendance}}{\text{Possible Student Attendance}} \times 100$$

# Factors to Analyze
# Attendance

1. What reasons do students give for being absent?

2. What programs are in place in the school to promote attendance? Are these programs working? Are other things needed?

3. What are the attitudes of our students toward school?

4. What services are in place to help students who have attendance problems? What are our intervention programs? Are they effective?

5. What programs are in place to help parents understand the importance of attendance? Are these programs effective?

# Data Analysis Questions
# Student Mobility

1. What is the mobility rate/index for the school?
2. Has the mobility rate changed over time?
3. What are the differences in student mobility when disaggregated by race/ethnicity, gender, and SES?
4. How does the student mobility rate or index compare to that of the school district? The state? The nation?
5. What percentage of students have been in the school since the first day of school? What percentage of students are in the school from the entering grade level (e.g., kindergarten) to the exiting grade level (e.g., grade 5)?
6. What are the differences in achievement between students who have been in the school since the first day of school and those students who moved in during the school year? ( Examples of achievement measures include the state's norm-referenced and criterion-referenced tests.)
7. What are the differences in disruptive behavior (e.g., suspensions, detentions) between students who have been in the school since the first day and those who moved in during the school year?

**School Mobility Index =** $\dfrac{\text{Students entering the school after the beginning of the school year} + \text{students withdrawing from school}}{\text{average daily membership}}$

This is one formula for school mobility. Your district or state may use another, and, if so, you'll want to use that.

# Factors to Analyze
# Student Mobility

1.  What are some of the consequences of students' frequently changing schools?  Are there problems with learning the school, district, or state standards?  Do students feel alienated?

2.  What are the challenges to teachers in dealing with a highly mobile population?  Is it more difficult to meet the academic and social needs of students?

3.  What processes are in place in the school to ensure that new students are positively acclimated to the school?

4.  What factors create the mobility rate?  Is there a high percentage of military students?  Is there a high percentage of students who move from one household to the next during the school year?  Does the school serve a transient population?  Is economic development bringing many new families to the community?

5.  How are teachers being supported in dealing with high mobility rates?

# Data Analysis Questions
# Paper/Pencil Tests

1.    How many students took the classroom achievement test?

2.    What are the characteristics (e.g., race/ethnicity, gender) of the students who took the test?

3.    What was the achievement level of students on this test? What percentage of students passed? What percentage of students failed? Is there **quality** in student achievement on this test?

4.    Did students consistently perform poorly on any of the test questions?

5.    Did students consistently perform well on any of the test questions?

6.    Were there any differences in how different classes (e.g., 4th period vs. 5th period) performed?

7.    Were there any differences in achievement disaggregated by student characteristics of race/ethnicity, gender (when appropriate to disaggregate)?

8.    How did the overall performance of students on this test compare to performance on other tests given in the course?

9.    What is the relationship between student results on classroom tests (grades) and passing the state's criterion-referenced test?

10.    What percentage of students got each question right? (For some test items, this tells you how easy or difficult each question was —generally, the higher the percentage, the easier the item. But the percentage of students getting a question right can also show how many students are learning the standards.)

# Factors to Analyze
# Paper/Pencil Tests

1. Does the classroom test appropriately measure the standards it was designed to measure? Was a paper/pencil test appropriate for the standards students were to learn? Was the test effective for determining this? Do the results of this test tell when a student has met the state/district standards?

2. Was the paper/pencil test of high quality and constructed well? Was it free of general flaws?

3. Did the test measure higher-level thinking and not just recall?

4. Where appropriate, did the test provide format practice for the state test (e.g., number of responses, placement of visuals)?

5. Where appropriate, did the testing conditions support that of the state test (e.g., calculators permitted, formula sheets, scratch paper)?

6. Overall, how did students respond to the test? What was their reaction? Did they think it was fair? Too long?

7. Can the test be used as a diagnostic tool as well as a tool for feedback? Did the test help guide students toward areas of needed improvement?

8. Are tests scored in a timely manner — so the results can be used with students for feedback and diagnosis?

# Data Analysis Questions
# Performance Tests

1.  Overall, how well did students achieve on the performance-based assessment? What percentage of students scored at the highest range? The mid range? The low range?
2.  On which parts of the assessment did students score best? Worst?
3.  What is the mean score for the entire class on the assessment? Is there **quality** in student achievement on this test?
4.  What number and percentage of the students met the level of expectation for the performance test?
5.  Were there any differences in how different classes (e.g., 4th period vs. 5th period) performed?
6.  Were there any differences in achievement disaggregated by student characteristics of race/ethnicity, gender or SES (when appropriate to disaggregate)? Was there **equity** on this test?
7.  How did the overall performance on this assessment compare to other types of assessments given in the course?
8.  What is the relationship between student results on this assessment and on similar tests administered by the state?

# Factors to Analyze
# Performance Tests

1. Were the learning targets clear? How do we know whether individual students are achieving the standards?
2. Was the rubric or assessment checklist clear and concise? Were students taught to use the rubric as a tool to analyze the quality of their own work? Was the rubric used as an instructional tool to help students in learning the standards?
3. Did the students have appropriate time to learn the standards measured by the performance assessment?
4. Were the materials and resources necessary for success available?
5. Does the assessment also serve as a diagnostic tool? Can the results noted in the rubric be used to guide students about what they need to do better next time?
6. Was the assessment aligned to state standards?
7. Is there a plan about what to do to help students who did not perform well on the assessments? Do students have a part in setting their own learning goals?
8. Are the assessments scored in a timely manner to ensure the results are available for feedback on achievement and diagnosis? Will students who need it be given additional time to learn the standards?
9. Did the performance assessment appropriately measure the standards it was designed to measure? Was the assessment task effective for doing this? Was the performance assessment tightly aligned to the state standards?

# Data Analysis Questions
## Curriculum

1. What is the quality of our curriculum guides by grade level and content area? What is the mean rating for each of our guides?

2. What number/percentage of objectives are there for each grade level and content area?

3. What percentage of the district curriculum is aligned to state standards? (The district curriculum may meet *and* exceed state standards.)

4. What percentage of the state standards are supported by the district/school curriculum?

5. What percentage of time does central office staff spend monitoring the curriculum?

6. What percentage of time does the principal and his or her assistants spend monitoring the curriculum?

7. What percentage of key instructional materials, such as the textbook, are tightly aligned to the district's curriculum?

8. What are the results of teacher feedback sheets related to the units in the curriculum guide?

9. What percentage of the curriculum is "fair game" for state tests?

10. What are the results of pacing guides? Do they provide on-target suggestions for helping students learn the standards?

11. What is the performance level of students on tests that accompany the curriculum?

# Factors to Analyze
# Curriculum

1. Do we have high academic standards for all the students we serve? Are the high academic standards clearly outlined in our curriculum guides?
2. Are the curriculum guides effective for communicating the standards to teachers?
3. How often is the curriculum reviewed and refined? Who makes suggestions for the revisions? What is the process for reviewing and refining the curriculum?
4. Are there enough objectives for students to learn the standards? Are there too many — so many that you couldn't possibly have time to teach them all?
5. Are the standards/objectives presented clearly and concisely? Is all that is embedded in the standards evident to the teachers — both the specific content and the processes that students are to learn?
6. What role does central office play in the implementation of the curriculum?
7. What methods are used to monitor the curriculum?
8. Do each of the guides include pacing guidelines and suggestions? Are these guidelines realistic with the standards and the time to teach them?
9. Does each guide include suggestions for assessment of the standards?
10. Does each guide provide connections to instructional materials and resources?
11. Does the guide provide clear direction about how to use the textbook? Does it indicate which chapters or sections are aligned to the standards?
12. Is professional development training provided to help teachers with the content in the curriculum guide? Does this training reflect standards-based instruction and assessment for the content area?
13. Have we constructed a curriculum map for each of the content areas we teach?
14. Have we talked about how to integrate the curriculum? Do we want to try this?
15. How do we communicate the curriculum to teachers? How do we communicate the curriculum to students and parents? Are our communication methods effective? What is the evidence of effectively communicating the curriculum to others?

# Data Analysis Questions
# Writing

1. How well do our students write on school writing tests? On state writing tests? Is there **quality** in student writing?

2. Are there differences in achievement between groups of students (e.g., race/ethnicity, gender)? Is there **equity** in student achievement in writing?

3. How does student achievement in writing compare among grade levels?

4. What percentage of students passed the state writing test? What percentage failed? How does this compare from year to year? Is there an increase? A decrease? Does the percentage stay the same?

5. What percentage of students passed the district's writing test? What percentage failed?

6. What percentage of students were in the proficient range? What percentage were in the advanced range?

7. In which domains of writing were students strongest? Weakest?

8. What percentage of our students enjoy writing?

9. What percentage of our teachers have been trained in the development and use of scoring rubrics and anchor papers for writing?

10. What is the relationship between the percentage of students who passed the school/district writing test and those who passed the state writing test?

11. What percentage of students received verified credits for English writing. (For example, in Virginia, a verified credit is defined as one in which a student has passed the high school English class plus the state's end-of-course assessment.)

# Factors to Analyze
# Writing

1. What are we already doing that supports the learning of writing skills?
2. What professional development offerings have we provided to help teachers teach writing better? What type of training have we provided? Have we provided training in the writing process for our teachers?
3. What effective teaching strategies do we regularly use to help students become good writers? Are these strategies aligned to our writing standards?
4. What makes the students in our top-scoring class write better than others?
5. Are our school/district writing objectives aligned to the state tests?
6. How have we paced our writing program? Do we have some sort of plan for teaching writing — such as a curriculum map? Have we thought about how we may want to integrate writing throughout the subject areas?
7. How would we describe our writing program to others?
8. Do we have a school writing rubric? Is it aligned to the district and state tests?
9. What resources do we have available for writing? Do we use what is available? Are there other resources we need?
10. Do our teachers like to teach writing?
11. What resources do we regularly use in our writing program?
12. Do we support writing with technology? If so, how? Do our students regularly use computers to produce a variety of writing?
13. What student evidences (e.g., assessments, products) do we have that the state and district objectives/standards are being taught?
14. What student evidences do we have that the state and district objectives/standards are being learned? If we don't currently have evidences in place, are we working on them?
15. In what ways do we support writing in the content areas?
16. What training (graduate or otherwise) do our teachers report they have had in the area of writing? What training (graduate or otherwise) do our teachers report they need in the area of writing? Do we have a plan for ensuring that teachers get the training they need?
17. Did we make enough time to teach writing? Did we give students enough time and experiences to learn to write effectively?
18. What support is provided to students who are struggling with writing? Is that support effective?
19. What percentage of time do students spend writing?

# Data Analysis Questions
# Science

1. What is the school mean score for the state science test and each reporting category/subtest on the test? Is there **quality** in student achievement?

2. How do our scores compare to the scores for the school division? The state?

3. In which science reporting categories did students perform worst? Best?

4. What is the pass rate of the students in our school for each of the science tests (i.e., 3rd grade, 5th grade, 8th grade, Earth Science, Biology, Chemistry)? How does this compare from year to year? How does the pass rate for each test compare to our district? The state?

5. How well do our students do on the state tests for science? Where are they in the proficient range? The advanced range? Are we barely making it? Strong results? Stellar results?

6. Are subgroups of students (e.g., race/ethnicity, gender, SES) performing at similar levels on the state science tests? Are there differences in achievement between groups of students? Is there **equity** in student achievement?

7. What are the enrollment patterns, including minority patterns, for students in science classes? How has the pattern changed over the years?

8. What percentage of our students score 3 or higher on science AP exams? Are subgroups of students (e.g., race/ethnicity, gender, SES) performing at similar levels on the AP exams?

9. What percentage of students are successful completers (i.e., grade of A, B, or C) in science classes? What percentage of students are not successful completers?

10. What percentage of minority students take advanced science classes? What has the percentage of students taking advanced science classes been over the past 3-5 years? What percentage of minority students take advanced science classes?

# Factors to Analyze
# Science

1. Is enough time spent on scientific investigation? Generally, do students have time to learn all the science standards?

2. Do our classrooms reflect student-centered, hands-on, minds-on teaching and learning? What are our evidences of this?

3. Are our classroom assessments aligned with the science standards? Do we have a comprehensive assessment program that provides a variety of assessment tools?

4. What steps do we take to ensure students register for science classes?

5. What is the district policy for science classes? What does the state require for graduation? Do we meet or exceed the requirements of the state?

6. Do we have the supplies and materials needed to teach the science curriculum? Are the supplies and materials organized so we can readily check them out and use them? Do we have a budget for consumable supplies? Do we know what to do with the supplies and materials that are available?

7. Has the textbook been reviewed to determine which parts of it support the teaching/learning of the district and state standards? Have we determined the alignment of the textbook to the district and state curriculum?

8. Have we talked about how we might structure our schedules and teaching to support the science standards? Does it make sense for us to team-teach?

9. At the elementary level, do we want to consider a science lab room?

10. Do we make use of computer simulation software in lieu of or complimentary to science labs?

11. What support is provided to students who are struggling in science? Is that support effective?

12. Are there areas in the science curriculum where additional teacher training is needed?

13. What programs are in place for parents, guardians, or caregivers to help them understand the science curriculum?

# Data Analysis Questions

# Title I

1. What percentage of our students receive Title I services?
2. What is the Title I enrollment trend over the past 3-5 years by grade level?
3. What is the Title I enrollment trend over the past 3-5 years at each organizational level (i.e., elementary, middle, high)?
4. What are the characteristics of our Title I students? What is the enrollment pattern over the past 3-5 years, disaggregated by student demographic characteristics of gender and race/ethnicity?
5. What is the enrollment pattern of the Title I program by school? How many and what percentage of students are served at each school?
6. How many and what percentage of teachers work as part of the Title I program?
7. What are the demographic characteristics (e.g., race/ethnicity, gender) of the Title I teaching staff?
8. What are the achievement results of students in the Title I program? How do the Title I students perform on the norm-referenced achievement tests?
9. How do students at different grade levels in Title I perform on norm-referenced achievement tests?
10. Are there any differences in achievement between different groups of students (e.g., race/ethnicity, gender) in the Title I program?
11. In which subtests on the norm-referenced achievement tests did students perform best? Worst?
12. How did the Title I students perform on the state's criterion-referenced tests? What were the strengths of the Title I students? The weaknesses?
13. How do the scores of Title I students compare to the scores of other students in the district?
14. How well do the Title I students write — as measured by the state's writing test?
15. What percentage of Title I students scored in each quartile on the norm-referenced test? How does this compare to previous years?

# Factors to Analyze
# Title I

1. What types of services do we provide for our Title I students? Are these services effective? How do we know?

2. How does the Title I program support students in learning state standards?

3. How is instruction different for students who are struggling in areas such as reading and mathematics?

4. What special training do Title I teachers have in providing significant remediation/acceleration services to students?

5. How are Title I services delivered? What evidences do we have that the delivery model is effective?

6. Is enough time spent with Title I students to make a difference in their meaning?

7. What additional support materials are available for helping struggling Title I students? How are these materials being used?

8. What programs are in place to fill the special needs Title I parents may have?

9. What are the collaboration efforts of the Title I teacher and the regular education teachers?

# Data Analysis Questions
# Special Education

1. What percentage of our students receive special education services?

2. What is the special education enrollment trend over the past 3-5 years by grade level?

3. What is the special education enrollment trend over the past 3-5 years at each organizational level (i.e., elementary, middle, high)?

4. What are the characteristics of our special education students? What is the enrollment pattern over the past 3-5 years, disaggregated by student demographic characteristics of gender and race/ethnicity?

5. What is the enrollment pattern of the special education program by school? How many and what percentage of students are served at each school?

6. How many and what percentage of teachers work as part of the special education program?

7. What are the demographic characteristics (e.g., race/ethnicity, gender) of the special education teaching staff?

8. What are the achievement results of students in the special education program? How do the special education students perform on the norm-referenced achievement tests?

9. How do students at different grade levels in special education perform on norm-referenced achievement tests?

10. Are there any differences in achievement between groups of students (e.g., race/ethnicity, gender) in the special education program?

11. In which subtests on the norm-referenced achievement tests did students perform the best? The worst?

12. How did the special education students perform on the state's criterion-referenced tests? What were the strengths of the special education students? The weaknesses?

13. How do the scores of special education students compare to other students in the district?

14. How well do the special education students write — as measured by the state's writing test?

# Data Analysis Questions
# Gifted & Talented

1. What percentage of our students are enrolled in our gifted and talented program? What is the overall enrollment?

2. What percentage of students, by grade level, are enrolled in the gifted and talented program?

3. What has been the trend in gifted and talented enrollment over the past five years by elementary, middle, and high school level students?

4. What are the enrollment patterns of students over the past five years? Have there been changes in the gender or race/ethnicity of the students?

5. What are the characteristics of our gifted and talented students? What is the enrollment pattern of students over the past 3-5 years, disaggregated by student demographic characteristics of race/ethnicity and gender?

6. What are the enrollment patterns of the gifted and talented program by school? How many and what percentage of students are served at each school?

7. What are the demographic characteristics (e.g., race/ethnicity, gender) of the gifted and talented teaching staff?

8. What are the achievement results of students in the gifted and talented program? How do the gifted and talented students perform on norm-referenced tests?

9. Are there any differences in achievement between different groups of students (e.g., race/ethnicity, gender) in the gifted and talented program?

10. In which subtests on the norm-referenced achievement tests did students perform best? Worst?

11. How did the gifted and talented students perform on the state's criterion-referenced tests? What were the strengths of the gifted and talented students? Weaknesses?

12. How do the scores of the gifted and talented students compare with other students in the district? The state?

13. How well do the gifted and talented students write, as measured by the state's writing test?

## Summary

This chapter has provided comprehensive lists of data analysis questions and accompanying factors to analyze. Both types of lists will help you organize and analyze your data. Once you have your data tables, charts, and graphs constructed, it's important to think about the data. The thinking part is what will guide you toward improved student learning. There is much to think about including factors in the area of curriculum, instruction, and assessment. The next chapter provides a framework for thinking about these three areas and gives several ideas of the kinds of data you may want to study related to these areas.

# 8 Chapter Eight
# The Path to
# Student Success

It would be great if a simple test score could provide enough information about what a school or district should do to improve student learning. That is simply not the case. If you want to get stellar results in student achievement, you'll want to look at data in the overall areas of the teaching process: curriculum, instruction, and assessment. In addition to curriculum, instruction, and assessment, there are certainly other things that influence student achievement in a school including student mobility, student attendance, socioeconomics of the community, parent involvement, and more. But remember, when you're working on improving student achievement, you've got to work in the areas for which you have the most control.

There are three key parts to *The Path to Student Success* model. The first part is getting to know the standards (curriculum). The second part is teaching the standards (instruction). The third part is assessing student achievement of the standards (assessment). When curriculum, instruction, and assessment are lined up and support one another, it's called alignment. Alignment is one of those things you're working toward when talking about improving student achievement.

The data you'll collect as a result of looking at information in this chapter is your process data. Remember, this is the type of data you can begin to look at that will lead you to changes — changes that will increase student achievement. Use data you collect from the various parts of *The Path to Student Success* model to determine some of the things you may want to work on in your school improvement plan. Paying attention to the data in each of these areas can bring big dividends in student learning. Let's take a look at each of the parts of my model, *The Path to Student Success*.

## Introduction to the Model

The first part of the model highlights that the *Path to Student Success* is as simple (although, not easy) as 1, 2, 3. These three parts include: 1. Get to know your standards; 2. Teach your standards; and 3. Assess your standards. Quickly review the visual of the overall model on the next page and then read about each of the parts of the model.

THE PATH TO STUDENT SUCCESS

.... can be as simple as 1, 2, 3

SCHOOL CLIMATE

SUCCESS

Leadership

Parent Involvement

Mobility Rates

# of Parents at Home

Socioeconomic Status of the Community

#1 Get to Know Your Standards

#2 Teach Your Standards

#3 Assess Your Standards

# Alignment of the Three Parts of the Model

Remember, when curriculum, instruction, and assessment all support one another, it's called alignment. Alignment is a good thing — and it's one of the areas a school should focus on to improve student achievement. You could even call this learning alignment. Remember, student achievement, at least partially, reflects the alignment of the teaching and learning process. So let's take a quick look at alignment of the three parts included in *The Path to Student Success* model.

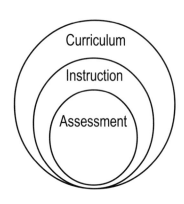

**Alignment of Curriculum, Instruction, and Assessment**

In the diagram to the left, all three components (curriculum, instruction, and assessment) of a learning framework are aligned. In this model, you would have a curriculum (learning targets) aligned to the state/district standards, you would be using specific strategies (instruction) to help students learn the curriculum, and then you would use appropriate assessment tools (assessment) to determine whether your students met the learning targets, or standards. As noted educator Fenwick English (1992) reminds us, alignment is critical to ensuring student success in school.

In this example, the parts of the teaching for learning process are not aligned. Curriculum and assessment are aligned, but the instruction is not. For some reason the right lessons aren't being delivered in the classroom. There may be a textbook problem. There may be teachers who aren't aware of the state frameworks. Who knows what it might be? But failure to ensure alignment here will most certainly influence the achievement scores of your students negatively.

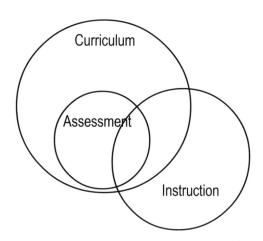

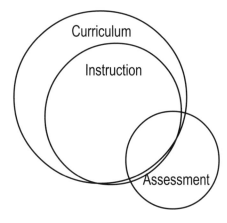

In this case — curriculum and instruction are aligned, but the assessment doesn't match. These assessments might be textbook assessments that aren't really aligned to the standards. They might also be classroom assessments that aren't really aligned to the standards. They might even be norm-referenced assessments, such as the *Iowa Tests of Basic Skills* or the *Stanford Achievement Tests*. (And these tests were not designed to measure your curriculum, so the tight alignment definitely won't be there!)

# THE PATH TO STUDENT SUCCESS

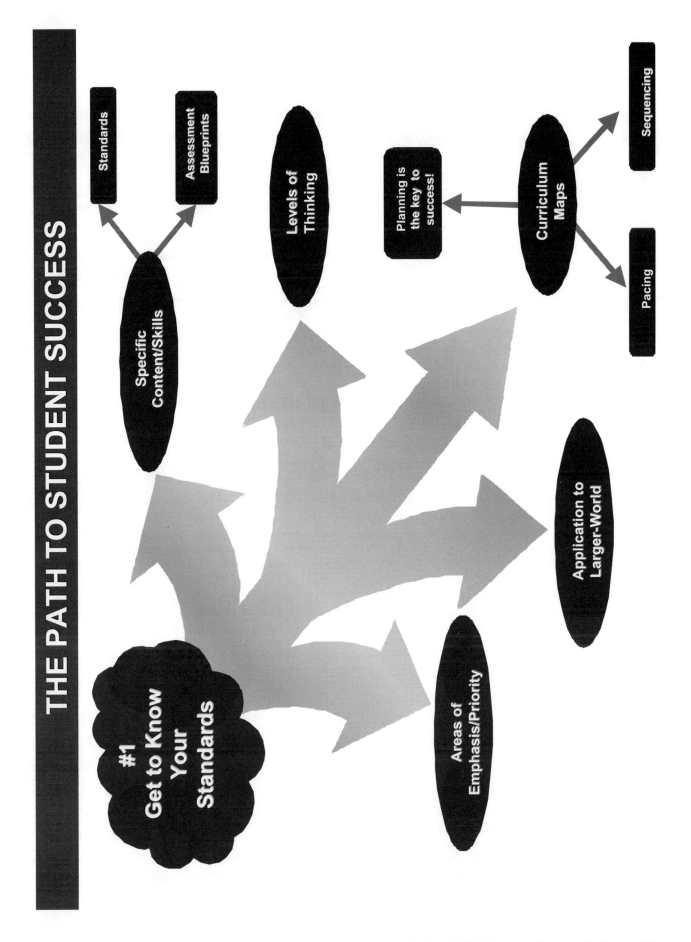

Standards

Assessment Blueprints

Specific Content/Skills

Levels of Thinking

Planning is the key to success!

Curriculum Maps

Sequencing

Pacing

#1 Get to Know Your Standards

Areas of Emphasis/Priority

Application to Larger-World

# #1: Get to Know Your Standards (Plan for Success)

Before you teach and subsequently assess standards, it's important to identify the intent of the content of the standards — and this should be clear to all who will use the standards (including the test-makers who design the tests for state standards).

Take a look at the standards below. As you read them, put yourself in the place of a teacher at the identified grade level.

---

History/Social Sciences, Grade 2

The student will study the contribution of ancient Egypt and China which have had an impact on world history, with emphasis on written language, laws, calendars, and architectural monuments such as the Pyramids and the Great Wall of China.

---

English, Grade 9

Read dramatic selections.
• Identify the two basic parts of drama.

*(This is a part of a standard.)*

---

History/Social Sciences, Grade 10

Analyze past and present trends in human migration and cultural interactions as they are influenced by social, economic, political, and environmental factors.

---

So, you're the teacher — what would you teach for each of these standards? What specifically is important for students to learn? What if there aren't materials readily available to help you? Where do you go? These examples are actual state standards. One of the first things a district needs to do with these standards is to help clarify the intent of the standards with teachers. **Standards need to be crystal clear to teachers. If the standards aren't clear, teachers can't make them clear to students. And if the standards aren't clear to students, it's less likely they will learn them.** (It's a funny thing about learning — when students know what they are supposed to learn, they learn better!)

Here's a problem you run into when the standards are not well defined, and there is a state assessment program in place. The standards are sent to testing companies to design test items. The purpose of the tests is to determine whether or not students have learned a standard. But, if the standard isn't clear, who do you think determines the specific content our students should have learned in the classroom? The Department of Education doesn't really determine this if the standards aren't clear. School divisions might "take a stab" at interpreting the standards — but different districts may interpret the standards in different ways. If the standards are not clear and well-defined, our teachers may also interpret the standards differently. If a standard is not clear but is being used by the testing company as a basis for writing test items — the people who write the test items determine what should have been taught. (And of course, they also probably have their own interpretations.)

I've worked with thousands of teachers in implementing standards — and here's something I consistently hear: "Just tell us what to teach and we'll be happy to teach it." Teachers want to know the specifics of their standards.

If we want to help our students be successful in learning standards, we must be absolutely clear what the intent of the standard is. What do you do if a standard isn't clear? First of all, check with the staff of the Department of Education for clarity about the standard. You'd probably go to the instructional side of the Department of Education for this. Some states release past versions of tests — you could also look to some of these for clarification. Use your assessment blueprints or frameworks to give you additional information about the standard. Some states have examples of student tasks that help teachers understand the intent of the standards. Use these too! When your Department of Education offers resources and materials related to the standards, take advantage of them. Take whatever time it takes to get clarification for your standards. It's really that important!

## Levels of Thinking

When reviewing your standards, identify the levels of thinking required by the standard. Does the standard call primarily for recall types of learning targets? Does the standard require a performance of some type from the student? Does the standard require various levels of thinking? Understanding the levels of thinking related to the standard is critical for making sound instructional and assessment choices. I certainly recommend that schools and teachers have a model they can follow to help identify the levels and types of thinking required by a standard. Examples of instructional models include Bloom's Taxonomy (Bloom, 1956), Dimensions of Learning (Marzano, 1992), Teaching Styles and Strategies (Hanson, 1986) or even my model, called the Comprehensive Learning Framework.

Understanding the level of thinking within a standard is critical — it's one of the ways we make choices about how to teach and assess the standards. You might call this learning alignment!

## Curriculum Maps

At some point, you've got to sit down and work with the data that describes how, over the course of the year, you're going to help students learn the standards. Heidi Hayes Jacobs (1997) promotes curriculum maps as a tool for pacing, sequencing, and aligning instruction and assessment to the standards. A curriculum map is a tool to let you find out where gaps and repetitions are in the curriculum at the school or district level. A curriculum map lets you learn the path that students are actually taking as they move through your school division, K-12. This could be some of the most important data you collect for curriculum.

## Application to the Larger World

The purpose of standards is to provide a high quality education for all the students served by a school, district, or state. This education serves as an enabler for students to become whoever in life they would like to become. Believe it or not, there is a reason for state standards other than to provide test scores. The purpose of standards is to ensure that students graduate with the knowledge and skills needed to thrive in today's world.

## Areas of Emphasis and Priority

Many districts and schools design programs that not only meet, but exceed state requirements. When getting to know your standards, you'll also want to pay close attention to these priorities. Does your district have an emphasis on technology? How about school-to-work programs? Perhaps a priority in your district is character education. Your district priorities should also be yours.

## Data Tools for Getting to Know Your Standards

There are many kinds of data and data collection tools you can use to get to know the curriculum better. I have used a variety of data tools to help me when getting to know the curriculum in a school or school district. I've included the following in this book:

Individual Standards Analysis
Curriculum Guide Rating Sheets
Scope and Sequence of Tests
Unit Review Sheets

## Individual Standards Analysis

The Individual Standards Analysis data collection tool gives you a format for reviewing each individual standard and learning what you have and what you need for each one. The chart gives you a place to make notations related to some important parts of getting to know the standard. I've included information on the chart about the type of information you use to complete the chart. (Please see the example on page 155.)

You may want to conduct this analysis only on the standards in which student achievement is not as high as you might like. If achievement toward a standard is progressing well for your school or district, just keep on doing the things you've been doing.  Use the Individual Standards Analysis form to collect data for standards in which student achievement needs to be improved.  This analysis is also helpful if you're working with standards for the first time.

# Individual Standards Analysis of What's Needed
## Time • Treasure • Talent

**Content Area:**

| Standards | Textbook Support? | Resources? | Time to Teach? | Integration Possible? | Content Training? | Strategies Training? |
|---|---|---|---|---|---|---|
| Write the standards you want to study more closely here. (You could also add bench-marks or objectives to this section.) | Is the textbook series you're using really tightly aligned to the state standards? Doing a comprehensive textbook alignment analysis will give you invaluable information. | Do you have the resources for you to teach the standards and for students to learn them? What is available? What is not available? | Do teachers feel that they have enough time to teach the standard? If not, what are the obstacles to having the time they need? | Integration can be a nice delivery and learning model. Does this standard lend itself to integration? | Is content training for this standard needed by 25 percent or more of your staff? If so, you may want to host the content training on-site. If it's less than 25 percent, you may want to help teachers find courses and workshops that will help them with the content. | Do teachers want or need strategies training for this standard? |

# Individual Standards Analysis of What's Needed
## Time • Treasure • Talent

**Content Area:**

| Standards | Textbook Support? | Resources? | Time to Teach? | Integration Possible? | Content Training? | Strategies Training? |
|-----------|-------------------|------------|----------------|-----------------------|-------------------|----------------------|
|           |                   |            |                |                       |                   |                      |

# Curriculum Guide Rating Sheets

I have adapted the curriculum guide rating sheets from a week-long training program, Curriculum Auditing (English, 1988), a course I took many years ago through AASA (American Association of School Administrators). I have seen several adaptations of the rating materials, but this is one that I have used over the course of the past seven years — and really like. You'll find it easy to use, and you'll also get a lot of good data related to your curriculum from these sheets. The next page gives you an overview of how to use the Curriculum Guide Rating Sheets and the data collection form that follows. Use both of these sheets as you look at the data related to curriculum.

These sheets can be used to "score" curriculum guides that have already been developed, but they're also very useful as a rubric for designing brand new curriculum guides. These sheets can be used at the school or the district level.

# Rating Curriculum Guides

Here's an analysis you may have never done before — but it's certainly a useful one, especially at the district level. In this part of the analysis of curriculum, you'll have a chance to check the "fitness" of your guide in terms of being a tool that provides the framework for the curriculum that is taught in the classroom. The purpose of a curriculum guide is to provide direction to teachers about what to teach, but as you already know, guides vary in their usefulness as tools for implementing standards in the classroom. We know what kinds of things make a guide useful, and these are listed below:

- Useful guides provide clear direction about the intent for each of the standards. The standards are clearly stated. The standards include enabling objectives that help teachers know all that is embedded in students learning a standard.
- The standards are keyed to district and state tests.
- The curriculum guide explains clearly the prerequisite skills that are needed to learn a standard.
- The curriculum guide provides information about resources, and these are matched to the standards.
- The guide provides specific examples about how to approach the standards.

Generally, it is the responsibility of the local school district to design and develop guides that are aligned to the state standards.

A district has the responsibility of ensuring that the district's curriculum is aligned to the state standards. In other words, if a teacher is using the district's curriculum guide, then he or she should feel confident that the standards are being taught.

**How to Use The Rating Rubrics:** You'll want to use one Rating Rubric for each curriculum guide you're reviewing. If there are five guides for elementary science, then you'd use five rating sheets. If there are six guides for elementary language arts, you'll use six rating guides. If your district includes K-5 in a single guide, then count this as a single guide for rating purposes.

The lower the score, the more work you need to do in the area of curriculum. Use the rating sheets to guide you toward what to improve in your curricular documents.

Note: The forms, *Rating of Curriculum Guides as a Tool for Implementing Standards* and *Summary Rating of Curriculum Guides As An Adequate Tool for Implementing Standards*, have been adapted from the ideas of Fenwick English and his work with curriculum auditing.

# Rating of Curriculum Guides as a Tool for Implementing Standards

Curriculum Guide _____

Grade Levels (circle all that apply)

K 1 2 3 4 5 6 7 8 9 10 11 12

Reviewer's Signature _____

Total Score 25 pts possible _____

Mean Score Total/5

| Criteria | 0 | 1 | 3 | 5 |
|---|---|---|---|---|
| **The standards are clearly stated.** | No goals/standards/objectives present. | Includes the standards, but the intent of what to teach is not really consistent or clear. | States the standards as indicated in the state framework. | States the standard and refines where necessary. Provides suggestions for sequencing and pacing. |
| **The standards are aligned to assessment.** | No evaluation or assessment approach stated. | Some approach toward the evaluation or assessment stated. | The standards are keyed to state tests, but there are no examples. | The standards are keyed to state and/or district tests. There are examples of assessment items for each standard. |
| **The skills needed to teach the standards are clear.** | Enabling objectives are not included. | Enabling objectives are included, but they do not match the standards. | Provides some enabling objectives, but not enough to clarify the intent of the standard. | Provides specific enabling objectives that clearly indicate what students should learn in the standard. |
| **Resource materials are aligned to the standards.** | Does not list the basic or supplementary materials. | Names the basic materials that should be used. | Names basic *and* supplementary materials. | Provides a tight match between resources, materials and standards. |
| **There are specific examples of how to teach the standards.** | Does not provide examples of how to approach the standards in the classroom. | Overall, has vague statements about how to teach the standards. | Provides general suggestions about instructional approaches. | Provides specific examples on how to teach key concept/skills in the classroom. |

# Unit Review

A Unit Review is a way to collect data from teachers about how their curriculum is being implemented in the classroom. The review sheets can be included with the curriculum guide, but they could also be completed at a curriculum work session with teachers. The purpose of the unit review is to find out information that will let your school or district staff make changes that will lead to improved delivery and learning of the curriculum.

The unit review can contain a variety of things, but ideally it should be kept simple. The review is a way for teachers to reflect on how easy or difficult the unit was for them to teach and students to learn — and then pass that information along. Teachers have wonderful ideas about what to do to improve the curriculum — and this is a way for you to collect those ideas. An example of a unit review, courtesy of Newport News Public Schools, Newport News, Virginia, shows how simple a unit review can be. As you review the feedback form, notice the kinds of data it provides for improving the delivery of standards in the district.

# History/Social Science and English Feedback Sheet

Please complete and send a copy of this Feedback Sheet to the Reading Office after each Work Plan has been taught.

Name_____ School _____ Date _____

Umbrella Title _____ Grade Level _____ Date _____

Work Plan # & Title _____

1. Did the document(s) provide an effective summary/overview of the History/Social Science and English Curriculum? _____ Yes _____ No
   Comment:

2. Did the work plan support the students' mastery of the SOLs? _____ Yes _____ No
   Comment:

3. Was the TIME Range adequate? _____adequate _____too short _____ too long
   Comment:

4. Did the activities engage students? _____Y es _____No
   Comment:

5. Were strategies for Quality Work evident in the TASKS and PRODUCT FOCUS?
   _____ Yes _____No  Comment:

6. Was the materials list adequate? _____ Yes _____ No
   Comment:

7. Please provide a list of any additional materials you have found which support this work plan or any additional tasks that you used. One goal of the curriculum writers was to provide you with SAMPLE work plans to teach the SOLs. We want to encourage you to develop other work plans to teach the Umbrella Statements to be included in this Resource Guide in the future. Please attach any new work plans to this sheet. These will be added as you and your colleagues continue to create Knowledge Work. Also, feel free to list any other suggestions or comments you may have.

# THE PATH TO STUDENT SUCCESS

**Textbook Alignment** → **Loose or Tight?**

**Research-Based Strategies**

**Resources**

**Align Strategies with Standards**

**Student-Centered Instruction**

**#2 Teach Your Standards**

**Integrate Where it Works**

# #2:  Teach Your Standards — Teach for Success

When investigating how to improve student achievement, you may be tempted to begin here.  But don't.  Begin with the curriculum piece, and make sure it is as tight as can be.  You want to begin with "the what" of teaching before you examine "the how." Pay attention to the standards, and make sure they're taught.  There's more than just good teaching in instruction.  The "what" matters.  Remember, you can teach the wrong things really, really well.  So, one of the things you'll want to do is to make sure you're teaching the standards and not just whatever is in the textbook or what you've taught in the past.  New state standards have changed the look of district curricula across the country.

## Align Strategies With Standards

When getting to know the content, you clarified the levels of thinking required to attain a standard.  One purpose for doing this is to make good instructional choices about what strategies to use to help students learn the standards.  Will student learning focus on recall objectives?  Will students have higher-order thinking objectives?  Are some objectives performance-based? How do you know which strategies to use to teach the parts of a standard?

Bring an instructional model into play here.  Does your school (or district) use one?  Perhaps you're organizing learning around the fine work in teaching strategies (Hanson, 1986).  Perhaps you use the Dimensions of Learning model (Marzano, 1992).  Perhaps you use Bloom's Taxonomy.  I personally don't think it matters too much which model you use — just that you use one.  The purpose of using one any one of these models is to ensure the alignment of curriculum, instruction, and assessment.

I've included my Comprehensive Learning Framework here.  I've put this together over the course of the years and synthesized ideas from several models for this framework.  It works for me, and it will work for you, too.

# Comprehensive Learning Framework

| Levels of Thinking | Key Question | Examples of Verbs | Examples of Learning Targets/Standards | Examples of Instructional Strategies | Examples of Classroom Assessment Tools |
|---|---|---|---|---|---|
| **Recall** | Do the students know the information? | Define<br>Demonstrate<br>Identify<br>Who<br>What<br>Where<br>When<br>Observe<br>Recall | Identify and draw the following polygons: pentagon, hexagon, heptagon, octagon, nonagon, and decagon.<br><br>Identify the parts of the solar system (sun, moon, Earth, other planets and their moons, meteors, asteroids, and comets). | Brainstorming<br>Mindmapping<br>Two-Column Notetaking<br>Drawing-to-Learn Strategies<br>Mnemonics<br>Concept Attainment<br>Graphic Organizers<br>Pair Review Strategies | Paper and Pencil Tests Including: Multiple Choice, Matching, Fill-in-the-Blanks, Short Answer, and Essay. |
| **Relate** | Can the students personalize the information? | Reflect<br>Share<br>Tell<br>Analyze<br>Approve<br>Initiate<br>Help | Analyze oral participation in small-group activities.<br><br>Evaluate own contributions to discussions. | Peer Editing<br>Pair Review Strategies<br>Cooperative Learning Activities<br>Small-Group Discussions<br>Think/Pair/Share<br>Goal Setting<br>Reflection | Observation Checklists<br>Goal Setting Sheets<br>Self-Evaluation Sheets<br>Interviews<br>Cooperative Learning Logs<br>Reading Logs<br>Reaction Pieces |
| **Connect** | Can the students connect the information to something else? | Analyze<br>Classify<br>Compare/Contrast<br>Explain<br>Generalize<br>Interpret<br>Prioritize | Analyze the relationship between an author's style, literary form, and intended impact on reader.<br><br>Compare the American political and economic system to systems of other nations, including Japan, China, and Western European nations. | Writing-to-Learn Strategies<br>Analogies<br>Metaphors<br>Inductive Thinking Activities<br>Making Patterns and Abstractions<br>Error Analysis<br>Graphic Organizers | Classification Tasks<br>Lab Reports<br>Graphing Tasks<br>Explanations for Solving Problems<br>Writing Samples<br>Summarizations<br>Compare and Contrast Tasks |
| **Create** | Can the students do something new and different with the information? | Create<br>Design<br>Develop<br>Generate<br>Imagine<br>Propose<br>Suggest | Plan and conduct an experimental investigation.<br><br>Write documented research papers.<br><br>Design, write, test, debug, and document a completed structured computer program. | Decision-Making<br>Inventions<br>Investigations<br>Problem Solving<br>Creative Thinking<br>Experimental Inquiry | Research Papers<br>Multi-part Projects<br>Artwork Exhibits<br>Video Projects<br>Written Reports<br>Oral Reports<br>Portfolios<br>Products |

# Research-Based Strategies

There is an overwhelming amount of research that provides us with great data for improving instruction. Are you using that data?

Try taking this little quiz to find out if each item is a TRUE/FALSE for improving student achievement.

T  F  1.    It's not important to grade student homework; it's just important for students to do homework.

T  F  2.    Time on task is important to student achievement.

T  F  3.    Using assessments included with a textbook series is adequate for determining whether or not a student has met the state standards.

T  F  4.    Pausing after asking a question in the classroom results in an increase in student achievement.

T  F  5.    When we give students opportunities to construct their own meanings, they learn more.

There are literally hundreds of research-based strategies we can use and the data related to these strategies point to how successful the strategies can be in our classrooms. While it's always good to look at primary research, there are some terrific resources to help you with the data. The answers to these five questions can be found in *The Handbook for Improving Student Achievement* (Cawelti, 1995). In my workshops, we review the data related to improved student learning — and guess what? Many of my participants comment that it's nice to be reminded of some of the techniques that we know improves student achievement.

So how might you look at the data in research as a way to move toward school improvement? Here's a technique to get you started. First of all, list 25 statements of fact that support student learning in the classroom. Second, have teachers note which of the 25 strategies they regularly and consistently use. Tally the data. Then use the information to set goals about which strategies might need additional attention in the classroom. Have teachers review the strategies they may not consistently use and decide which of these they'd like to practice in the classroom.

## <u>Resources</u>

Let's talk about the data related to resources we use to help students learn standards — especially the Number One resource: textbooks.

Tight alignment of textbooks to the state and local standards is a good thing. Loose alignment is not. Tight alignment means that, when a textbook company gives itself credit for aligning to the standards, there is enough for the teacher to teach the standards and for the students to learn the standards. Loose alignment means that the standard is supported, but there are not enough background readings, materials, or activities for the teacher to teach the standard or the student to learn it.

How important is the data related to textbook alignment? When you consider that for many teachers the textbook is the curriculum document of choice, it's incredibly important! I often ask people if they think their textbooks are tightly aligned to state standards. For the most part, except for math, they say "no." If the textbooks are not tightly aligned to state standards, but are being used as a key curricular document in the classroom, what does that say for teaching the right thing — the state and district standards?

Each year, your school or district is probably involved in the adoption and purchase of a textbook series. Do you rely entirely on the alignment reports provided to you by textbook companies or do you review the data yourself? I encourage you to collect textbook alignment data for every new book you adopt. The next few pages provide you with data collection tools for doing this. You'll find a template for conducting a single textbook analysis to the state standards on pages 159-162. On page 163, you'll find a template that lets you compare three textbooks to the district standards.

# Textbook Alignment Analysis

There are a couple of ways to check the alignment of the textbook to the standards. In the Textbook Alignment Analysis, you'll be collecting data to determine the answer to a simple question: Does this textbook adequately support the teaching of the standards for this course and grade level?

For the data collection related to textbook alignment, you'll need a copy of your state standards/district curriculum and the textbook for which you're checking the alignment.

Under the column, **Standards**, simply list the standards to which you're aligning the textbook. I recommend that you write the whole standard out — and not just the number of the standard. It will make your job much easier as you're collecting your data.

Under the column, **Textbook References**, list specific pages in the book that support each of the standards. As you're doing this, also make note of a very important issue: Does the textbook include enough information so that a teacher can teach the standard and a student can learn the standard? We'll call this tight alignment.

When you have finished checking the pages of the textbook for each standard, then review the list of standards and make a professional judgment about the tightness or looseness of the text to the standard. Use the chart below to determine the level of alignment (i.e., tight, loose, none) the book has toward the standards.

| Tight | Loose | None |
|---|---|---|
| You could teach this standard with information provided in the text. You wouldn't need any other texts to fill in the gaps. | The textbook has parts that certainly help you teach the standards, but you would need additional resources to do this well. | The book doesn't cover this standard. |

# Textbook Alignment Analysis

Textbook Name _____

Author _____

Publisher _____ Copyright Date _____

Content Area _____ Grade Level _____

| State Standards | Textbook References |
|---|---|
|  |  |

# Textbook Alignment Analysis

| State Standards | Textbook References |
| --- | --- |
| | |

Now, you've gone through your textbook piece by piece, page by page, to determine which parts of the text are aligned to the state standards or district curriculum.  Use the data you've collected to answer the following questions:

1.      How many objectives or standards were you reviewing for your course or content area? _____

2.      How many of the standards have a tight alignment of the textbook? _____  What percentage of the standards does this represent? _____ (Just divide the number of tightly aligned standards by the total number of standards and multiply by 100.)

3.      How many of the standards have low or no alignment of the textbook? _____  What percentage of the standards does this represent? _____ (Just divide the number of loosely aligned standards by the total standards and multiply by 100.)

4.      Is this adequate for textbook alignment to the standards?

5.      What is your overall recommendation about this textbook as it relates to alignment?  (Remember, it doesn't matter how pretty the pictures are or how big or beautiful the book is.  If it's not aligned, it's not going to do the job for you.)

# Textbook Alignment Analysis

Content Area _____ Grade Level _____

| State/District Standards | Textbook 1 | Textbook 2 | Textbook 3 |
|---|---|---|---|
|  |  |  |  |

## Student-Centered Instruction

The students are at the center of learning. There is much data and information that speaks to student-centered learning. I've included this piece in the *Path to Student Success* model as a reminder that learning takes place only when a student does it. We can't lecture our way to student success. What we're looking for are teacher facilitators who provide active and engaging learning experiences for students.

As you collect data in your classrooms, who is doing the work — the teachers or the students? How are students learning? Are they working together? Is there plenty of interaction? Do students have opportunities to talk about what they're learning? Are they engaged in problem-based projects?

## Integration

Integration can be a nice delivery model for many standards and can help students learn information in a way that makes sense to them. At the very least, we should strive to integrate the basic skills of reading, writing, speaking, listening, and thinking into our content areas. We don't have to stop there. We can also integrate across subject or content areas. There are many natural connections between reading, writing, mathematics, science, social studies, music, and art. It's just a matter of determining if and how to integrate. If your teachers have collaborative planning time, integration between content areas is more likely. Teachers need time to talk about their approaches. Heidi Hayes Jacobs (1989) has written some excellent materials on the topic of curriculum integration. Check the *Resources and References* section for ideas that will help you integrate the curriculum.

## Content and Format Alignment of Practice Tests

Schools all over the country purchase practice tests to help students perform well on tests, especially if they have high-stakes tests in place. School personnel purchase the tests and wonder, "Will the practice tests really do the job we think they will do?" All you have to do is collect data for the practice tests, and you can easily determine whether they'll work for you. It's cost-effective to conduct this analysis *before* your order practice tests, not after.

Ideally, a practice test will do two things for you. First, it will support the state standards by having items that are directly tied to the state standards. Second, it will provide format practice for students in taking the state standards tests. This familiarity gives students and teachers confidence and helps reduce test anxiety.

The following pages provide an explanation of how to collect and organize data for each type of alignment (i.e., content and format/ context) for practice tests. (I've designed these pages to stand alone — it will make your work easier when you conduct a context and content alignment of the practice tests.)

# Format Alignment of Commercial Practice Tests to the State Tests

Alignment of instructional materials is important when we want students to succeed in learning standards.  One type of instructional material used by many schools and divisions is the practice test.  Practice tests, if formatted similarly to the state tests, can provide context, or format, alignment.

During a format analysis of a state test, you'll be determining what types of thinking are included and how questions are asked.  In addition, look for features in the format of the test questions that would be useful for you to remember as you design your own tests.  Please remember that you're not reviewing content here — that's a separate alignment check.

For this analysis, you'll need a copy of your state standards, the assessment blueprints/ frameworks/test specifications, sample tests for your state and whichever practice test you are reviewing.

1.      Use the handout, *Format Alignment of Commercial Practice Tests to the State Tests*, to list the features of the test format you are reviewing.  (You may want to begin with the assessment blueprints and then review the sample test items.)

2.      Now use the list of features as a comparison for each of the practice tests you are reviewing.  The blank template has room for you to compare three different practice tests.

3.      Use the information from the comparison chart to determine the **format alignment** of the practice tests to the State test you are analyzing.

**Analysis Questions:**  Are most of the format features of the state test also on the practice test? (The more format features that are included, the stronger the format alignment.)  If the alignment is not strong, is this practice test still worth using?  Why or why not?

# Format Alignment of Commercial Practice Tests to the Virginia Standards of Learning Tests

## Standards of Learning Test: Mathematics, Grade 3  EXAMPLE

| SOL Test Features | Commercial Practice Tests | | | SF | |
|---|---|---|---|---|---|
| multiple choice format | | | | yes | |
| use of rulers | | | | yes | |
| use of leading 0 | | | | yes | |
| use of pictures | | | | yes | |
| right answer always there | | | | yes | |
| item stems are complete questions or sentences | | | | yes | |
| emphasizes negative key words | | | | na | |
| commas for numbers with 4 digits or more | | | | yes | |
| fraction denominators 10 or less | | | | yes | |
| fractions written vertically | | | | yes | |
| decimals have 1 decimal place (except money) | | | | uses 1 + 2 dec. places | |
| sums & dilfferences don't exceed 5 digits | | | | yes | |
| multipliers will not exceed 5 | | | | yes | |
| multiplicands will not exceed 99 | | | | yes | |
| quotients and divisors whole numbers less than 10 | | | | | |
| no more than 4 categories on line or bar graphs | | | | 4 + 5 categories | |
| no more than 5 categories for pictographs | | | | yes | |
| even # items F, G, H, J | | | | yes | |
| length of test | | | | yes | |

> Use this column to identify, in whatever way you wish, whether or not the format features are supported by the practice test.

> Include features for your own state tests. You'll find most of these features in the assessment blueprints. You can also get ideas for the features from sample test items.

# Format Alignment of Commercial Practice Tests to the State Tests

**State Test:**

| State Test Features | Commercial Practice Tests | | |
|---|---|---|---|
| | | | |
| | | | |
| | | | |
| | | | |
| | | | |
| | | | |
| | | | |
| | | | |
| | | | |
| | | | |
| | | | |
| | | | |
| | | | |
| | | | |
| | | | |
| | | | |
| | | | |
| | | | |
| | | | |
| | | | |
| | | | |
| | | | |
| | | | |
| | | | |
| | | | |
| | | | |

# Content Alignment of Commercial Practice Tests to the State Standards

For this analysis, you'll be conducting a content analysis of the practice test compared to the state standards. Ideally, a practice test provides format familiarity *plus* supports the standards we want students to learn in our classrooms.

For this analysis, you'll need a copy of your state standards, the assessment blueprints (test specifications), state sample tests, and whatever practice test you are reviewing.

1.    Use the handout, *Content Alignment of Commercial Practice Tests to the State Tests*. List the standards numbers along the left-hand column for whichever test area you are analyzing.

2.    Now go through each and every practice test item to see which standards they support. There's a place to write the question numbers on the comparison chart. (Look under Commercial Practice Tests to see where to place your question numbers.)

3.    Use the information from the comparison chart to determine the **content alignment** of the practice tests to the standards you are analyzing.

**Analysis:** Are all standards included with items from the practice tests? If not, what percentage of the standards are included? Are there items in the practice book that are not related to the state standards? If so, what percentage are not related to the state standards? What can we say about the content alignment of these materials to the state standards? As a benchmark: a 0-40 percent match is loose alignment; 41-70 percent is medium alignment; and 71-100 percent is tight alignment.

By the way, does a single practice test have to assess all of the state standards? Probably not.

# Content Alignment of Commercial Practice Tests to Virginia's Standards of Learning Tests (SOL)

## SOL Content Area and Grade Level:  Grade 3 Mathematics  EXAMPLE

| Standards of Learning | Commercial Practice Tests | | | SF |
|---|---|---|---|---|
| Number/Number Sense  3.1 | | | | 3, 6, 14 |
| 3.2 | | | | 8, 16 |
| 3.3 | | | | 1, 9 |
| 3.4 | | | | 12 |
| 3.5 | | | | 11 |
| 3.6 | | | | 13, 25 |
| 3.7 | | | | 7, 17, 26 |
| Computation/Estimation  3.8 | | | | 15,18,19,20, 24,34 |
| 3.9 | | | | |
| 3.10 | | | | 30, 31 |
| 3.11 | | | | 10, 32 |
| 3.12 | | | | 27 |
| 3.13 | | | | 28, 29 |
| Measurement  3.14 | nothing included for liquids/volume or weight/mass | | | 37, 39 |
| 3.15 | | | | 33, 35 |
| 3.16 | | | | |
| 3.17 | | | | 36, 38 |
| Geometry  3.18 | | | | 40, 42, 43, 44 |
| 3.19 | | | | |
| 3.20 | | | | 41 |
| Probability  3.21 | | | | |
| 3.22 | | | | 21, 22, 48, 49, 50, 51, 52, 54, 55, 56 |
| 3.23 | | | | 23, 47, 53 |
| Patterns, Functions, Alg  3.24 | | | | 57, 58, 59, 60 |
| 3.25 | | | | |

*Callout (pointing to left column):* List the state standards in the column on the left.  You can list these by number or write the actual standard.

*Callout (pointing to right column):* Write the question numbers that support the standards.  Watch for patterns and trends.  Are all of the standards included?  Most?  Some?

# Content Alignment of Commercial Practice Tests to the State Tests

**State Content Area and Grade Level:** _____

| | Commercial Practice Tests | | |
|---|---|---|---|
| Standards | | | |
| | | | |
| | | | |
| | | | |
| | | | |
| | | | |
| | | | |
| | | | |
| | | | |
| | | | |
| | | | |
| | | | |
| | | | |
| | | | |
| | | | |
| | | | |
| | | | |
| | | | |
| | | | |
| | | | |
| | | | |
| | | | |
| | | | |
| | | | |
| | | | |
| | | | |

# THE PATH TO STUDENT SUCCESS

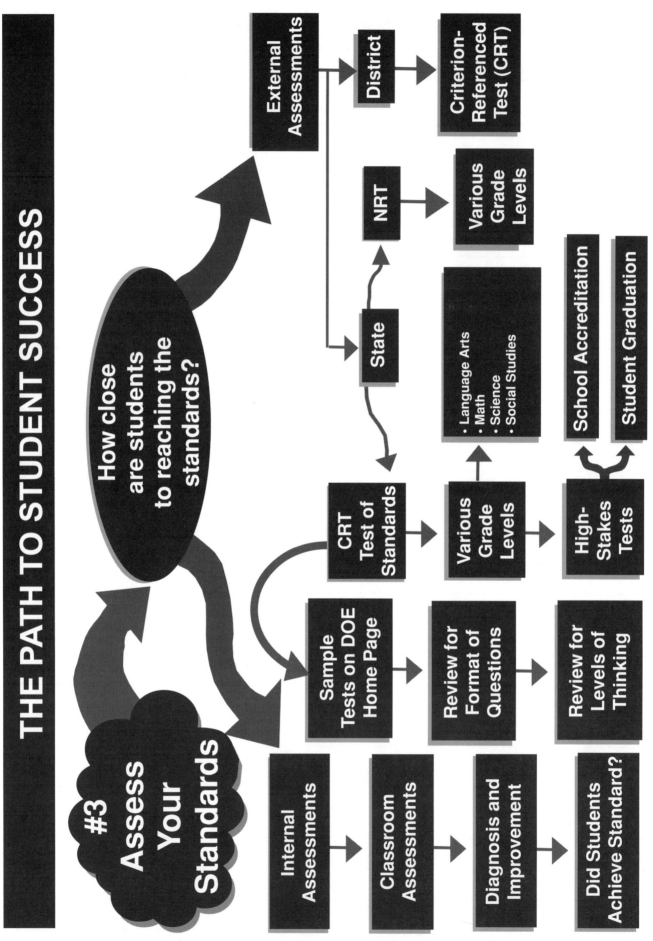

**How close are students to reaching the standards?**

**#3 Assess Your Standards**

External Assessments
- District → Criterion-Referenced Test (CRT)
- State → NRT → Various Grade Levels

CRT Test of Standards → Various Grade Levels
- Language Arts
- Math
- Science
- Social Studies

Various Grade Levels → High-Stakes Tests → School Accreditation / Student Graduation

Sample Tests on DOE Home Page → Review for Format of Questions → Review for Levels of Thinking

Internal Assessments → Classroom Assessments → Diagnosis and Improvement → Did Students Achieve Standard?

## #3: Assess Your Standards — Assess for Success

There are two basic types of assessments: internal and external. Ideally, both are designed to show how close are students to reaching the standards, but that's not really the case — and that's why we have to pay attention to data here.

## External Assessments

External assessments are those that you probably wouldn't be giving if someone didn't say you had to give them. How many of us would administer the *Stanford Achievement Test*, the *Iowa Tests of Basic Skills* or any of the state tests if we didn't have to?

There is some dislike for many external tests because teachers know the tests usually don't adequately measure achievement of the standards. We get test scores, but do they really tell us which standards students have or have not mastered? The commercially published norm-referenced tests have not been designed to fully assess the standards in any state. Those tests have been designed to tell you how students are performing in relation to other students (the norming group) who took the same test under the same conditions. So while the emphasis given to many norm-referenced tests may make you feel that there must be alignment, do remember that these tests haven't been designed for any one state.

External tests are a way of life in our public schools, so we need to get to know them also.

## Internal Assessments — Classroom Assessments

There is power in good assessment tools and in a balanced assessment program in our classrooms. Good assessments let us assess for success: to assess for diagnosis and improvement as well as to see whether students are achieving a standard.

Pay a lot of attention to good classroom assessment! Remember that most state standards assessments don't tell you which standards students have met. Textbooks, because they're not tightly aligned to state standards, don't have assessments that really reveal whether or not a student is achieving a standard. **The only way to know whether your students are achieving a standard is through good, balanced classroom assessment: comprehensive classroom assessment.**

If you're not convinced yet of the importance of good classroom assessment, review the checklist, *What's the Best Way to Monitor the Curriculum?* Along the left side of the checklist are examples of ways that we monitor the curriculum in our districts and schools. There are two key reasons we monitor the curriculum: to find out whether teachers are teaching the curriculum and to find out whether students are learning the curriculum. By the way, which one do you think is most important? Participants in my workshops identify that finding out whether students are learning the curriculum is most important to them. When we work through the checklist, they often discover that the data reveals the traditional methods of monitoring the curriculum don't really tell us if students are learning. Observations of teachers tell us if teachers are teaching the curriculum, but not if students are learning the curriculum. Having a checklist for teachers to check off when they teach the standards does not tell us if students are learning the standards. Collaborative planning time is an effective way for teachers to self-monitor teaching the curriculum. But, unless they talk about student achievement and how students are progressing toward the standards, it's not an effective way to determine whether or not students are learning the curriculum.

So how do we know if students are learning the curriculum? It's the data we collect through our classroom assessments that tell us whether or not students are learning standards. Classroom assessments provide some of the most important data of all.

As you work to use data to improve student achievement, see if you need to have a more comprehensive approach to classroom assessment in your school or district. (There are a number of assessment resources listed in the References and Resources section of this guide to help you with this important journey.)

# What's the Best Way to Monitor the Curriculum?

| Examples of Ways We Monitor the Curriculum | Are Teachers Teaching the Standards? | Are Students Learning the Standards? |
|---|---|---|
| Standards on Chalkboard | yes | |
| Lesson Plans | yes | |
| Teacher Checklist | yes | |
| Document in Curriculum Guide | yes | |
| Mentoring Program | yes | |
| Collaborative Planning Time | yes | |
| Teacher Evaluation | yes | |
| Central Office Supervision | yes | |
| Achievement Meetings With Teachers | yes | yes |
| Bank of Tests Aligned With Standards | yes | yes |
| School Writing Prompts/Rubrics | yes | yes |
| Other Assessments of the Standards | yes | yes |
| | | |
| | | |

# Get to Know Your State Assessments, Too

You want to know how to assess student learning in the classroom, but you'll also want to be very familiar with your state assessment program. You can't know too much about how your students are assessed from the state level. As with other parts of the *Path to Student Success* model, there's some important data here.

See if you can answer the following questions about your own state's assessment program.

1.   How many tests are included in the state assessment program? What kinds of tests (i.e., criterion, norm-referenced) tests are given?
2.   Which content areas are assessed?
3.   In which grade levels are the tests given?
4.   For each of the state tests, how are scores reported?
5.   What is a passing score for each of the tests?
6.   What is the impact on students if they do not do well on the tests? Do the tests change or influence student grades? Do the tests change graduation plans? Do students have to participate in remediation programs?
7.   Do students retake the state tests if they fail?
8.   What is the impact on the school faculty if students do not do well on the tests?
9.   What is the format of the tests? Are they all multiple choice? Are some of the items short answer? Is there a writing portion of the test? Are there performance-based assessments?
10.  When do students take the tests? How long does it take for students to get their results?
11.  Are there any rewards or consequences to schools based on student performance on the tests?
12.  Are there assessment blueprints, test specifications, or assessment frameworks available?
13.  If there is a writing test, how is it scored? Is there a rubric for the writing portion of the test?

Could you answer all of the questions? If not, it's not too late to explore your state assessment program further.

# 9 Chapter Nine
# More Analysis Tools

I've already discussed graphs, charts and data organizers with you.
These are all data tools that can help you organize and analyze your
data. But I do want to provide you with a few other analysis tools.
These tools and strategies will help you look even more closely at
your data and take your analysis to another level.

A number of ready-to-use strategies and tools are provided in this
section. These include:

  Data Analysis Map
  Success Path Summary
  Data Findings Map
  Achievement Think Sheets
  Criteria Matrix
  MultiVoting

## Variety of Data Analysis Tools and Methods

There are many ways to think about data — you've got charts,
graphs, data tables and a whole host of other data analysis tools.
In this chapter, I share some of my favorite analysis techniques
and hope you'll find them as useful as I do.

# Data Analysis Map

A Data Analysis Map is a mind map for a piece of data you want to analyze. (Refer to the diagram below to get an idea of how to set up the Data Analysis Map.) Get yourself a huge sheet of easel paper and the charts and graphs you want to analyze. Then, tape the charts and graphs onto separate sheets of paper. Then, write areas of analysis around the charts or graphs and brainstorm all the factors you can that influence the data in the center.

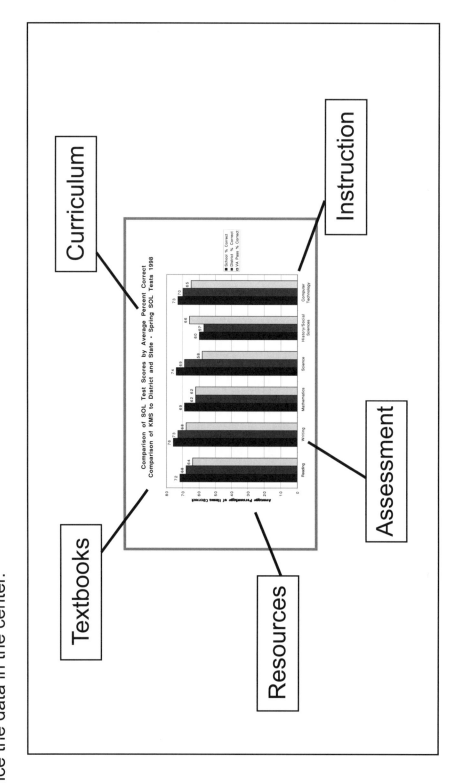

# Success Path Summary

*Factors Related to SOL*, located on page 189, is an example of how you might look at the big picture of where you are in a content area — and then use the information to determine what to do next. If you've ever looked at your scores and wondered what to do first to move toward improvement, then this tool might be just the right thing for you. In this example, you'll see the results of the research in the area of Social Studies that a school team put together. (They did much of this analysis based on the work from *Path to Student Success*, in Chapter 8.) The school improvement team members collected data in the areas of the teaching and learning process: curriculum, instruction, and assessment.

SOL in this example means "standards of learning." Just substitute whatever you call your own state or district standards when you do the Success Path Summary for your own school or district. The chart, *Factors Related to SOL*, lists several factors and data related to SOL achievement. These include: SOL Scale Score, % Passing This Test, Alignment of the Curriculum, Instructional Strategies for Implementing the SOL, Classroom Assessment, Textbook Alignment, % SES in School, and Mobility.

Review the data below and then see how it is plotted on the chart entitled, *Factors Related to SOL*. (I've also included the follow-up questions that I might use with this chart.)

**SOL Test Mean Scaled Score for Social Studies**: 365
**Percentage of Students Passing This Test:** 47%
**School Percent SES (students on free/reduced lunch)**: 76%
**Mobility Rate:** 15%

**Level of Curriculum Alignment**
The teachers conducted a curriculum alignment of this curriculum to the state standards. They made a couple of important observations. The first was that the district curriculum was not quite aligned to the standards and the state tests. Certainly some parts were aligned, but the alignment overall was low. The second thing they observed was that the curriculum didn't clearly enough describe "the what." Teachers noted that there were some broad standards open to interpretation by different people teaching them. They had great concerns about this — their thinking was, "Be clear about what you want to make sure our students learn and we can help them get there. But we must know for what we are being held accountable."

## Instructional Strategies for the SOL

This faculty certainly recognizes the importance of being well-trained to help students learn the content of the standards. They also noted that training for other content areas was more comprehensive than for this area. For this content area, the faculty had participated in some training, but not very much. They are faced with the issue of having only two inservice days during the school year, and they recognize that staff development needs to be continuous and ongoing — not just a one-shot approach. This is an area they want to work on in their next school improvement plan.

## Classroom Assessment of the SOL

This was a really interesting area for the teachers. First, they determined that the state tests do not really tell them which standards the students do or do not know. When reviewing state test data, they knew the reporting category where they were lowest, but they didn't really know which standards they needed to pay more attention to — and they found this to be quite frustrating. They also found that the assessments for the textbooks just weren't working to properly assess achievement of the standards. But, because of the time constraints of trying to get everything in, they were using the assessments with the textbooks just to make sure they had grades for students. Plus, the textbook assessments did assess some of the information in the textbook.

## Textbook Alignment

This was a huge surprise to this faculty. They sat down and did an alignment check of their textbook to the state standards. Guess what? They found that only 35 percent of their textbook was tightly aligned to the state standards. They instantly recognized the importance of not teaching everything in the textbook. Now they are wondering what other resources they can use to teach the standards.

# Factors Related to SOL

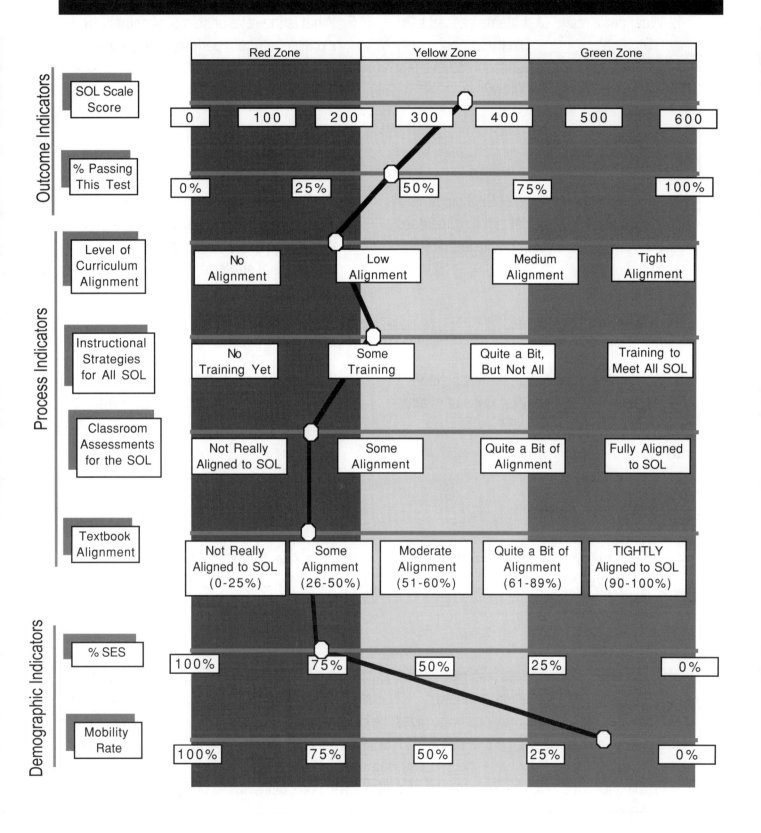

**Now connect the plots and make a vertical line graph. Then use the graph to answer the questions that follow.**

1.  What percentage of students passed this SOL test? _____ Did the school meet its pass score for accreditation on this test? _____ How do you know?

2.  What is the percentage of SES students in this school? _____ What significance does this have in terms of students learning the SOL?

3.  What is the mobility rate for this school? What is mobility and what kinds of effects does it have on a school?

4.  What is the level of curriculum alignment for this SOL test? _____

5.  What is the relationship of alignment to excellent student performance on the SOL test?

6.  What role do various instructional strategies play in implementing the SOL? What should this school do about instructional strategies?

7.  What role does classroom assessment have in implementing the SOL? What should this school do about classroom assessment?

8.  What role do textbooks have in implementing the SOL? What should this school do about textbooks?

After members of the school staff plotted their data and answered the above questions, there was one more important question to answer. *What should the school tackle first in its improvement efforts?* The chart on the previous page gives the clue. You see, a school has control over many of its process indicators. Since this school's level of curriculum alignment is in the red zone, they'll want to start here. They have the process data that indicates the need to begin here and it is something for which they have quite a bit of control. The curriculum has to be right before focusing on everything else!

# Data Findings Map

## Summary

Write a summary statement of key data in this block. The summary statement should include the three pieces of data listed below.

**Supporting Data Source 1**

**Supporting Data Source 2**

**Supporting Data Source 3**

If you're working on evidences of need, these should be outcome indicators. If you're working on other data related to student achievement, you might list process data here.

# Achievement Think Sheets

The *Achievement Think Sheets* are simply tools for doing some additional thinking about your school or district data and why you're getting the results you are getting. There are two sheets to this analysis, and you would use both for each content objective area (e.g., reading, writing, mathematics, science, social studies) you are trying to improve.

## How to Use the Achievement Think Sheets

Review the data for the objective area you are studying. List the key performance indicators you uncovered during your data search that point to success for this objective area. Consider listing three or more data pieces (remember the concept of *triangulation*?) After you've listed the data, take some time to reflect on (and list on the sheet) your ideas about what contributed to success. You may have implemented a new reading program and you think it's leading you to your better test scores. So list it. You may have introduced a new program in your school that requires all students to read a minimum of 45 minutes a day. List that, too. Whatever points to your success, list it.

Now, go back to the data and list the data pieces that you're not so happy with. Place these under the examples of weaknesses column of the second page. It's time to think again — what are some of the things going on in your school that you think contribute to the weaknesses? List these in appropriate column. Perhaps you've had an abundance of assembly programs during the morning hours, when most language arts is done. Whatever your ideas are, list them. After you've listed your ideas about what has contributed to the weakness, ask yourself an important question, "Why are we still doing these things?" There will be items on this list you can do something about — so do something about them.

# Achievement Think Sheet

Goal Area _____

Objective Area _____

| List specific data examples of SUCCESS for this objective area. | List your ideas about what contributed to this list of SUCCESSES. |
|---|---|
| Key Performance Indicators | |
| Data Source | |

# Achievement Think Sheet

## Goal Area _____  Objective Area _____

| List specific data examples of **WEAKNESSES** for this objective area. | | List your ideas about what contributed to this list of **WEAKNESSES**. |
|---|---|---|
| **Key Performance Indicators** | | |
| Data Source | | |
| | | |

# Criteria Matrix

One data collection tool that is very useful in making school improvement decisions is the criteria matrix. Use the criteria matrix when you're determining what strategies you want to include in your school improvement plan.

Here's how to use the matrix. First of all, determine the criteria you want to use as the checkpoint for each of your strategies. Do you want the strategies to be research-based? Do you want the strategies to be implemented within your budget constraints? Do you want human resources to support and successfully implement the strategies? Do the strategies represent "out-of-the-box" thinking? Will the strategies help move you toward your school mission and goals? List, across the top of the matrix, whatever criteria you want to use.

Second, brainstorm a list of all of the strategies you're considering for your school improvement plan. These strategies will most likely fall under the categories of curriculum, instruction, and assessment. (See the example for ideas of how to list these.)

Then, using the criteria, go through each strategy and place a check or other marker in the block for each criterion the strategy meets. Then, look for the patterns. Do you have strategies without any checks or markers? Do you have strategies that you cannot afford to implement? Do you have strategies for which you don't have a support system to implement?

# Criteria Matrix
## for Selecting
## Improvement Strategies

| | There is evidence that the strategy provides the success we are after. | The strategy can be implemented within our budget constraints. | We have the human resources and support to successfully implement the strategy. | The strategy represents "out-of-the-box" thinking for us — it's not just listing what we're already doing. | The strategy will help us move toward our school mission and learning targets. | | |
|---|---|---|---|---|---|---|---|
| 1. Design a school writing rubric aligned to state and district standards. | YES | YES | YES | NO | YES | | |
| 2. Provide a variety of formats for students to write. | YES | YES | YES | NO | YES | | |
| 3. Assess student responses to writing prompts three times each year (September, January, May). | YES | YES | YES | NO | YES | | |
| 4. Provide laptop computers for each teacher. | NO | NO | NO | YES | YES | | |
| 5. Provide writing process training for all teachers on the staff. | YES | YES | YES | NO | YES | | |
| 6. Teach students to assess their own writing. | YES | YES | YES | NO | YES | | |
| | | | | | | | |
| | | | | | | | |

# Criteria Matrix for Selecting Improvement Strategies

| | | | | | | | |
|---|---|---|---|---|---|---|---|
| | | | | | | | |
| | | | | | | | |
| | | | | | | | |
| | | | | | | | |
| | | | | | | | |

# MultiVoting

MultiVoting is a way to get everyone on a committee or team to select important items from a list, with limited difficulty. A series of votes reduces the size of the list to those items that are most important to the members of the group.

## How to MultiVote

1.  Generate a list of items. Use an individual or group brainstorming session to do this.
2.  Reduce the individual lists to one master list. Do this round-robin style. Start with group one, and have a team member read off the first item on the list. (Team members from other groups mark off this item, if it is on their list.) Go to the next team and have them read the first item on their list. Continue the process until every team has had a chance to share every item on their list. This is called list reduction.
3.  Review the new master list with the entire group. Provide time for clarification of the items on the list.
4.  Provide each participant with "voting dots." (You could also use self-stick notes.) Give them a set number of votes to use. Ask participants to use their dots to show the importance they place on items in the master list.
5.  After participants have voted, review the top four or five items. Voting can be done a second time if the list needs to be reduced to fewer than four or five items.

## When to Use MultiVoting

Use MultiVoting anytime you want to bring school members together to show their priorities. You'll find it to be a fast and efficient way to collect data from a team!

# 10 Chapter Ten
# Data-Based Plans

## Data-Based Plans Are a Tool of the Improvement Process

Student success must be planned! It doesn't occur by happenstance. Data should be an integral part of the school or program improvement process because you'll have information that will point you in the right direction when determining what to do to make your school a better place than it already is. Use data, and you'll be more focused in your school improvement work. Use data, and you'll be able to verify what is/is not working in your school or program. Use data, and you'll gain insights into the root causes of the weaker areas of your programs. Use data, and you'll make better decisions.

One of the tools for creating and managing change in the school is the school improvement plan. You'll find a template for a data-based school improvement plan with a *portion* of a plan completed to give you an idea of how to complete this type of plan.

While I provide you with this planning tool, I don't focus on the school improvement process here. But, please note that the process of involving a team to make decisions about what the improvement efforts are is critical. For more information about the overall school improvement process, I recommend that you review the school improvement process designed by Larry Lezotte and Barbara Jacoby (Lezotte, 1990).

School improvement teams can use data as an integral part of the school improvement process, and the data shows up in the plans. I am often asked what I recommend for formatting data-based plans and the like. This chapter provides information about what you may want to include in a data-based school improvement plan.

Remember that a school improvement plan is a tool — designed and developed by a school team — to identify priorities for a given period and to state what actions staff members will be taking to address priorities. The plan tells you the *who, what, when, where*, and *why* of the efforts you are committing to for the school year.

## Categories in a School/District Improvement Plan

There are many formats for a school plans. The format I've chosen to include in this book is one that I have refined from a variety of sources. When I offer options of different plan formats to school teams, this is the one that is selected for use by 98 percent of the teams. It works! I love the simplicity of this format, and I think you will, too. But remember, it doesn't matter what format you choose, there are some key parts to a school improvement plan. You'll want to know each part!

## Goal Area

This is where you list your overall goal. What is the goal area? Student achievement? School climate? Community relations? High expectations? Student safety? Leadership? The goal area should be aligned to the priorities and goals of the school division.

## Objectives

Tell what it is you're working to improve. Is it reading? Writing? Mathematics? Social Studies? Science? School climate? Write this in clear and concise language. You'll see in my example that I encourage you to do this differently from how you've probably been taught to do this in the past. I'm asking you to break out of the box of how you may have learned to write objectives (for improvement purposes) in the past. Please know, though, that I've included all those good things you've learned — I just organize it differently.

Another note on objectives: Most, if not all, of the objectives should be related to student achievement and should be chosen based on student performance data. The objectives should be reasonable in number (three to five) and should get at the essence of improvement. They should be more than "improve our score" objectives.

## Evidences of Need

What are the data pieces — key performance indicators — that show a need to spend time, energy, and resources on this particular objective? You'll want to triangulate here. Usually, one piece of data is not enough to help you make decisions about improving student achievement in your school. Your Evidences of Need show where your weak areas are, but they also give information you need for improvement. When listing data sources as Evidences of Need, you'll probably use outcome and demographic data.

## Evidences of Success

Key performance indicators serve as performance targets. What will your data look like if you've been successful? Here's where you set your measurement goals. (This piece is sometimes included as a part of the improvement objective, but it's easier to track and monitor if you separate it out.)

You'll want to triangulate your data here, unless you really want the success of your plan to fall on just one piece of data. Remember that triangulation means using multiple measures, different pieces of data. In your Evidences of Success, you'll have a number of indicators that point toward your success.

Your Evidences of Success can show whether you have equity in quality. Your data pieces will show how well you did — the quality piece. Often, your Evidences of Success will also include disaggregated data to determine the answers to the questions, *Is there learning for all? Is there equity in learning for different subgroups of students?*

## Action Strategies

What tasks will you need to complete in order to meet your improvement objectives? The action strategies should be written clearly and concisely — and I like writing them so they begin with verbs. That shows the action in the strategy! The strategies should be tightly aligned to the improvement area, and there should be enough of them to make a difference! Consider organizing your strategies around the three parts of the teaching for learning process: curriculum, instruction, and assessment. Alignment of the action strategies to the improvement objectives is important.

When you organize your strategies around curriculum, instruction, and assessment, this also keeps you from doing something that is commonly done: rushing to include strategies in a school improvement plan. You see, strategies may not be the problem. It may be curriculum or assessment. If you need ideas about the kinds of work to conduct in each strategy, you may want to revisit Chapter 8, *Path to Success*, for ideas.

## Person Responsible For Implementing Strategy

Remember, if someone is not in charge of implementing the strategy, it probably won't get implemented. Who's going to head up the implementation of the strategy? List specific names here. Put someone in charge, or no one is in charge. Check to be sure that no one person is overwhelmed with tasks and that everyone who should be is involved.

## Resources Needed to Complete Task

What are the resources needed to successfully implement the action strategies? Do you need to review curriculum materials? How about information related to your state's test? Do you need other people as resources? Are there supplies and materials that you need? Make a list of resources needed for each strategy. You'll find that the person responsible for completing the task will have a running start. You're providing information that will help someone do his or her job better.

## Budget Implications

So what is each of your strategies going to cost? Include this in your plan — some things do take money to implement. If professional development training is included, put in all of the costs related to the training.

## Dates of Activity

Not everything has to start in September and end in June. When do the activities really need to start and end? Some activities will take a week to complete, some a month, and some the whole year. Remember to put a start and an end date for every activity.

## Monitoring Dates

If you want to make sure that your plan is implemented as scheduled, you'll want to monitor it frequently. Commit to dates when you'll hear a report or look at progress toward the goals. Monitor the plan frequently.

## Monitoring Indicators

These are indicators that point to success at the end of an action strategy. These data indicators will most likely be process indicators. These indicators also help you monitor a plan and give you information about the success of the individual strategies along the way of implementing your plan!

# Improvement Plan

## District Goal Area — Student Achievement

## School Objective — Improve Writing Skills

### Evidences of Need

Key Performance Indicators that show a need to spend time, energy, and resources on this particular objective.

- 68% of the fifth-grade students passed the Direct Writing portion of the English SOL test (spring administration). The minimum pass rate for school accreditation is 70% of the students passing the test.

- 55% of the fifth-grade students scored below 5 points on the composition domain on the SOL writing test. 45% scored a 5 or above on the composition domain.

- 52% of the fifth-grade students scored below 5 points on the written expression domain on the SOL writing test. 48% scored a 5 or above on the written expression domain.

- 62% of the fifth-grade students passed the school-wide writing prompt.

- 48% of the fifth-grade students demonstrated improvement in writing during the school year (September - May).

### Evidences of Success in Improvement

Key Performance Indicators/Performance Targets that point to success at year-end review.

- Increase in the percent of fifth-grade students passing the SOL writing test from 68% to 80%.

- Increase in the percent of fifth-grade students scoring 5 points or above on the composition domain from 45% to 55%.

- Increase in the percent of fifth-grade students scoring 5 points or above on the written expression domain from 48% to 55%.

- Increase in the percentage of fifth-grade students passing the school-wide writing prompt from 62% to 80%.

- Increase in the percentage of fifth-grade students demonstrating improvement in writing during the school year from 48% to 60%.

| Action Strategies (Tasks) | Person Responsible for Implementing Strategy | Resources Needed to Complete Task | Budget Implications | Dates of Activity (start-to-end) | Monitoring Dates | Monitoring Indicators Indicators that point to success at the end of a strategy. |
|---|---|---|---|---|---|---|
| **Curriculum**<br>1.1 Determine the alignment between the writing skills in the district curriculum and those tested on the writing portion of the state tests. | B. Hicks | • Curriculum guides for language arts<br>• SOL state assessment blueprints | • No additional funding needed | August 1999 (begin)<br><br>September 1999 (end) | Team Meeting (August update item on agenda)<br><br>September 21 (due date) | • Completed alignment report<br>• Percentage of objectives related to SOL<br>• Results of writing assessments (skill areas) |
| 1.2 Recommend writing objectives considered to be essential for meeting the achievement goals measured by the state tests. | G. Barnes | • Curriculum guides for language arts<br>• SOL state assessment blueprints | • No additional funding needed | September 22 (begin)<br><br>October 15 (end) | October 15 | • Completed report<br>• Master listing, by grade level, of essential objectives<br>• Committee recommendation about which objectives are priority (including rationale) |
| 1.3 Review a variety of commercial writing programs or programs tried with success in other schools, to determine whether they provide the standards for writing defined by the state and district. | D. Tyler Committee | • Writing-in-the-Content Area Program<br>• Tidewater Writing Project<br>• Writers' Workshop | • No additional funding needed | October (begin)<br><br>December (end) | December | • Completed alignment report by grade level |

| Action Strategies (Tasks) | Person Responsible for Implementing Strategy | Resources Needed to Complete Task | Budget Implications | Dates of Activity (start-to-end) | Monitoring Dates | Monitoring Indicators<br>Indicators that point to success at the end of a strategy. |
|---|---|---|---|---|---|---|
| 1.4 Examine the new reading textbook (which includes writing) to identify strategies which specifically support the domains of composition and style. | W. Bryan | • Textbook series teacher's manual and assessment resources<br>• Textbook company consultant | • No additional funding needed | September (begin)<br><br>October 1 (deadline) | October | • Completed alignment report by grade level |
| **INSTRUCTION**<br>1.5 Examine the latest research and best practices in effective writing techniques. | M. Wahlstrom | • State Department of Education<br>• Northwest Regional Laboratory<br>• University of Illinois Professional Library<br>• Best Practices from Other Schools<br>• Internet | • Professional development books related to writing and writing assessment $450.00 | September (begin)<br><br>January (end) | October 15 | • Completed research report<br>• Committee recommendations, including rationale, for staff training in writing techniques |
| 1.6 Provide format writing practice for students, similar to the writing portion of the SOL tests. | A. March | • Textbook assessment materials, including prompts<br>• School writing rubrics | • No additional funding needed | September (prompt 1)<br><br>January (prompt 2)<br><br>May (prompt 3) | September (prompt 1 results)<br><br>January (prompt 2 results)<br><br>May (prompt 3 results) | • Results of student writing assessments from the textbook series |

| Action Strategies (Tasks) | Person Responsible for Implementing Strategy | Resources Needed to Complete Task | Budget Implications | Dates of Activity (start-to-end) | Monitoring Dates | Monitoring Indicators *Indicators that point to success at the end of a strategy.* |
|---|---|---|---|---|---|---|
| 1.7 Identify at-risk writers and provide tutoring sessions or additional assistance for each. | M. Wahlstrom | • Computer software, Writers' Workshop • Volunteers | • No additional funding needed | September (and ongoing all year) | Monthly (September through the end of the school year) | • Master listing of students by grade level • Log of assistance provided to students • Evidence of writing improvement |
| 1.8 Provide a variety of ways for students to write. | A. Dickason | • Textbook assessment materials, including prompts • School writing rubrics | • No additional funding needed | September (and ongoing all year) | Monthly (September through the end of the school year) | • Master listing of types of writing assignments given to students • Results of student performance on various types of writing |
| 1.9 Teach students how to use graphic organizers as a tool for writing. | D. Holland | • Graphic organizers provided with textbook series | • No additional funding needed | September (and ongoing throughout the school year) | November January March | • Results of student portfolios |
| **ASSESSMENT** 1.10 Provide training for teachers to ensure they are familiar with the SOL tests. | B. Williams | • State Department of Education, research representative • Central office representative • State assessment blueprints | • No additional funding needed — central office staff members will conduct the training session | October | October | • Agendas from training sessions • Evaluation form results from training sessions • Results from student writing assessments at the beginning, middle, and end of the school year |

| Action Strategies (Tasks) | Person Responsible for Implementing Strategy | Resources Needed to Complete Task | Budget Implications | Dates of Activity (start-to-end) | Monitoring Dates | Monitoring Indicators *Indicators that point to success at the end of a strategy.* |
|---|---|---|---|---|---|---|
| 1.11 Provide scoring training for assessing student work with the criteria expected on the SOL tests. | W. Bryan | • State Department of Education, research representative<br>• Central office representative<br>• State assessment blueprints<br>• School writing rubrics | • Scoring training for teachers, Assess for Success. Consultant fees and expenses $2,000.00 | October 17-18 | October | • Agenda from training session<br>• Results of student writing assessments at the beginning, middle, and end of school year |
| 1.12 Design writing prompts to be given at the beginning, middle, and end of the school year. These prompts will be scored by a locally-developed rubric aligned with the state's rubric. | M. Wahlstrom | • Reading series assessment materials<br>• School-wide writing rubrics | • No additional funding needed — training in designing writing prompts included in the above workshop | September | September (prompt 1)<br><br>January (prompt 2)<br><br>May (prompt 3) | • Results of student writing assessments<br>• Comparison of school rubric to state rubric (to see if school rubric will serve as a predictor) |
| **GENERAL**<br>1.13 Verify the effectiveness of instructional strategies. | B. Dickason | • No special resources needed | • Training: How to Assess Instructional Strategies — after school workshops $800.00 | Training Date November 17, 1999<br><br>Monthly Team Meetings | • Strategies updates as agenda items on faculty council agendas<br>• Results of effectiveness of training | • Results of student writing assessments from the textbook series |
| 1.14 Communicate to parents and students the district's learning targets (writing skills and objectives). | D. Wahlstrom | • Printed materials<br>• Software for designing newsletter<br>• School writing rubrics | • Printed materials for parents, $500.00<br>• Standards for Student Notebooks, $800.00<br>• Posters with Learning Targets, $150.00 | September (and ongoing throughout the school year) | • Quarterly newsletter: September December March June | • School newsletter<br>• Writing booklet (for parents)<br>• Learning targets posted in each classroom |

# Improvement Plan

District Goal Area _____

School Objective _____

## Evidences of Need

Key Performance Indicators that show a need to spend time, energy, and resources on this particular objective.

## Evidences of Success in Improvement

Key Performance Indicators/Performance Targets that point to success at year-end review.

| Action Strategies (Tasks) | Person Responsible for Implementing Strategy | Resources Needed to Complete Task | Budget Implications | Dates of Activity (start-to-end) | Monitoring Dates | Monitoring Indicators Indicators that point to success at the end of a strategy. |
|---|---|---|---|---|---|---|
|  |  |  |  |  |  |  |
|  |  |  |  |  |  |  |
|  |  |  |  |  |  |  |

| Action Strategies (Tasks) | Person Responsible for Implementing Strategy | Resources Needed to Complete Task | Budget Implications | Dates of Activity (start-to-end) | Monitoring Dates | Monitoring Indicators *Indicators that point to success at the end of a strategy.* |
|---|---|---|---|---|---|---|
| | | | | | | |
| | | | | | | |
| | | | | | | |

# Writing the Key Performance Indicators (KPIs)

Many school districts require staff to write data-based plans. And there is an expectation that the effectiveness of the plan can be measured. This measurement piece is done with key performance indicators (performance or outcome indicators) in the Evidence of Success part of your plan. Learning to write KPIs is yet another important data skill. And learning to write them correctly will save you many hours during the school year — and will also make it easy for you to determine the results of your improvement plans fairly quickly. (You can quickly see how they are written in the sample format of the school improvement plan, but more information about writing them is included here.)

When you begin to write key performance indicators, you might be inclined to write something like the following:

> Students passing the writing test.

That's a fair start, but the next example is better:

> The percentage of 6th grade students passing the state writing test.

Remember, KPIs are used in two ways: as indicators of need and/or indicators of success. How you write the KPI will depend on whether the item is being used as an evidence of need or success. As with everything else, generally you will choose whether something is an indicator of need or of success. You'll use your professional judgment about where to place the KPI. Suppose I told you that students in the school got a mean percentile score of 43 on the Stanford Achievement Test, 9th Edition (or other norm-referenced test). Would you put that KPI as an indicator of need or an indicator of success? (Chances are you'd put that under indicator of need.) What if I told you that during the previous year in the same school the students earned a percentile score of 34 on the same test? Now what do you think? You may now be thinking that the percentile score of 43 is now an evidence of success. (Even though you'd still want to see continuing improvement.)

So let's review how to write KPIs for baseline data. (Baseline data is when you're collecting the information for the first time — or it's the starting point of where you're looking at student achievement.)

## Writing KPIs as Evidences of Need

When you're writing KPIs as **Evidences of Need**, write them like this:

> 32% of the third-grade students passed the writing portion of the Virginia Standards of Learning test.

> 50% of the third-grade students indicated they enjoy writing, as indicated by the school's writing interest survey.

## Writing KPIs as Evidences of Success

The **Evidences of Success** part of your school plan points to your improvement goals — your measures of success. When you're writing KPIs as Evidences of Success for the end of the school year, write them like this:

> **Increase** in the percent of students scoring 3 or higher on the composing domain of the writing test from **32% to 50%**.

> **Increase** in the percentage of students indicating they enjoy writing from **50% to 90%**.

Notice that I recommend you begin writing your Evidences of Success with a verb. Do you want your measurement piece to show an increase? A decrease? Use a verb to help describe exactly what you hope will happen. Also, notice that I encourage you to build in the actual measurement amount at the end of the statement. Many schools do not build in the improvement target as a part of writing the success indicators. Schools may have written that they would like to increase the percentage of students by a achieving at a certain level (increase by 5 percent).

Knowing how to write these KPIs will save you much time and energy. Everything you need to determine whether or not you've met your objectives will be in the plan; and at the end of the year, all you'll have to do is get the final data pieces and compare them to the Evidences of Success in your plan.

## Setting Improvement Goals

You may have wondered in the past how much of an improvement goal you should set. Is five percent enough? Should it be from three to ten percent? Well, it depends.

Katherine Divine, while working for Portsmouth Public Schools in Virginia, described how to determine how much growth is sufficient to target in a school improvement objective.

There are two key types of improvement goals: (1) percent of students change and (2) percent of students achieving a standard.

If you are looking at the percent of students change, a goal of a 10-25% increase is appropriate.

If you are looking at the percent of students achieving a standard, that goal should be 75-80% attainment for all students.

On the next page you'll find an overview of information related to setting worthy increases or levels of achievement.

I often see schools with this improvement objective: *Improve the test scores.* I prefer to use the improvement of the test scores as an indicator of success or need. I think what we're improving are skills and knowledge such as writing, reading, math, science, and social studies. If we are doing a better job with these areas, we'll see it in the results of the test scores — those evidences of success!

# What is a worthy increase or level of achievement when setting improvement goals?

## % of Students Change

**Looking for increases or decreases in the percentage of students**

**Examples:**
- Decrease in the percentage of students with discipline referrals.

- Increase in the percentage of students scoring at or above the 50th percentile.

**Goal: 10-25% of the group you're trying to move.**

## % of Students Achieving a Standard

**Looking for increases in the percentage of students meeting standards**

**Examples:**
- Increase in the percentage of students passing the state writing test.

- Increase in the percentage of students achieving mastery in a science class.

**Goal: 75-80% mastery for all students.**

# Make Your School Plan Work For You

Don't let the school improvement plan just sit on a shelf. After all the work you've put into collecting, organizing, and analyzing data, use your plan. Using a school improvement plan on a regular basis takes discipline and practice, but it gets the results you want. Here are a few ideas for using your school improvement plan.

1. Write the school plan so it is usable. Use language that is clear and concise. Write to express, not impress.

2. Make time every day (10 minutes) to review your school improvement plan. Keep your eye on the game. Keep your plan in front of you.

3. Highlight key parts of your plan. Use post-it notes to note the key pages, and refer to these pages often.

4. Put progress reports for individual strategies on the planning team agenda.

5. Make a master calendar from the dates of implementation for the key strategies in the plan.

6. Place extra copies of your school plan on the counter in the office. Share your plan with central office staff members. (Many of them will be resources in helping you implement your plan.)

7. Post your school improvement plan — and progress towards each piece — on your school's website.

8. Celebrate all of the small steps along the way. At the end of the year, celebrate BIG!

So there you have it. Data can be an important part of your school improvement plan. Use it to determine the priority areas for improvement for your school. Use outcome and demographic data to determine your evidences of success — your improvement indicators. Use outcome, demographic, and process data to help you monitor your plan along the way.

## Improvement Plan Rubric

If you want a quick check on whether or not you're including key components in your plan, just use the Improvement Plan Rubric on the next page.

# Improvement Plan Rubric

|  | Publishable<br>(It's a Wrap!) | On the Way | Not Yet<br>(Back to the Planning Board) |
|---|---|---|---|
| **Improvement Objectives** | The improvement plan has objectives that are clear and concise.<br><br>The objectives are aligned with the school district's goals, mission, vision, and priorities.<br><br>The objectives are related to student achievement.<br><br>The improvement objectives have been chosen based on student performance data.<br><br>The objectives are written so that they are measurable.<br><br>The objectives reflect the school's learning questions.<br><br>The objectives are reasonable in number (3-5).<br><br>The objectives get at the essence of improvement; they're content or process objectives and not just data improvement objective — "improve our score" objectives. | The plan has objectives, but they're not clear or concise.<br><br>The objectives are aligned with school district goals, mission, and vision.<br><br>The objectives are not measurable.<br><br>The objectives don't reflect the school's learning questions.<br><br>The objectives are scant (2).<br><br>The objectives tell how much the scores are going to go up rather than just what is going to improve (e.g., reading, writing, math, science, social studies). | The plan has fewer than three objectives, and they're not written clearly and concisely.<br><br>The objectives aren't aligned with the district goals, mission, and vision.<br><br>The objectives aren't measurable.<br><br>The objectives don't reflect the school's learning questions.<br><br>The objectives tell how much the scores are going to go up rather than just what is going to improve (e.g., reading, writing, math, science, social studies.) |
| **Key Performance Indicators** | The key performance indicators are aligned with the improvement objectives.<br><br>At least three Evidences of Need have been included to validate why time, energy, and resources should be spent on this area.<br><br>At least three Evidences of Success have been included.<br><br>The Evidences of Success provide the performance target.<br><br>The Evidences of Success include more than just standardized test scores.<br><br>The Key Performance Indicators provide disaggregated data measures, where appropriate. | Most of the KPIs are aligned with the improvement objectives.<br><br>There are 1 or 2 Evidences of Need.<br><br>There are 2 Evidences of Success.<br><br>The Evidences of Success provide the improvement piece, but they are not written clearly.<br><br>The Evidences of Success are the standardized test scores.<br><br>The KPIs do not provide disaggregated data measures. | Most of the KPIs are aligned with the improvement objectives.<br><br>No Evidences of Need have been included.<br><br>There is only one Evidence of Success.<br><br>The Evidences of Success do not provide the improvement piece.<br><br>The Evidence of Success is the standardized test scores.<br><br>The KPI does not provide disaggregated data measures. |

|  | Publishable (It's a Wrap!) | On the Way | Not Yet (Back to the Planning Board) |
|---|---|---|---|
| **Strategies** | The action strategies are written clearly and concisely.<br><br>The strategies are tightly aligned to the improvement objective.<br><br>The action plans contain new strategies — and not just a repeat of what's been done already — that support the improvement of the objectives in the plan.<br><br>There are enough strategies to make a difference in the improvement area.<br><br>The action strategies contain items in curriculum, instruction, and assessment.<br><br>The action strategies have costs attached to them.<br><br>The strategies list key resources (e.g., materials, people).<br><br>Each strategy has a monitoring date.<br><br>Each strategy has an implementation date.<br><br>Each strategy identifies a person who will "head up" the strategy.<br><br>Each strategy is doable — within the constraints of the school year, the budget, and other resources. | The action plans are organized.<br><br>The action plans contain strategies, but they're the strategies already being done.<br><br>The improvement objectives have strategies, but there are so many that it's unlikely that all of the strategies get completed.<br><br>The strategies are not designed around the teaching and learning process: curriculum, instruction, and assessment.<br><br>The strategies have a cost, but it's not clear where the costs came from.<br><br>The key resources are listed, but in a way that is not really useful.<br><br>Action plans have monitoring dates, but no details.<br><br>Implementation dates are included.<br><br>Specific people are not included.<br><br>Most of the strategies are doable. | The action plans are neat and organized.<br><br>The improvement objectives have strategies, but they're not sufficient to ensure improvement.<br><br>There is no cost attached to the strategy.<br><br>Key resources are not listed. |
| **General** | The school improvement plan has a cover with school and district names.<br><br>There is a page that identifies the names of the school planning team members.<br><br>There is a page that describes the process the faculty used in developing its school improvement plan, including how faculty approval was attained. | | |

## Summary

A school improvement plan is a critical tool for creating and managing changes that lead toward improved student achievement. Data plays a role in the development of school improvement plans. Data is used to determine where the school is in the area of student achievement and is also used to set measurement indicators for the plan.

# Appendix
# A Analysis Guide

One technique for working with and thinking about data is to create analysis guides. These guides walk you through the key pieces of your data and help to make sure you look at everything you may need to review.

## Parts of An Analysis Guide

Analysis guides can be as extensive or as brief as you'd like. I've designed guides that are comprehensive, taking you through the test frameworks all the way to the results of the assessments. My guides often include pieces from *Data Analysis Questions* and *Factors to Analyze* — then everything goes into a workbook format.

## Example Portion of An Analysis Guide

In this appendix, I've put a piece of an overall analysis guide. The entire guide includes the following components: Reporting Categories, Data Analysis, Curriculum Analysis, Instruction Analysis, and Assessment Analysis. Together, these parts give a really good picture of what's working and what's not working in a school, district, or program. Please note that the example in Appendix A is only one part of the overall guide, just to give you an idea of how you might organize a guide yourself.

## Other Areas for Analysis Guides

Analysis guides can be created for any tests or types of assessments. I've created these for the *Stanford 9*, the *Iowa Tests of Basic Skills*, different state assessments, and assessments in general. School teams usually enjoy "working through the guide" to look at and think about their data.

## Data Analysis Section for a State Test

Remember, the information in this appendix is only one part of a more comprehensive guide. As you preview the information, you'll notice templates for data tables and a variety of charts and graphs. Also notice that some state tests simply don't provide enough data for use in improving instruction. That's why there have been so many other data pieces for you to think about in this book. By the way, many of our state tests are designed as tests of accountability and not tests which provide diagnostic information about what to do to help students achieve at higher levels. So don't try to read more into the data related to your state tests than you should. There is an exception to this though. In many of the writing tests that various states give, there is enough information to improve instruction, and you'll certainly want to take a hard look at that data.

# SOL Analysis Guide

### for Virginia SOL Tests

## Section 2
# Data Analysis — Writing

# Direct Writing Analysis, Grades 5, 8, 11

Use the template on the following page to graph the percentage of students you have scoring in each of the domain areas. (Remember to go to your School Summary Reports to find this information.) Then answer the questions that follow.

The Direct Writing portion of the SOL tests is given in grades 5, 8, and 11. Students are asked to respond to a prompt, and their papers are scored using a rubric. (An adapted copy of the assessment blueprint rubrics is included in this section.)

When student scores come back, you get information about how students did in each of the domains (i.e., composing, sentence formation, mechanics). This information can be found in your School Summary Report. (Of course, individual student information can be located on the Student List Report.) Reviewing this information can be useful in helping students improve.

Here's the good news: With the data by domain area, you can make adjustments in writing instruction. Here's more good news: The School Summary Report tells you what percentage of students are in each level of control for each domain area.

There are four levels of control:

1    Little or No Control
2    Inconsistent Control
3    Reasonable Control
4    Consistent Control

# Percent of Students Earning Each Domain Score
## SOL Direct Writing Test

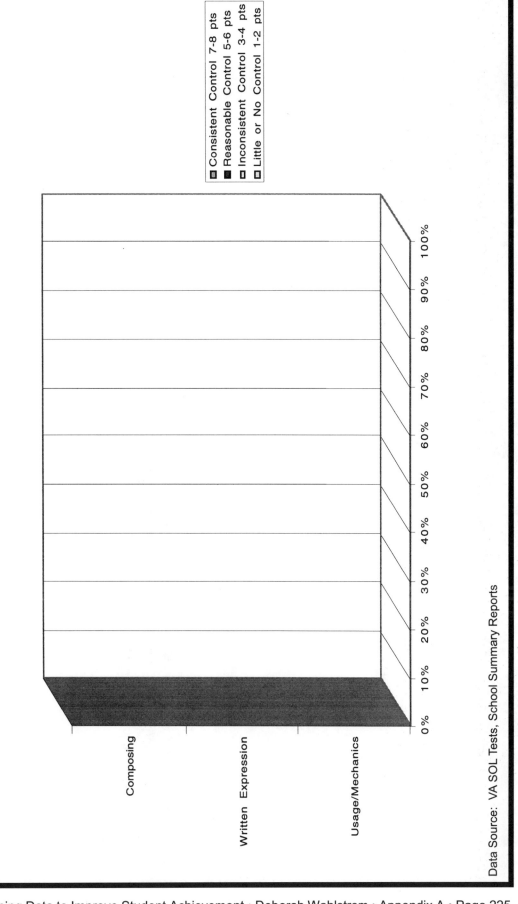

Composing

Written Expression

Usage/Mechanics

0%  10%  20%  30%  40%  50%  60%  70%  80%  90%  100%

- Consistent Control 7-8 pts
- Reasonable Control 5-6 pts
- Inconsistent Control 3-4 pts
- Little or No Control 1-2 pts

Data Source: VA SOL Tests, School Summary Reports

# Analysis Questions for Domains of Writing

1. In which domain did your school/district have the highest percentage of students achieving consistent and reasonable control? (You'll add these two percentages together.)

2. What factors in your school or district led to this success? (What are some of the good things you are implementing that help students achieve at this level?)

3. In which domain did your school/district have the highest percentage of students scoring at little/ no control and inconsistent control? (You'll add these two percentages together.)

# Disaggregation of Mean Scaled Scores by Gender

The SOL score report, Analysis of Subgroup Performance, provides information that is useful in determining whether or not there is "learning for all" in your school. The SOL score reports provide subgroup data for gender and race/ethnicity. Use the score report to fill in the data on the table at the right.

|  | Total | Females | Males | Gap |
|---|---|---|---|---|
| Mean Scaled Score |  |  |  |  |

## Analysis Questions

1. What was the total mean score for students taking this test? Is there **quality** on the achievement levels of this test? _____ If so, why? If not, why not?

2. Who achieved a greater score, the males or the females? What were the scores for each?

3. Is there gender **equity** on this assessment? Is there a gap in achievement between the scores of the males and females? (The difference in the scores between males and females is the gap.)

4. Why is it important to look at gaps in the achievement levels between different subgroups of students?

# Disaggregation of SOL Test by Gender

The SOL score report, Analysis of Subgroup Performance, also provides information about subgroups of students and their overall achievement on the SOL tests. Use the Analysis of Subgroup Performance to complete the data table at the right.

| | Total Summary | | Females | | Males | | Gap | |
|---|---|---|---|---|---|---|---|---|
| | # | % | # | % | # | % | # | % |
| Students Tested | | | | | | | na | na |
| **Proficiency Levels** | | | | | | | | |
| Failing/Does Not Meet | | | | | | | | |
| Pass/Proficient | | | | | | | | |
| Pass/Advanced | | | | | | | | |
| Pass Rate (% Passing) | | | | | | | | |

## Analysis Questions

1. What is the total number of students who took this test? _____ This number represents _____ % of the students in the school.

2. What was the percent passing rate for the total group? _____ What was the percent passing rate for the females? _____ What was the percent passing rate for the males? _____

3. Is there **quality** on this test? _____ If so, why? If not, why not? (Use the percent pass rate to make your decision.)

4. What is the gap between the passing rate for males and females on this SOL test? _____ Is this a gap for which you should be concerned? _____ If so, why?

**Continued on Next Page**

5. Is there **gender** equity on this test? (Use the gap percentages to make your decision.)

6. What percentage of students attained a Failing/ Does Not Meet proficiency level (scaled score of 0-399)? _____ How many students does this represent? _____

7. What other areas of disaggregation might be appropriate for your school? Race/ethnicity? Socioeconomic status?

# Disaggregation of Mean Scaled Scores by Race

The SOL score report, Analysis of Subgroup Performance, provides information that is useful in determining whether or not there is "learning for all" in your school. The SOL score reports provide subgroup data for gender and race/ethnicity. Use the score report to fill in your race/ethnicity data on the table at the right.

| | Total | American Indian/Alaskan Native | Asian or Pacific Islander | Black | Hispanic | White |
|---|---|---|---|---|---|---|
| Mean Scaled Score | | | | | | |

# Analysis Questions

1. What was the total mean score for students taking this test? Is there **quality** on the achievement levels of this test? _____ If so, why? If not, why not?

2. Who achieved a greater score, the minority students or white students? What were the scores for each?

3. Is there race/ethnicity **equity** on this assessment? Is there a gap in achievement between the scores of the different races? (The difference in the scores between minority students and white students is the gap.)

4. Why is it important to look at gaps in the achievement levels between different subgroups of students?

# Disaggregation of SOL Test by Race/Ethnicity

The SOL score report, Analysis of Subgroup Performance, also provides information about subgroups of students and their overall achievement on the SOL tests. Use the Analysis of Subgroup Performance to complete the data table at the right.

| | Total Summary | | American Indian/Alaskan Native | | Asian or Pacific Islander | | Black | | Hispanic | | White | |
|---|---|---|---|---|---|---|---|---|---|---|---|---|
| | # | % | # | % | # | % | # | % | # | % | # | % |
| Students Tested | | | | | | | | | | | | |
| **Proficiency Levels** | | | | | | | | | | | | |
| Failing/Does Not Meet | | | | | | | | | | | | |
| Pass/Proficient | | | | | | | | | | | | |
| Pass/Advanced | | | | | | | | | | | | |
| Pass Rate (% Passing) | | | | | | | | | | | | |

## Analysis Questions

1. What is the total number of students who took this test? _____ This number represents _____ % of the students in the school.

2. What was the percent passing rate for the total group? _____ What was the percent passing rate for the black students? _____ What was the percent passing rate for the white students? _____

3. Is there **quality** on this test? _____ If so, why? If not, why not? (Use the percent pass rate to make your decision.)

4. What is the gap between the passing rate for minority and white students on this SOL test? _____ Is this a gap for which you should be concerned? _____ If so, why?

5. Is there **race/ethnicity** equity on this test? (Use the gap percentages to make your decision.)

6. What percentage of students attained a Failing/Does Not Meet proficiency level (scaled score of 0-399)? _____ How many students does this represent? _____

7. What other areas of disaggregation might be appropriate for your school? Gender? Socioeconomic status? Mobility? Attendance? Special education students?

# SOL Test Summary Sheet

## for SOL Test:

## Test Date:

Number of Students Taking This SOL Test

Percent Pass Rate for This SOL Test

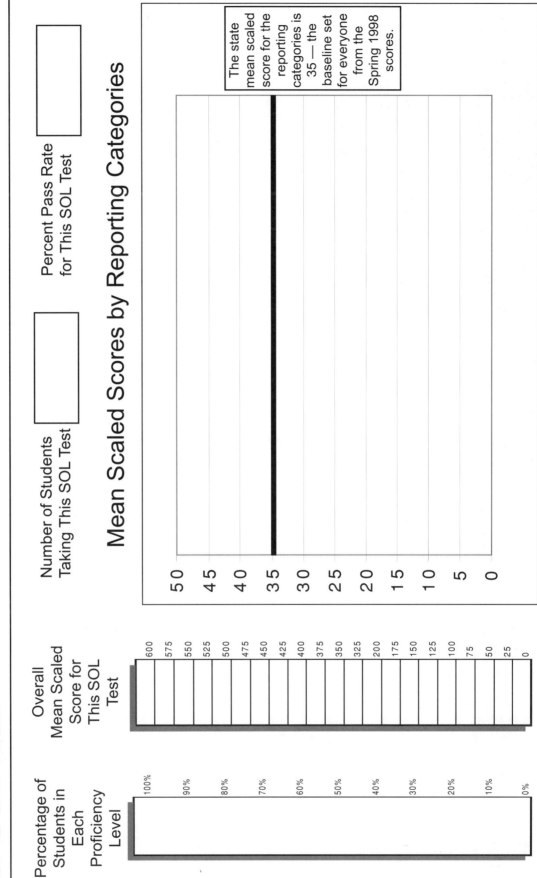

Overall Mean Scaled Score for This SOL Test

600
575
550
525
500
475
450
425
400
375
350
325
200
175
150
125
100
75
50
25
0

Percentage of Students in Each Proficiency Level

100%
90%
80%
70%
60%
50%
40%
30%
20%
10%
0%

### Mean Scaled Scores by Reporting Categories

50
45
40
35
30
25
20
15
10
5
0

The state mean scaled score for the reporting categories is 35 — the baseline set for everyone from the Spring 1998 scores.

# SOL Test Summary Sheets • Spring 1998

## Analysis Questions

Use the information on the SOL Test Summary Sheet to help you answer the questions that follow.

1.  How many students took this SOL test? _____ What percentage of the students overall does this represent? _____

2.  Why might the percentage of students who took the test be less than 100%?

3.  What number and percentage of students attained a Pass/Proficient level (scaled score of 400–499) of achievement on this SOL test?

4.  What number and percentage of students attained a Pass/Advanced level (scaled score of 500–600) of achievement on this SOL test?

5.  What number and percentage of students attained a passing score (a scaled score of 400 or greater) on this test? (This will be the number of students who attained a Pass/Proficient level of achievement + students who attained a Pass/Advanced level of achievement).

6.  What is the school mean scaled score for this SOL test? _____

# Mean Scaled Scores for Reporting Categories

## Analysis Questions

1. Rank the reporting categories for this test from high to low, based on the mean scaled scores.

---

**Ranking of Reporting Categories by Mean Scaled Scores**

---

2. In which reporting category did students in the school do best? In which category did students in the district do best?

| School | District |
|--------|----------|
|        |          |

3. Think about your school. What are some of the factors that have led to this success?

4. In which reporting category did students in your school perform worst? What factors may have led to this?

# Data Analysis Section of Guide

**Weaknesses**

**Strengths**

# Appendix B Implementing Standards Checklist

Data can be a useful tool for making decisions about implementing standards. There are so many things to think about in a variety of different areas. The following checklist provides a quick view of things a school administrator or improvement team may want to consider when implementing state standards.

The checklist is organized to help you think about data through the following lenses:

Using Data
Curriculum
Instruction
Assessment
Communications
School Improvement Plans

# Administrator's Checklist
## For Implementing State Standards

## Using Data

1. We have collected a variety of data about our school.

   ❐ outcome

   ❐ demographic

   ❐ process

2. We have organized and analyzed the following state-mandated achievement data:

   ❐ norm-referenced test results

   ❐ state criterion-referenced test results

3. In addition to the achievement data above, we have organized and analyzed our state report card data:

   ❐ attendance

   ❐ promotion/retention rates

   ❐ professional training index

   ❐ diploma types (high school)

   ❐ advanced placement results (high school)

   ❐ mobility ratings

   ❐ _____

   ❐ _____

   ❐ _____

   ❐ _____

   ❐ _____

4. We have organized and analyzed other data useful for understanding achievement in our school:

   ❐ student grades in courses

   ❐ percentage of students performing on grade level

   ❐ climate surveys

   ❐ _____

5.   We have disaggregated, where appropriate, our data based on:
   ❒   race/ethnicity
   ❒   gender
   ❒   SES
   ❒   mobility index
   ❒   attendance
   ❒   _____
   ❒   _____

6.   We have completed Achievement Profiles to get the big picture of each of the core content areas:
   ❒   English/Language Arts/Reading/Writing
   ❒   Science
   ❒   Math
   ❒   Social Studies
   ❒   _____

7.   We have determined areas of focus for the upcoming school year — based on the data we've reviewed and analyzed.  We have discussed factors that may have contributed to the achievement level.

8.   We have designed a school improvement plan based upon our data.  In this plan we have also set high targets for student achievement.  We have talked about what we need to do to help students who aren't learning as well as expected.  Our plans have addressed the needs of our school through the lenses of curriculum, instruction, and assessment.

# Curriculum

1. We have thoroughly reviewed the state/district assessment blueprints to find out:
   - ☐ which objectives/standards ARE on the state test.
   - ☐ which objectives/standards ARE *NOT* on the state test.
   - ☐ the reporting categories/subtests.
   - ☐ the number of questions in each category.
   - ☐ the percentage of the curriculum in each reporting category.

2. For each of the district's curriculum objectives and standards, we have:
   - ☐ Determined how to help the student learn the objectives/standards.
   - ☐ Determined how to assess the objectives/standards in the classroom.

3. We have looked at the state reports and compared the scores we achieved to the possible scores.
   - ☐ We have identified the reporting categories/subtests in which we're weakest.
   - ☐ We have identified the reporting categories/subtests in which we're strongest.
   - ☐ We have "pulled out" the standards and objectives for weak areas. We've brainstormed reasons for the weaknesses.

4. We have developed a process for ensuring that teachers understand how to implement the standards.

5. We have had teachers create a classroom curriculum map for the school year.
   - ☐ We have provided training for curriculum mapping, if needed.
   - ☐ We have evidence of curriculum maps for each of the core content areas.
   - ☐ We have verified the curriculum maps to ensure the percentage of time teachers plan to teach the different parts of the curriculum reflects the percentages in the assessments, where appropriate.
   - ☐ We have determined how to handle standards that are skills that should be taught and reinforced during the entire school year.
   - ☐ We have discussed ways to integrate the curriculum, where appropriate.
   - ☐ We have discussed how to pace the teaching and learning of the district curriculum for the block schedule, if appropriate.

6. We have determined how to monitor the teaching and learning of the standards and the district's curriculum.
   - ☐ We have provided training for this, if needed.

# Instruction

1. We have looked at the data and the curriculum to determine areas where we might need a renewed emphasis on learning strategies that will help the students learn the objectives/standards.

2. We have determined what types of strategies support the learning of different standards. (Not all standards are alike.)

3. We have surveyed teachers to determine their levels of expertise in key instructional strategies. We have prioritized these and chosen those that will make the most difference in helping students learn the targets.

4. We have conducted a strategy search:
   - ❒ research-based strategies and evidences
   - ❒ internal trainers/experts
   - ❒ external experts
   - ❒ books
   - ❒ videos
   - ❒ site visits to successful programs
   - ❒ courses
   - ❒ workshops

5. We have determined professional development activities, and have made plans to provide them where appropriate.

6. We have a plan to encourage teachers to participate in professional development opportunities that are not provided by the school (e.g., workshops, college courses).

7. We have included the training and monitoring of these strategies in our school improvement plan.

8. We have identified research-based strategies and plan to use them consistently in the classroom.

9. We have conducted a textbook alignment analysis for new textbooks we're adopting or purchasing.

10. We have identified supplementary resources and materials that support the teaching and learning process.

# Assessment

1.  Since we don't want to wait until students have taken the state tests to determine their achievement levels toward the standards, we have discussed and planned for ways to assess their achievement of the standards in the classroom.

2.  We have thoroughly reviewed the assessment blueprints or frameworks to determine the helpful hints for taking the state test. We have a plan for sharing this with our students and their parents.

3.  We know how to assess each of the standards in our classrooms. (We know which standards require paper/pencil tests and which standards require performance assessment.)

4.  We know how to use the results of assessment to improve student learning.

5.  We have a plan/ideas for helping students deal with test anxiety, student motivation when taking tests, and testwiseness — not just for the state tests, but for tests in general. (The purpose of this component is to help students become confident test takers.)

6.  We have conducted a format analysis of practice tests, comparing them to our state test.

7.  We have conducted a content analysis of practice tests, comparing them to our state/district standards.

# Communications

1. We have a plan for communicating the expectations we have for achievement to our faculty and students.

2. We have a plan for sharing data, addressing the state tests, and studying the assessment blueprints with our faculty.

3. We have determined how to communicate the standards to our students and parents.

4. We have determined how to communicate information about the state assessments to students and parents.

5. We have a plan for answering questions from the media about our state assessment results. We have anticipated questions the media may ask and are prepared to respond to them.

6. We have some sort of written communication that provides achievement results to our students, staff, parents, and community (e.g, school lunch menu, school newsletter, PTA newsletter, school profile of achievement, executive summary).

# School Improvement Plans

1.     We have developed a data-based school improvement plan.

2.     We have designed a plan in which there is alignment of the goals, objectives, and strategies, all based on our data.

3.     We have written excellent statements for the objectives in our plan.  Our objectives are:
   - ❐   clear and concise.
   - ❐   aligned with the school district's goals, mission, vision, and priorities.
   - ❐   measurable.
   - ❐   reflective of our data.
   - ❐   reasonable in number (3-5 objectives).
   - ❐   included to get at the essence of improvement.  (They're content or process objectives and not just raise-our-test-scores objectives.)

4.     Our key performance indicators are aligned with the improvement objectives.
   - ❐   We have included at least three evidences of need, where appropriate.
   - ❐   We have included at least three evidences of success, where appropriate.
   - ❐   The evidence of success provides the improvement measurement piece.
   - ❐   The evidences of success include more than just standardized test scores.
   - ❐   Our key performance indicators, including evidences of need and success, provide disaggregated data measures, where appropriate.

5.     We have designed action plans that we can use to implement and monitor ourselves during the year.
   - ❐   The action plans are organized.
   - ❐   The action plans contain strategies that support the improvement of the objectives in the plan.
   - ❐   Each improvement objective has sufficient action strategies.
   - ❐   The action strategies have a cost attached to them.
   - ❐   The action plan lists key resources (e.g, materials, people).
   - ❐   Each strategy has an implementation date.
   - ❐   Each strategy identifies a person who will be responsible for the implementation of the strategy.
   - ❐   Each strategy is doable — within the constraints of the school year, the budget, and other resources.

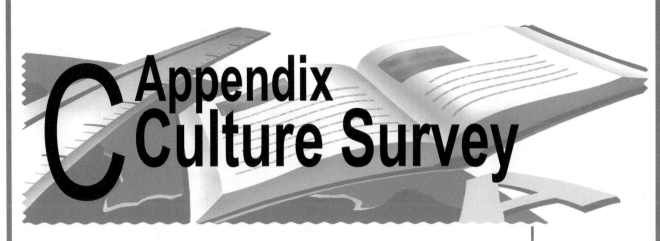

# Appendix C Culture Survey

## What is a School Culture Survey?

School culture surveys are useful tools for determining overall culture as part of a school effectiveness evaluation. As I work with schools, staff members often ask me for an economical survey that can be used to gather more data about the culture of the school. This chapter contains a battery of school culture surveys that you are welcome to use. (All I request is that you keep the credit at the bottom of the survey pages.)

There are two forms to this survey: one for teachers and one for students. These forms may be photocopied and administered in groups or individually. Instructions for administering and scoring the survey are included. I hope this will be a useful tool to many of you in learning more about the climate of your school.

# School Culture Survey Battery Data Sheet

**Authors:**            Deborah Wahlstrom, Ph.D.
                        Alfred P. Rovai, Ph.D.

**Purpose:**            To sample teachers and students using the survey method in order to assess school culture as part of a school effectiveness evaluation.

**Population:**         Elementary, middle, and secondary classroom teachers and middle and secondary students.

**Forms:**              Teacher Survey of School Culture - 1st Edition (TSSC-1) and Student Survey of School Culture - 1st Edition (SSSC-1).

**Administration:**     Survey forms may be photocopied and administered in groups or individually.

**Time:**               Administration time is approximately 10 - 15 minutes.

**Scales:**             General school culture score and the following subscores: teacher perspective and student perspective (student perspective available only for middle and secondary schools at present).

**Validity:**           The authors assess the School Culture Survey Battery to have high face validity. Content validity will be determined by a panel of experts.

**Reliability:**        Internal consistencies for the TSSC-1 range from .89 to .97. Reliability data for the SSSC-1 has not yet been determined.

**Norms:**              To be determined.

The School Culture Survey Battery consists of two survey instruments: the *Teacher Survey of School Culture - 1st Edition* (TSSC-1) and the *Student Survey of School Culture* - 1st Edition (SSSC-1). Each survey is four pages long and follows this User's Manual. The surveys are not to be modified in any way. To do so will invalidate the battery norms and the evidence of survey validity and reliability.

The battery was created to provide an easy method of measuring school culture based on the inputs of classroom teachers and students. The TSSC-1 can be administered to teachers in elementary, middle, and high schools. The SSSC-1 is appropriate for middle and high school students only. There is no form presently available in this test battery for elementary school students.

Copyright notice

These surveys are copyrighted. Purchasers of this book are granted a license to photocopy and administer the surveys for their schools only. This license does not extend to the publication and/or further distribution of these surveys by book, magazine, electronic media, etc.

Sampling

In order to minimize the threat of bias, the following sampling techniques should be closely followed.

■ TSSC-1: administer the survey to all of the classroom teachers present at school on the day the survey is administered.

■ SSSC-1: administer the survey to either 100 students or 25% of the students present at school on the day the survey is administered, whichever figure yields the higher number of completed surveys. These numbers are minimums. Higher numbers may be used. STUDENTS MUST BE SELECTED AT RANDOM; and, if truly random procedures are used the selected students will represent a cross-section of the school ( e.g., by grade, by race, by sex, by achievement, by socioeconomic status).

The importance of using random sampling procedures cannot be overstated. For example, if surveys are distributed evenly by teacher and teachers are told to randomly administer the surveys to their students, some teachers may only administer surveys to their best students. Such a practice will result in bias and misleading results. The best method is for the school's administrative office to randomly select the names of students to complete the survey from the school roster.

Procedures

The survey should be administered by a nonthreatening individual. (This person is called the survey administrator.) The school principal or assistant principals should not be present. The survey administrator should assemble the respondents, distribute the survey, read aloud the following directions, and collect the survey as respondents finish. ADDITIONAL DIRECTIONS SHOULD NOT BE PROVIDED.

Directions

The following directions are to be read to respondents:

> The survey you have in front of you consists of four pages and should only take a few minutes for you to complete. You may use either pen or pencil. The purpose of this survey is to help us make your school a better place to teach and learn. Your honest responses to each question will help us achieve this purpose.
>
> Your responses will be kept absolutely confidential. The first page includes some information about yourself. Please note that we are not asking you to place your name on this survey. Therefore your responses will remain anonymous.
>
> The survey includes a number of statements with each statement followed by one or more scales. Take a look at the example statement and scale near the bottom of the first page of the survey.
>
> [PAUSE for a moment or two]
>
> Each scale consist of pairs of words separated by five spaces that are numbered zero through four. The numbers are there to help you identify the spaces. The statement in this example is *Taking a test.* The scale consists of the words *nervous* and *relaxed* separated by five spaces. The idea is for you to place an "X" in the appropriate space to show how you feel about the statement. For example, if taking a test makes you feel very nervous, you would place an "X" in the space marked with a zero. If taking a test makes you somewhat nervous, you would mark the scale in the space marked with a one, as shown in the next example. Naturally, if you are very comfortable about taking a test, you would mark the space marked with a four on the "relaxed" side of the scale. If you can't decide, or if you feel midway or neutral between the two words, you should place an "X" in the middle space marked with a two.
>
> As you complete this survey please make sure you place an "X" in the appropriate space on all scales. You may now start.

Scoring

The TSSC-1 consists of 42 numbered statements, each followed by one or more scales for a total of

65 scales. The SSSC-1 consists of 39 numbered statements, also followed by one or more scales for a total of 65 scales. Both surveys are scored in the same manner.

Before scoring either the TSSC-1 or SSSC-1, check for blank scales. Do not count blank scales as zero! If over two scales are left blank, the survey should be treated as invalid, and the survey results for that respondent should be discarded. If one or two scales have been left blank, the scorer may insert a substitute score of "4" for the blank scales.

Scores for each scale are determined in accordance with the template provided with each scale. For example:

**1. Professional development opportunities available to teachers at my school**
           **rare**        ( 0 )  ( 1 )  ( 2 )  ( 3 )  ( 4 )        **frequent**

A score of 2 will be given for this scale if the respondent answered in the middle space.

Score each scale, then add all scores on each survey to obtain the overall score. The minimum possible score for the TSSC-1 and the SSSC-1 is 0, and the maximum possible score for each survey is 260.

The following scores for your school can now be calculated:

■   Teacher perspective school culture score (range: 0 to 260): the mean TSSC-1 score for your school.

■   Student perspective school culture score (range: 0 to 260): the mean SSSC-1 score for your school.

■   Overall school culture score (range: 0 to 260): the arithmetic average of the mean TSSC-1 score and the mean SSSC-1 score.

Reliability

Internal consistencies for the TSSC-1 range from .89 to .97. The SSSC-1 has not yet been checked for reliability.

Evidence of validity

The authors assess the School Culture Survey Battery to have high face validity. Content validity will be determined by a panel of experts.

Norms

To be developed

# Teacher Survey of School Culture - 1st Edition (TSSC-1)

The purpose of this survey is to obtain information concerning teacher perceptions of school culture. It should take only a few minutes to complete. All responses will be kept confidential.

Please complete the following items.

1. Age: **( 1 )** 25 or less      ( 2 ) 26 - 30      ( 3 ) 31 - 40      ( 4 ) 41 - 50      ( 5 ) over 50

2. Sex: **( 1 )** Male      ( 2 ) Female

3. Race or ethnic group: **( 1 )** White (includes Arabian)   ( 2 ) Black   ( 3 ) Hispanic
   ( 4 ) Asian (includes Pacific Islanders)   ( 5 ) Native American   ( 6 ) Bi-racial

4. Highest degree earned: **( 1 )** Bachelor's ( 2 ) Master's ( 3 ) Master's + ( 4 ) Doctorate

5. Number of years of full-time teaching:      ( 1 ) 3 or fewer            ( 2 ) between 4 and 10
   ( 3 ) between 11 and 20   ( 4 ) over 20

6. Number of years employed at your present school: ( 1 ) 1 or less      ( 2 ) between 2 and 3
   ( 3 ) between 4 and 10   ( 4 ) over 10

7. Are you presently endorsed for the grade-level or content area you teach? **( 1 )** Yes ( 2 ) No

# Directions

This survey consists of 42 statements. Each statement is followed by one or more scales that consist of pairs of words separated by five spaces. Place an "X" in the appropriate space between words to show how you feel about the statement. For example, consider the statement "Taking a test." If taking a test makes you feel very nervous, you would mark the scale like this:

Taking a test
   nervous        (**X**) ( 1 ) ( 2 ) ( 3 ) ( 4 )      relaxed

If taking a test makes you somewhat nervous, you would mark the scale like this:

   nervous        ( 0 ) (**X**) ( 2 ) ( 3 ) ( 4 )      relaxed

Naturally, if you are comfortable about taking a test, you would mark on the "relaxed" side of the scale. If you can't decide, or if you feel midway or neutral between the two words, you should mark the middle space. PLEASE ENTER A RESPONSE ON ALL SCALES.

# Teacher Survey

1. Professional development opportunities available to teachers at my school

   rare           ( 0 )   ( 1 )   ( 2 )   ( 3 )   ( 4 )      frequent

   waste of time ( 0 )   ( 1 )   ( 2 )   ( 3 )   ( 4 )      beneficial

2. Extent to which my needs and concerns are addressed by inservice programs

   small         ( 0 )   ( 1 )   ( 2 )   ( 3 )   ( 4 )      large

3. Teacher morale at my school

   low           ( 0 )   ( 1 )   ( 2 )   ( 3 )   ( 4 )      high

4. Rewards and acknowledgments received for my knowledge, skills, and performance

   scarce        ( 0 )   ( 1 )   ( 2 )   ( 3 )   ( 4 )      abundant

5. Professional interactions and collaborations among teachers

   rare           ( 0 )   ( 1 )   ( 2 )   ( 3 )   ( 4 )      frequent

   unproductive ( 0 )   ( 1 )   ( 2 )   ( 3 )   ( 4 )      productive

6. Professional interactions between teachers and school administrators

   rare           ( 0 )   ( 1 )   ( 2 )   ( 3 )   ( 4 )      frequent

   unproductive ( 0 )   ( 1 )   ( 2 )   ( 3 )   ( 4 )      productive

7. My expectations of support from the principal

   low           ( 0 )   ( 1 )   ( 2 )   ( 3 )   ( 4 )      high

8. Professional interactions between teachers and other school staff

   rare           ( 0 )   ( 1 )   ( 2 )   ( 3 )   ( 4 )      frequent

   unproductive ( 0 )   ( 1 )   ( 2 )   ( 3 )   ( 4 )      productive

9. Professional interactions between teachers and parents

   rare           ( 0 )   ( 1 )   ( 2 )   ( 3 )   ( 4 )      frequent

   unproductive ( 0 )   ( 1 )   ( 2 )   ( 3 )   ( 4 )      productive

10. Parental involvement and support at my school

    low           ( 0 )   ( 1 )   ( 2 )   ( 3 )   ( 4 )      high

11. Professional interactions between teachers and students

    unproductive ( 0 )   ( 1 )   ( 2 )   ( 3 )   ( 4 )      productive

12. My principal's responses to student academic achievement and good deeds

    scarce        ( 0 )   ( 1 )   ( 2 )   ( 3 )   ( 4 )      abundant

    inconsistent ( 0 )   ( 1 )   ( 2 )   ( 3 )   ( 4 )      consistent

13. Disruptive classroom behavior by students in my classroom

    prevalent     ( 0 )   ( 1 )   ( 2 )   ( 3 )   ( 4 )      rare

14. My principal's response to student misconduct

    inconsistent ( 0 )   ( 1 )   ( 2 )   ( 3 )   ( 4 )      consistent

    slack         ( 0 )   ( 1 )   ( 2 )   ( 3 )   ( 4 )      firm

Continued on next page

15. Responses by other teachers to student misconduct

        inconsistent  ( 0 )  ( 1 )  ( 2 )  ( 3 )  ( 4 )    consistent

        slack  ( 0 )  ( 1 )  ( 2 )  ( 3 )  ( 4 )    firm

16. The extent to which teachers lower grades in response to student misconduct

        frequent  ( 0 )  ( 1 )  ( 2 )  ( 3 )  ( 4 )    not at all

17. My school environment

        unsafe  ( 0 )  ( 1 )  ( 2 )  ( 3 )  ( 4 )    safe

        unfocused  ( 0 )  ( 1 )  ( 2 )  ( 3 )  ( 4 )    focused

        disorderly  ( 0 )  ( 1 )  ( 2 )  ( 3 )  ( 4 )    orderly

        unpleasant  ( 0 )  ( 1 )  ( 2 )  ( 3 )  ( 4 )    pleasant

        neglecting  ( 0 )  ( 1 )  ( 2 )  ( 3 )  ( 4 )    nurturing

        disinviting  ( 0 )  ( 1 )  ( 2 )  ( 3 )  ( 4 )    inviting

18. The way students are treated at my school

        disrespectful  ( 0 )  ( 1 )  ( 2 )  ( 3 )  ( 4 )    respectful

19. Racial tensions at my school

        high  ( 0 )  ( 1 )  ( 2 )  ( 3 )  ( 4 )    low

20. Non-teaching duties assigned to teachers at my school

        excessive  ( 0 )  ( 1 )  ( 2 )  ( 3 )  ( 4 )    reasonable

        trivial  ( 0 )  ( 1 )  ( 2 )  ( 3 )  ( 4 )    meaningful

21. My principal as a resource provider

        meager  ( 0 )  ( 1 )  ( 2 )  ( 3 )  ( 4 )    ample

22. My principal as an instructional resource

        inactive  ( 0 )  ( 1 )  ( 2 )  ( 3 )  ( 4 )    active

        useless  ( 0 )  ( 1 )  ( 2 )  ( 3 )  ( 4 )    useful

23. My principal as a communicator

        inarticulate  ( 0 )  ( 1 )  ( 2 )  ( 3 )  ( 4 )    articulate

        one-way  ( 0 )  ( 1 )  ( 2 )  ( 3 )  ( 4 )    two-way

        top down  ( 0 )  ( 1 )  ( 2 )  ( 3 )  ( 4 )    top down + bottom up

24. Visible presence of my principal

        rare  ( 0 )  ( 1 )  ( 2 )  ( 3 )  ( 4 )    frequent

25. The feedback I receive after a classroom observation by my principal

        none  ( 0 )  ( 1 )  ( 2 )  ( 3 )  ( 4 )    substantial

26. Leadership and decision-making at my school

        sluggish  ( 0 )  ( 1 )  ( 2 )  ( 3 )  ( 4 )    energetic

        unfocused  ( 0 )  ( 1 )  ( 2 )  ( 3 )  ( 4 )    achievement-oriented

27. Staff and faculty meetings

        rare  ( 0 )  ( 1 )  ( 2 )  ( 3 )  ( 4 )    frequent

        unproductive  ( 0 )  ( 1 )  ( 2 )  ( 3 )  ( 4 )    productive

        one-way  ( 0 )  ( 1 )  ( 2 )  ( 3 )  ( 4 )    two-way

Continued on next page

28. Departmental meetings
   rare          ( 0 )   ( 1 )   ( 2 )   ( 3 )   ( 4 )      frequent
   unproductive ( 0 )   ( 1 )   ( 2 )   ( 3 )   ( 4 )      productive

29. The extent to which school meetings I attend address instructional concerns
   low          ( 0 )   ( 1 )   ( 2 )   ( 3 )   ( 4 )      high

30. The extent to which students at my school participate in school decisions
   low          ( 0 )   ( 1 )   ( 2 )   ( 3 )   ( 4 )      high

31. School vision, goals, and objectives
   ambiguous ( 0 )   ( 1 )   ( 2 )   ( 3 )   ( 4 )      clear

32. Expectations for my students
   unsuccessful ( 0 )   ( 1 )   ( 2 )   ( 3 )   ( 4 )      successful
   break rules   ( 0 )   ( 1 )   ( 2 )   ( 3 )   ( 4 )      follow rules

33. My use of incentives and rewards for students to promote academic excellence
   seldom       ( 0 )   ( 1 )   ( 2 )   ( 3 )   ( 4 )      often

34. Opportunities for teachers at my school to help students attain mastery of basic skills
   low          ( 0 )   ( 1 )   ( 2 )   ( 3 )   ( 4 )      high

35. Opportunities for teachers at my school to help students attain high academic achievement
   low          ( 0 )   ( 1 )   ( 2 )   ( 3 )   ( 4 )      high

36. The typical percentage of students expected to master basic skills at each grade level
   0%          ( 0 )   ( 1 )   ( 2 )   ( 3 )   ( 4 )      100%

37. Academic mastery of basic skills does not vary by socioeconomic status at my school
   disagree     ( 0 )   ( 1 )   ( 2 )   ( 3 )   ( 4 )      agree

38. Teacher use of a variety of assessment tools to track learning targets and student performance
   rare          ( 0 )   ( 1 )   ( 2 )   ( 3 )   ( 4 )      prevalent

39. Decisions and actions concerning student learning is based on data analysis
   rarely        ( 0 )   ( 1 )   ( 2 )   ( 3 )   ( 4 )      frequently

40. Teacher monitoring of student progress at my school
   infrequent   ( 0 )   ( 1 )   ( 2 )   ( 3 )   ( 4 )      frequent
   one source   ( 0 )   ( 1 )   ( 2 )   ( 3 )   ( 4 )      many sources

41. School-provided feedback to teachers on how well each student is progressing
   inadequate   ( 0 )   ( 1 )   ( 2 )   ( 3 )   ( 4 )      adequate

42. Homework
   not required ( 0 )   ( 1 )   ( 2 )   ( 3 )   ( 4 )      required
   ungraded    ( 0 )   ( 1 )   ( 2 )   ( 3 )   ( 4 )      graded

## End of Survey

# Student Survey of School Culture - 1st Edition
# (SSSC-1)

The purpose of this survey is to obtain information concerning student perceptions of school culture. It should take only a few minutes to complete. All responses will be kept confidential.

Please complete the following items.

1. Age: _____

2. Sex:         ( 1 ) Male     ( 2 ) Female

3. Race or ethnic group:   ( 1 ) White (includes Arabian)     ( 2 ) Black     ( 3 ) Hispanic

          ( 4 ) Asian (includes Pacific Islanders)  ( 5 ) Native American    ( 6 ) Bi-racial

4. Grade: _____

5. Number of years you attended this school:   ( 1 ) less than one year       ( 2 ) 1 - 2 years

( 3 ) 3 - 4 years         ( 4 ) over 4 years

6. Number of years you lived in this school district:   ( 1 ) less than one year      ( 2 ) 1 - 3 years

( 3 ) 4 - 6 years         ( 4 ) 7 - 10 years         ( 5 ) over 10 years

# Directions

This survey consists of 39 statements. Each statement is followed by one or more scales that consist of pairs of words separated by five spaces. Place an "X" in the appropriate space between words to show how you feel about the statement. For example, consider the statement "Taking a test." If taking a test makes you feel very nervous, you would mark the scale like this:

Taking a test

    nervous         ( **X** ) ( 1 ) ( 2 ) ( 3 ) ( 4 )         relaxed

If taking a test makes you somewhat nervous, you would mark the scale like this:

    nervous         ( 0 ) ( **X** ) ( 2 ) ( 3 ) ( 4 )         relaxed

Naturally, if you are comfortable about taking a test, you would mark on the "relaxed" side of the scale. If you can't decide, or if you feel midway or neutral between the two words, you should mark the middle space. PLEASE ENTER A RESPONSE ON ALL SCALES.

# Student Survey

1. How I feel about my school

| | | | | | | |
|---|---|---|---|---|---|---|
| dislike | ( 0 ) | ( 1 ) | ( 2 ) | ( 3 ) | ( 4 ) | like |
| unsafe | ( 0 ) | ( 1 ) | ( 2 ) | ( 3 ) | ( 4 ) | safe |
| disorderly | ( 0 ) | ( 1 ) | ( 2 ) | ( 3 ) | ( 4 ) | orderly |
| unpleasant | ( 0 ) | ( 1 ) | ( 2 ) | ( 3 ) | ( 4 ) | pleasant |
| boring | ( 0 ) | ( 1 ) | ( 2 ) | ( 3 ) | ( 4 ) | interesting |
| simple | ( 0 ) | ( 1 ) | ( 2 ) | ( 3 ) | ( 4 ) | challenging |
| not belonging | ( 0 ) | ( 1 ) | ( 2 ) | ( 3 ) | ( 4 ) | belonging |

2. Racial tensions at my school

| | | | | | | |
|---|---|---|---|---|---|---|
| high | ( 0 ) | ( 1 ) | ( 2 ) | ( 3 ) | ( 4 ) | low |

3. The manner in which students of different races are treated at my school

| | | | | | | |
|---|---|---|---|---|---|---|
| unfairly | ( 0 ) | ( 1 ) | ( 2 ) | ( 3 ) | ( 4 ) | fairly |

4. How I am treated at school by teachers and others in authority

| | | | | | | |
|---|---|---|---|---|---|---|
| no respect | ( 0 ) | ( 1 ) | ( 2 ) | ( 3 ) | ( 4 ) | with dignity |

5. My school building and facilities

| | | | | | | |
|---|---|---|---|---|---|---|
| dirty | ( 0 ) | ( 1 ) | ( 2 ) | ( 3 ) | ( 4 ) | clean |
| miserable | ( 0 ) | ( 1 ) | ( 2 ) | ( 3 ) | ( 4 ) | comfortable |
| drab | ( 0 ) | ( 1 ) | ( 2 ) | ( 3 ) | ( 4 ) | bright |
| inadequate | ( 0 ) | ( 1 ) | ( 2 ) | ( 3 ) | ( 4 ) | adequate |

6. The extent to which students cut classes at my school

| | | | | | | |
|---|---|---|---|---|---|---|
| frequent | ( 0 ) | ( 1 ) | ( 2 ) | ( 3 ) | ( 4 ) | rare |

7. My knowledge of school rules and consequences for their violation

| | | | | | | |
|---|---|---|---|---|---|---|
| low | ( 0 ) | ( 1 ) | ( 2 ) | ( 3 ) | ( 4 ) | high |

8. Rules at my school

| | | | | | | |
|---|---|---|---|---|---|---|
| unclear | ( 0 ) | ( 1 ) | ( 2 ) | ( 3 ) | ( 4 ) | clear |
| unreasonable | ( 0 ) | ( 1 ) | ( 2 ) | ( 3 ) | ( 4 ) | reasonable |

9. Enforcement of rules at my school

| | | | | | | |
|---|---|---|---|---|---|---|
| slack | ( 0 ) | ( 1 ) | ( 2 ) | ( 3 ) | ( 4 ) | strict |
| unfair | ( 0 ) | ( 1 ) | ( 2 ) | ( 3 ) | ( 4 ) | fair |

10. Disruptive classroom behavior by students at my school

| | | | | | | |
|---|---|---|---|---|---|---|
| frequent | ( 0 ) | ( 1 ) | ( 2 ) | ( 3 ) | ( 4 ) | rare |

11. The extent to which my friends get into trouble at school

| | | | | | | |
|---|---|---|---|---|---|---|
| high | ( 0 ) | ( 1 ) | ( 2 ) | ( 3 ) | ( 4 ) | low |

12. The extent to which drugs and/or alcohol are used by students

| | | | | | | |
|---|---|---|---|---|---|---|
| high | ( 0 ) | ( 1 ) | ( 2 ) | ( 3 ) | ( 4 ) | low |

Continued on next page

13. The extent to which students bring weapons (e.g., guns, knives) to school
high ( 0 ) ( 1 ) ( 2 ) ( 3 ) ( 4 ) low

14. My principal's acknowledgments of student academic excellence and good deeds
rare ( 0 ) ( 1 ) ( 2 ) ( 3 ) ( 4 ) frequent
inconsistent ( 0 ) ( 1 ) ( 2 ) ( 3 ) ( 4 ) consistent

15. My teachers' acknowledgements of student academic excellence and good deeds
rare ( 0 ) ( 1 ) ( 2 ) ( 3 ) ( 4 ) frequent
inconsistent ( 0 ) ( 1 ) ( 2 ) ( 3 ) ( 4 ) consistent

16. The extent to which students participate in school decision-making
low ( 0 ) ( 1 ) ( 2 ) ( 3 ) ( 4 ) high

17. The ability of students at my school to bring about desired changes in school practices
low ( 0 ) ( 1 ) ( 2 ) ( 3 ) ( 4 ) high

18. My principal
unfriendly ( 0 ) ( 1 ) ( 2 ) ( 3 ) ( 4 ) friendly
unsupportive ( 0 ) ( 1 ) ( 2 ) ( 3 ) ( 4 ) supportive
unhelpful ( 0 ) ( 1 ) ( 2 ) ( 3 ) ( 4 ) helpful
unfair ( 0 ) ( 1 ) ( 2 ) ( 3 ) ( 4 ) fair
disrespectful ( 0 ) ( 1 ) ( 2 ) ( 3 ) ( 4 ) respectful

19. How often I see the principal somewhere at school
rare ( 0 ) ( 1 ) ( 2 ) ( 3 ) ( 4 ) frequent

20. Teachers at my school
unfriendly ( 0 ) ( 1 ) ( 2 ) ( 3 ) ( 4 ) friendly
unsupportive ( 0 ) ( 1 ) ( 2 ) ( 3 ) ( 4 ) supportive
unhelpful ( 0 ) ( 1 ) ( 2 ) ( 3 ) ( 4 ) helpful
unfair ( 0 ) ( 1 ) ( 2 ) ( 3 ) ( 4 ) fair
disrespectful ( 0 ) ( 1 ) ( 2 ) ( 3 ) ( 4 ) respectful

21. Recognition of student academic achievement at my school
low ( 0 ) ( 1 ) ( 2 ) ( 3 ) ( 4 ) high

22. My expectation of support from my teachers
low ( 0 ) ( 1 ) ( 2 ) ( 3 ) ( 4 ) high

23. My expectation of getting high grades
low ( 0 ) ( 1 ) ( 2 ) ( 3 ) ( 4 ) high

24. My expectation of getting help from my teachers when I need it
rare ( 0 ) ( 1 ) ( 2 ) ( 3 ) ( 4 ) frequent

25. How I would describe teacher-student relations at my school
poor ( 0 ) ( 1 ) ( 2 ) ( 3 ) ( 4 ) excellent
restricted ( 0 ) ( 1 ) ( 2 ) ( 3 ) ( 4 ) open

Continued on next page

26. My expectation of support from the principal when I need it
  low ( 0 ) ( 1 ) ( 2 ) ( 3 ) ( 4 ) high

27. My expectation of support from my parents when I need it
  low ( 0 ) ( 1 ) ( 2 ) ( 3 ) ( 4 ) high

28. My teachers' expectations of me
  failure ( 0 ) ( 1 ) ( 2 ) ( 3 ) ( 4 ) successful
  untrustworthy ( 0 ) ( 1 ) ( 2 ) ( 3 ) ( 4 ) trustworthy

29. My parents' expectations of me
  failure ( 0 ) ( 1 ) ( 2 ) ( 3 ) ( 4 ) successful
  untrustworthy ( 0 ) ( 1 ) ( 2 ) ( 3 ) ( 4 ) trustworthy

30. The amount of effort I expend at doing my school work
  low ( 0 ) ( 1 ) ( 2 ) ( 3 ) ( 4 ) high

31. The amount of emphasis on learning and getting good grades at my school
  low ( 0 ) ( 1 ) ( 2 ) ( 3 ) ( 4 ) high

32. My understanding of what I am expected to learn
  low ( 0 ) ( 1 ) ( 2 ) ( 3 ) ( 4 ) high

33. Feedback I get from my teachers concerning my progress
  rare ( 0 ) ( 1 ) ( 2 ) ( 3 ) ( 4 ) frequent

34. Homework at my school
  rare ( 0 ) ( 1 ) ( 2 ) ( 3 ) ( 4 ) frequent
  ungraded ( 0 ) ( 1 ) ( 2 ) ( 3 ) ( 4 ) graded

35. The value to me after I graduate from this school of the majority of my courses
  low ( 0 ) ( 1 ) ( 2 ) ( 3 ) ( 4 ) high

36. The person most responsible for what I learn
  my teacher ( 0 ) ( 1 ) ( 2 ) ( 3 ) ( 4 ) me

37. Classroom instruction at my school
  unclear ( 0 ) ( 1 ) ( 2 ) ( 3 ) ( 4 ) clear
  unchallenging ( 0 ) ( 1 ) ( 2 ) ( 3 ) ( 4 ) challenging

38. Opportunities for group discussions and group projects during class
  low ( 0 ) ( 1 ) ( 2 ) ( 3 ) ( 4 ) high

39. Classroom procedures at my school
  inefficient ( 0 ) ( 1 ) ( 2 ) ( 3 ) ( 4 ) efficient

# End of Survey

# D Appendix
# Needs Assessment

A needs assessment is a useful tool to determine the needs of staff members in such areas as professional development needs, resource needs, time needs, and more. Needs assessment questionnaires can help you collect, organize, and analyze data related to the needs of people. As you work with implementing standards and improving achievement in your school, it is useful to have a handle on the instructional strategies which teachers are comfortable using — and which strategies they indicate a need to still learn or practice.

This chapter provides a needs assessment for instructional strategies training. As you work with classroom, school, district, and program improvement efforts, you will probably come to the conclusion that the learning strategies a teacher chooses to use in the classroom do make a difference in student achievement.

# Administering and Analyzing the Instructional Strategies Needs Assessment

## Purpose

The purpose of this needs assessment is to identify professional development needs of members of the staff in the area of instructional strategies likely to help students learn effectively in the classroom.

## Procedures

You may want to administer this survey at a faculty meeting. The approximate time to complete the needs assessment is 10 minutes.

- Give everyone a pencil.
- Explain the importance of the needs assessment and how you'll use the results in your school or district.
- Remind everyone that his or her responses will be kept confidential. (Provide envelopes in which people can place and seal their responses.)
- Read the directions to the respondents.
- Finally, remind everyone to respond to all 30 items on the assessment.

## Scoring

Information about setting up a database or completing the scoring manually is provided in this guide. In addition, there is information that should be helpful in interpreting the results of the needs assessment.

# Instructional Strategies Needs Assessment

We want your ideas about training that may be useful in doing the very best job you can do to implement standards in our school/district. This needs assessment has been designed to help us learn more about your professional development needs for a variety of promising classroom practices/instructional strategies. Please note that you do not need to place your name anywhere on the needs assessment sheet, and no signature is requested. Your openness and candor in completing this needs assessment will strengthen our professional development planning.

To complete this form, simply turn this paper over and mark your answers. When you finish, please return your needs assessment form by _____ to:

Please indicate the grade level you teach. (Circle all that apply.)

| | Elementary | | | | Middle | High |
|---|---|---|---|---|---|---|

**Pre K   K   1   2   3   4   5   6   7   8   9   10   11   12**

Please indicate the specific content/subject areas you teach. (Again, please circle *all* that apply.)

**Alternative Education**
**English/Language Arts**
**Fine Arts (i.e., Art, Music)**
**Foreign Language**
**Gifted and Talented**
**Mathematics**
**Physical Education**
**Pre-Kindergarten**
**Science**
**Social Studies**
**Special Education**
**Title I**
**Vocational/Technical**
**Other** _____

# Instructional Strategies Needs Assessment

**Directions:** The instructional/learning strategies we choose to use in the classroom can have great impact on student achievement. Please review the list of 30 strategies and make a judgment about your level of need for training for each strategy. You'll give yourself a score of 1-5 for each of the strategies.

**Introductory (1)** — Introductory-level training in the basics would be useful to you.

**Intermediate (3)** — You're familiar with the instructional strategy and possibly use it in the classroom, so intermediate-level training would be useful.

**Advanced SME (5)** — You're already very good with the instructional strategy (a subject matter expert or SME) and actually don't need additional training in using the strategy in the classroom. In fact, you know the strategy well enough to train other people how to do the strategy.

| Instructional Strategies | Introductory Level | | | Advanced SME Level | |
|---|---|---|---|---|---|
| | 1 | 2 | 3 | 4 | 5 |
| 1. Advance organizers | | | | | |
| 2. Alternative assessment techniques | | | | | |
| 3. Analogies | | | | | |
| 4. Assessing prior knowledge | | | | | |
| 5. Calculator problem-solving | | | | | |
| 6. Case studies/scenarios | | | | | |
| 7. Concept attainment | | | | | |
| 8. Cooperative learning | | | | | |
| 9. Demonstrating/modeling | | | | | |
| 10. Direct teaching | | | | | |
| 11. Generating/solving real-life problems | | | | | |
| 12. Graphic organizers/visual tools | | | | | |
| 13. Group projects | | | | | |
| 14. Individual projects | | | | | |
| 15. Library and research skills | | | | | |
| 16. Manipulatives/hands-on activities | | | | | |
| 17. Metacognition (thinking strategies) | | | | | |
| 18. Multiple intelligences | | | | | |
| 19. Problem-based learning | | | | | |
| 20. Questioning strategies | | | | | |
| 21. Reading strategies | | | | | |
| 22. Reciprocal learning | | | | | |
| 23. Review strategies | | | | | |
| 24. Student-led discussions/Socratic Seminars | | | | | |
| 25. Study skills (including test-taking skills) | | | | | |
| 26. Using technology to support learning | | | | | |
| 27. Thematic instruction | | | | | |
| 28. Whole-class discussions | | | | | |
| 29. Writing in the content area | | | | | |
| 30. Writing process strategies | | | | | |

Side 2 of Needs Assessment

# Design a Template Like This to Organize Your Data

| Instructional Strategies | 1 | 2 | 3 | 4 | 5 | 6 | 7 | 8 | 9 | 10 | 11 | 12 | 13 | 14 | 15 | Total | Mean |
|---|---|---|---|---|---|---|---|---|---|---|---|---|---|---|---|---|---|
| 1. Advance organizers | | | | | | | | | | | | | | | | | |
| 2. Alternative assessment techniques | | | | | | | | | | | | | | | | | |
| 3. Analogies | | | | | | | | | | | | | | | | | |
| 4. Assessing prior knowledge | | | | | | | | | | | | | | | | | |
| 5. Calculator problem-solving | | | | | | | | | | | | | | | | | |
| 6. Case studies/scenarios | | | | | | | | | | | | | | | | | |
| 7. Concept attainment | | | | | | | | | | | | | | | | | |
| 8. Cooperative learning | | | | | | | | | | | | | | | | | |
| 9. Demonstrating/modeling | | | | | | | | | | | | | | | | | |
| 10. Direct teaching | | | | | | | | | | | | | | | | | |
| 11. Generating/solving real-life problems | | | | | | | | | | | | | | | | | |
| 12. Graphic organizers/visual tools | | | | | | | | | | | | | | | | | |
| 13. Group projects | | | | | | | | | | | | | | | | | |
| 14. Individual projects | | | | | | | | | | | | | | | | | |
| 15. Library and research skills | | | | | | | | | | | | | | | | | |
| 16. Manipulatives/hands-on activities | | | | | | | | | | | | | | | | | |
| 17. Metacognition (thinking strategies) | | | | | | | | | | | | | | | | | |
| 18. Multiple intelligences | | | | | | | | | | | | | | | | | |
| 19. Problem-based learning | | | | | | | | | | | | | | | | | |
| 20. Questioning strategies | | | | | | | | | | | | | | | | | |
| 21. Reading strategies | | | | | | | | | | | | | | | | | |
| 22. Reciprocal learning | | | | | | | | | | | | | | | | | |
| 23. Review strategies | | | | | | | | | | | | | | | | | |
| 24. Student-led discussions | | | | | | | | | | | | | | | | | |
| 25. Study skills | | | | | | | | | | | | | | | | | |
| 26. Using technology | | | | | | | | | | | | | | | | | |
| 27. Thematic instruction | | | | | | | | | | | | | | | | | |
| 28. Whole-class discussions | | | | | | | | | | | | | | | | | |
| 29. Writing in the content area | | | | | | | | | | | | | | | | | |
| 30. Writing process strategies | | | | | | | | | | | | | | | | | |
| Column Total | | | | | | | | | | | | | | | | | |
| Column Mean | | | | | | | | | | | | | | | | | |

**Respondents**

You'll write the number indicated by the respondent in the blank cells. The number for each strategy will be a 1, 2, 3, 4, or 5.

You'll want to have as many columns as you have respondents. (I've included columns for 15 respondents.) If 110 people respond to the needs assessment, you'll have 110 columns (plus your columns and rows for Total and Mean).

Consider setting your data sheet up using a software program such as Microsoft Excel. This way, you can have the Totals and Mean for the columns and rows automatically calculated for you.

# Analyzing the Needs Assessment Results

| Instructional Strategies | 1 | 2 | 3 | 4 | 5 | 6 | 7 | 8 | 9 | 10 | 11 | 12 | 13 | 14 | 15 | Total | Mean |
|---|---|---|---|---|---|---|---|---|---|---|---|---|---|---|---|---|---|
| Advance organizers | 1 | 3 | 1 | 1 |  | 2 | 3 | 1 | 5 | 5 | 1 | 1 | 3 | 1 | 1 |  | 2.00 |
| Alternative assessment techniqu | 3 | 3 | 3 | 3 |  | 3 | 3 | 1 | 3 | 3 | 1 | 1 | 3 | 1 | 1 |  | 2.20 |
| Analogies | 1 |  |  |  |  |  |  |  |  | 3 | 1 | 1 | 3 |  |  |  |  |
| Assessing prior knowledge | 1 |  |  |  |  |  |  |  |  | 1 | 1 | 3 |  |  |  |  |  |
| Calculator problem-solving | 1 |  |  |  |  |  |  |  |  | 3 | 2 | 3 |  |  |  |  |  |
| Case studies/scenarios | 1 |  |  |  |  |  |  |  |  | 1 | 1 | 1 |  |  |  |  |  |
| Concept attainment | 1 |  |  |  |  |  |  |  |  | 5 | 3 | 1 |  |  |  |  |  |
| Cooperative learning | 5 | 5 | 5 | 5 | 5 | 5 | 5 | 5 | 5 | 5 | 5 | 5 |  |  |  |  |  |
| Demonstrating/modeling | 5 | 5 | 5 | 5 | 5 | 5 | 5 | 5 | 5 | 3 | 3 | 3 | 3 | 3 | 1 | 61 | 4.07 |
| Direct teaching | 3 | 2 | 3 | 2 | 3 | 2 | 3 | 1 | 5 | 1 | 3 | 5 | 2 | 3 | 1 | 39 | 2.60 |
| Generating/solving real-life probl | 1 | 1 | 1 | 1 |  |  |  |  |  |  |  |  |  |  | 1 | 19 | 1.27 |
| Graphic organizers/visual tools | 1 | 3 | 2 | 3 |  |  |  |  |  |  |  |  |  |  | 1 | 28 | 1.87 |
| Group projects | 5 | 5 | 5 | 3 |  |  |  |  |  |  |  |  |  |  |  |  | 3.53 |
| Individual projects | 3 | 3 | 3 | 3 |  |  |  |  |  |  |  |  |  | 3 |  | 50 | 3.33 |
| Library and research skills | 5 | 5 | 5 | 5 |  |  |  |  |  |  |  |  |  | 5 | 5 | 75 | 5.00 |
| Manipulatives/hands-on activitie | 3 | 1 | 1 | 1 | 3 | 3 | 3 | 3 | 5 | 3 | 3 | 3 | 3 | 3 | 3 | 41 | 2.73 |
| Metacognition (thinking strategie | 1 | 1 | 1 | 1 | 2 | 1 | 3 | 3 | 5 | 2 | 3 | 3 | 2 | 3 | 3 | 34 | 2.27 |
| Multiple intelligences | 1 | 1 | 1 | 1 |  |  |  |  |  |  |  |  |  |  | 3 | 37 | 2.47 |
| Problem-based learning | 1 | 1 | 1 | 1 |  |  |  |  |  |  |  |  |  |  | 3 | 39 | 2.60 |
| Questioning strategies | 3 | 3 | 3 | 1 |  |  |  |  |  |  |  |  |  |  |  |  | 2.07 |
| Reading strategies | 3 | 3 | 3 | 2 |  |  |  |  |  |  |  |  |  |  | 3 | 43 | 2.87 |
| Reciprocal learning | 1 | 1 | 1 | 1 | 3 | 3 | 3 | 3 | 5 | 3 | 3 | 3 | 1 | 1 | 3 | 35 | 2.33 |
| Review strategies | 3 | 3 | 3 | 4 | 3 | 5 | 5 | 5 | 5 | 3 | 5 | 5 | 5 | 5 | 3 | 62 | 4.13 |
| Student-led discussions | 1 | 1 | 1 | 1 | 1 | 3 | 3 | 3 | 5 | 5 | 5 | 3 | 3 | 5 | 5 | 45 | 3.00 |
| Study skills | 1 | 1 | 1 | 1 |  |  |  |  |  |  |  |  |  |  | 5 | 31 | 2.07 |
| Using technology | 1 | 2 | 1 | 1 |  |  |  |  |  |  |  |  |  |  | 1 | 21 | 1.40 |
| Thematic instruction | 1 | 3 | 3 | 3 |  |  |  |  |  |  |  |  |  |  | 3 | 37 | 2.47 |
| Whole-class discussions | 3 | 3 | 5 | 5 |  |  |  |  |  |  |  |  |  |  | 5 | 59 | 3.93 |
| Writing in the content area | 1 | 1 | 1 | 1 |  |  |  |  |  |  |  |  |  | 1 | 1 | 31 | 2.07 |
| Writing process strategies | 1 | 1 | 1 | 1 | 3 | 3 | 3 | 5 |  | 1 | 1 | 3 | 1 | 1 | 1 | 31 | 2.07 |
| **Column Total** | 62 | 66 | 69 | 65 | 70 | 77 | 86 | 80 |  | 83 | 74 | 77 | 76 | 72 | 70 | 1175 | 78.33 |
| **Column Mean** | 2.07 | 2.20 | 2.30 | 2.17 | 2.33 | 2.57 | 2.87 | 2.67 | 4.93 | 2.77 | 2.47 | 2.57 | 2.53 | 2.40 | 2.33 | 39.17 | 2.61 |

The respondents are the people who responded to the needs assessment. This analysis template uses numbers instead of names to maintain confidentiality.

To get the total, just add all of the numbers in the row. (Of course, if you have more than 15 respondents, you'll have more than 15 numbers to add.)

To get the mean, divide the number in the total column by the number of respondents (in this example, 15). In this needs assessment, the higher the mean, the more the teachers feel they know about the strategy.

A low mean may alert you to the fact that this is an area where staff members may need introductory-level training for the strategy.

Respondent number nine has identified that he or she is practically a subject-matter expert in everything, and doesn't need additional training.

# Ranking the Instructional Strategies

NOTE: This school has student achievement results which indicate a need for students to write better — especially in the composing and written expression domains. This school may, when training is provided to staff, want to ensure that teachers get a good background in these strategies. (Of course, the alternative assessment training includes the use of rubrics to score student writing.)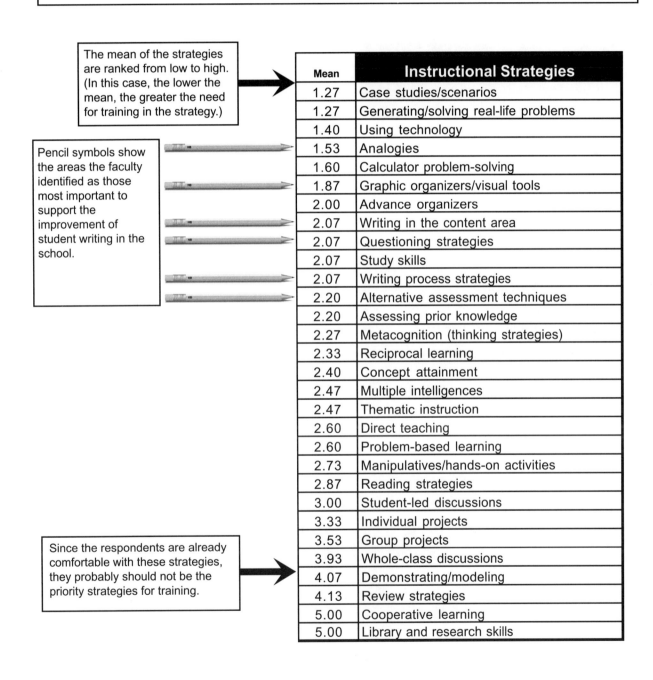

The mean of the strategies are ranked from low to high. (In this case, the lower the mean, the greater the need for training in the strategy.)

Pencil symbols show the areas the faculty identified as those most important to support the improvement of student writing in the school.

| Mean | Instructional Strategies |
|------|--------------------------|
| 1.27 | Case studies/scenarios |
| 1.27 | Generating/solving real-life problems |
| 1.40 | Using technology |
| 1.53 | Analogies |
| 1.60 | Calculator problem-solving |
| 1.87 | Graphic organizers/visual tools |
| 2.00 | Advance organizers |
| 2.07 | Writing in the content area |
| 2.07 | Questioning strategies |
| 2.07 | Study skills |
| 2.07 | Writing process strategies |
| 2.20 | Alternative assessment techniques |
| 2.20 | Assessing prior knowledge |
| 2.27 | Metacognition (thinking strategies) |
| 2.33 | Reciprocal learning |
| 2.40 | Concept attainment |
| 2.47 | Multiple intelligences |
| 2.47 | Thematic instruction |
| 2.60 | Direct teaching |
| 2.60 | Problem-based learning |
| 2.73 | Manipulatives/hands-on activities |
| 2.87 | Reading strategies |
| 3.00 | Student-led discussions |
| 3.33 | Individual projects |
| 3.53 | Group projects |
| 3.93 | Whole-class discussions |
| 4.07 | Demonstrating/modeling |
| 4.13 | Review strategies |
| 5.00 | Cooperative learning |
| 5.00 | Library and research skills |

Since the respondents are already comfortable with these strategies, they probably should not be the priority strategies for training.

# E Appendix Media Relations

## Celebrate Progress

It is important to communicate your school/district progress toward standards and other school goals. Some states help you do this by issuing report cards about your school. School reports usually provide information about how your students are doing on state tests, but often they provide other kinds of information: school attendance data, mobility rates, and school demographics. As student achievement in your school or district continues to rise, share the news!

## Talking With the Media

Because accountability is such a priority in most states, the media reviews and analyzes state assessment data, usually in the newspaper and television. I am often asked for tips on dealing effectively with the media when talking about achievement results.

On the following pages, you'll find some quick tips for dealing effectively with the media.

# T•H•E
# Golden Rules
## for Dealing Effectively With the Media

### Professional Image

Be calm, caring, and credible. Let the professional in you shine.

Credibility is important. Our public puts a lot of weight on sincerity and caring.

Act confidently. Be poised. You are the expert. Remember that you'll usually know more about the topic than the reporter does.

### Preparation

There are some media opportunities you will know about (e.g., when test results are announced.) Preparation and planning are critical. Think about how you'll respond to different media situations, and plan to deal with each.

Include a summary of statistics related to your test results. Share this information in an easy-to-understand way. Provide media with advance copies of news releases and other important information.

Write your own news release. Use this with the media, and then place copies on the counter in the front office of the school or district.

Anticipate questions the media will ask: *How are your test scores? Why did they go up/down? What plan of action will you be taking? Why are your scores higher/lower than neighboring schools?*

Review the *who, what, when, where,* and *why* of the topic for which you're being interviewed.  Do you know the background of the testing program?  Can you answer questions about the scores?

When the scores are down . . .
"Yes, they are much lower than we expected.  We already have a plan in place — let me tell you about it."

Include your business card and the correct spelling of your name and title.  You'll most likely be a quotable notable.


## Responding

Respond to media calls quickly, accurately, and caringly.  Reporters usually have very tight deadlines.

Be clear and concise with your answers.  Watch the use of educational jargon. Don't tell the media how to build the clock when all they want is the time.

Be accurate with your responses and make sure everything you share is correct.

Be available to work with the media.  Since the media helps to shape the image for a school or district, it's in your best interest to work with them.

If you don't know the answer to something, say so.  Offer to call back as soon as you get an answer.

Remember that any time you are working with media, everything is "on-the-record."

Don't be flip, sarcastic, or humorous when talking with the media.

Before talking with the media, think of two or three points you want to make and weave them into your responses.

Don't say "No comment."  When you agree to talk with the media, you're agreeing to talk.

Be honest and base your responses on facts.

Be willing to admit mistakes, problems, or concerns. Be up front about the realities of your school. Remember to share what your plan of action is.

Remember that much of the information you deal with is public information. You have a responsibility to provide this information when it is requested.

## Media Relationships

If possible, build a good working relationship with the newspaper and television reporters who cover your school or district. A personal relationship is one of the most important factors in dealing with the media.

Reporters aren't the bad guys. (And they don't get everything wrong.) The journalists are professionals who are doing their job — which is to look at the good, the bad, and the interesting in our schools and districts.

Ask reporters what information you can provide to make their job easier. Back-up material may be useful to the reporter.

*Thank* reporters for a job well done.

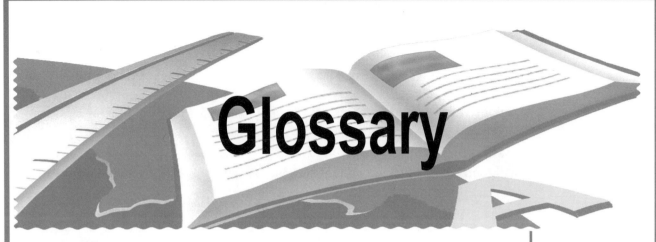

# Glossary

**Accountability**

The process of setting and being held responsible for defined and measured expectations. These expectations can be set at the classroom, school, district, and/or state levels. (For example, there is accountability in classrooms and schools when you hold students to high standards.)

**Achievement Test**

An objective or performance-based test that measures educationally relevant skills or knowledge about such subjects as reading, writing, mathematics, science, and social studies. Achievement tests can be developed commercially, districtwide, or at the classroom level.

**Alignment**

The process of assuring a match between the written, the taught, and the tested curricula.

**Age Norms**

Values or numbers which represent typical or average performance by age groups. The distribution of test scores by age of test takers.

**Anecdotal Data**

Data obtained from a written description of a specific incident or pattern in an individual's behavior (an anecdotal record).

**Assessment**

Collecting, analyzing, and using information to make informed decisions about student achievement. Assessments may include norm-referenced tests, criterion-referenced tests, anecdotal records, classroom tests, projects, portfolios, and other forms of data collection (Logan, 1997).

**Average/Mean**

A statistic that refers to the sum of a set of scores divided by the number of scores in the set.

### School Report Card

A report card for a school or district. Report cards contain a variety of data for a school or district including performance/outcome indicators, demographics, and process indicators. The purpose of a school report card is to communicate school achievement and other indicators of school success to the public.

### Battery

A group of tests that are administered to a given population. When a state or district gives tests that include a variety of tests, they are giving a battery of tests or assessments.

### Bar Graph

A pictorial representation that includes bars to display the percent or frequency of data. If the bars on the graph are placed vertically, the graph may be referred to as a vertical bar graph. If the bars on the graph are placed horizontally, the graph may be referred to as a horizontal bar graph.

### Box-and-Whisker-Plot

A type of visual for summarizing and displaying a distribution of scores. A box-and-whisker plot is made of a rectangular box with horizontal lines (called "whiskers") extending from both ends of the box. A box-and-whisker plot provides a visual summary of the 25th, 50th, and 75th percentiles of a score distribution and the highest and lowest scores.

### Criteria Matrix

A visual tool or graphic organizer that is useful when making decisions based upon criteria. This organizer provides a way to analyze and think about choices.

### Criterion-Referenced Test

A test that assesses specific instructional objectives or standards. Results from criterion-referenced tests reveal what it is that students know and what they are able to do with what they know. Criterion-referenced tests may be traditional tests, such as paper-and-pencil tests, but they may also be alternative types of tests.

In a criterion-referenced test, the focus is on performance of an individual as measured against a standard or criterion rather than against performance of others who take the same test, as with norm-referenced tests.

### Curriculum Map

A tool and a way of collecting data for aligning, pacing, and sequencing instruction and assessment in a classroom, grade level, content area, school, district, or all. Curriculum maps, which are calendar based, show what students are learning in classrooms. Curriculum maps can be used to ensure vertical and horizontal alignment of a school or district curriculum.

## Cutoff Score

A cutoff score, or cut score, is the lowest score on a selection device that contributes to a positive selection. So if a cutoff score on a test is 400, then 400 would be the lowest score a student could obtain to pass the test.

## Data

Information, especially information organized for analysis or used as the basis for decision making. Data can be the numbers that provide numerical values for a characteristic in a population, but data doesn't have to be only numbers.

## Data Table

A table or chart that contains numerical data. Data tables can be easily analyzed in the table format, but can also be turned into charts and graphs for easier interpretation of the data.

## Data-Based Decisions

Decisions based upon the analysis of data. Decisions can be made based on different types of data: outcome, demographic, or process data.

## Deviation Scores (x)

A deviation score is how far away the score is — how much the score deviates — from the mean. The score for an individual minus the mean score for the group.

## Demographics

The statistical characteristics of human populations (e.g., age, race/ethnicity, experience, socioeconomic status). These statistics help describe the students who receive the outcome/performance scores.

## Disaggregation

The process of breaking data into smaller subsets in order to more closely analyze performance. Disaggregation is an analysis tool that lets you determine whether there is equity on outcome measures, whether different groups of students are performing similarly on the outcomes.

## Distractors/Distracters

An incorrect choice in a multiple choice or matching item (also called a foil).

## Equity in Quality

From the Effective Schools literature, *equity in quality* is an indicator of an improving school (Lezotte, 1990). *Quality* refers to how well students are achieving. *Equity* refers to which students are achieving — and ideally there are not huge gaps in the achievement levels between different groups of students.

### Frequency

The number of times a given score (or set of scores in an interval grouping) occurs in a distribution. Frequency data is compiled in a special data table or chart called a frequency table.

### Frequency Distribution

A tabulation of scores in ascending or descending order showing the number of individuals who obtain each score or fall within each score interval (HBEM, 1998).

### Histogram

A graphic display of data which shows the amount of variation in the data. A histogram (commonly called a bar chart) is a picture of a grouped frequency distribution.

### Gain Score

A gain score is a score that represents the difference between a posttest score and a pretest score.

### Grade-Equivalent Scores

Grade-equivalent scores are used to relate a given student's test score to the average score of other students who took the test based on grade and month.

### Graph

A graph is a pictorial representation of a set of data. Popular graphs include bar graphs, line graphs, stacked bar graphs, pie charts, Pareto charts, and box-and-whisker plots. Just as a "picture is worth a thousand words," a good graph is worth at least 10,000 numbers in a table (Jaeger, 1993). Well-constructed graphs provide a quick view of the overall features of a set of data.

### Improvement Plan

A plan, ideally developed with significant input from staff and community, designed to lead toward improvements in the school. An improvement plan is a tool for creating and managing change.

### Item

An individual question or exercise in a test or evaluative instrument.

### J Curve

A J curve describes a student's standing in relation to learning designated standards. J curves are based on the notion that given enough time and support, students can have higher achievement.

## Key Performance Indicators (KPIs)
Data points that are used as a measure of success or need. Also referred to as outcome or performance indicators. Data sources you choose to tell whether or not a program is working.

## Line Graph
A line graph is a type of graph that lets you look at data over time. Instead of using bars to represent the data, a line graph uses points, connected by a line.

## Maximum
The highest score on a test.

## Mean
The average score in a set of scores. You compute the mean by adding all of the scores then dividing the sum by the total number of scores. The most frequently used indicator of the middle of a score or distribution.

## Median
The score that falls in the exact middle of a range of scores. To find the median, sort the scores from lowest to highest — or highest to lowest. If the number of scores is odd, the median is the middle value. If the number of scores is even, then the median is the average of the two middle values. The median is the score point that divides a group into two equal parts — the 50th percentile. Half the scores are below the median, and half are above it (HBEM, 1998). The median is another name for the 50th percentile.

## Minimum
The lowest score on a test.

## Mobility Index
An index used to reference the movement of students in and out of a school or division.

## Mode
The score that occurs with the greatest frequency in a distribution of scores.

## MultiVoting
A technique which includes a series of votes to reduce the size of a list to those items that are most important to the members of a group.

## N (Number of Students)
The number of students who took a particular test. N is the symbol commonly used to represent the number of cases in a group. If 75 students took a test, then the N = 75.

### Normal Curve

The normal curve is the bell-shaped curve that results when a normal distribution of scores is graphed. In this normal curve, the mean, median, and mode are the middle of the distribution with half the scores on one side and half the scores on the other.

### Normal Curve Equivalent (NCE)

Normal curve equivalent (NCE) scores are standard scores based on the normal curve. NCEs have a standard deviation of approximately 21 so that the range of probable scores is 1-99. NCEs are commonly used with the measurement of performance in federal programs such as Title I.

### Norming Group

The group of students who took a test and thus serve as the basis of comparison for other students taking the same test. A norming group may be a national sample of students at a specified grade level, but a norming group can also be a local sample of students.

### Norm-Referenced Test

Tests that are designed to determine the performance of an individual in comparison to other individuals in the norming group. Norm-referenced tests describe how a student performs in relation to the performance of the norming group of students. Scores on a norm-referenced test are based on the normal curve, the bell-shaped curve.

### Norms

The distribution of test scores for a norming group. Norms are the test results achieved by the norming group.

### Outcome Indicator

Data that reports the outcomes or performance of the achievement results of students.

### Pareto Chart

A Pareto chart is a special form of a vertical bar graph that helps determine which problems to solve and in which order.

### Percent Correct Scores

Scores that represent the percentage of test items a student answers correctly. Percent correct scores are calculated by dividing the number of questions a student answered correctly by the number of questions he or she could have answered correctly and then multiplying by 100.

## Percent Passing Scores

Percent passing scores represent the percentage of students who passed a particular test.

## Percentile

A percentile is a point on a score scale that divides a score distribution into two parts: the part equal to or below the score — and the part above. There are 99 different percentiles — the 1st percentile, the 2nd percentile, and so on, up to the 99th percentile. Together the percentiles divide a score distribution into 100 parts. For example, the 40th percentile is the point on the score scale where exactly 40 percent of the scores in a distribution either equal it or fall below it.

## Percentile Rank

Percentile ranks express the percentage of scores in the norming group that are less than or equal to the raw score. Percentile scores are among the most commonly reported scores and are best used to describe a student's standing in relation to the norming group at the time of testing. National Percentile Rank is a score that shows how a student performed in relation to a group of students who were tested under the same conditions at the same time of the year during national standardization.

If a student received a percentile rank of 68 on a nationally normed test, the student scored at or better than 68 percent of the individuals in the norm group.

## Pie Chart

A pie chart is a type of graph used to display the percentage data in different categories. It is a circular graph with wedges that represent each of the categories. The width of each wedge is proportional to the percentage of cases that fall into its corresponding category. Thus a category that contained 20 percent of all cases would have a wedge that was twice as wide as the wedge of a category that contained only 10 percent of all the cases (Jaeger, 1993).

## Process Indicators

Data pieces that get at the essence of change because they represent whatever is producing the outcome data/indicators. Examples of process indicators include curriculum alignment results, percentage of teachers trained in a specialized strategy, amount of time students spend learning, and more.

## Quartiles

Quartiles split the frequency distribution of scores into four segments, each containing one-fourth of the data. Q1 is the first (bottom) quartile and contains scores from 1-25. Q2 is the second quartile and contains scores from 26-50. Q3 is the third quartile and contains scores from 51-75. Q4 is the fourth (top) quartile and contains scores from 76-99.

### Range

The measure of the spread of scores between the lowest and the highest scores in a distribution. To get the range, just subtract the lowest score from the highest score. If the top score on a test was 100 and the lowest 65, the range would be 35 (100-65 = 35).

### Raw Scores

The number of questions or items that a student answers correctly on a test. A score that has not had anything done to it — has not been converted or transformed to any other scoring system. Raw scores are converted to other scoring systems such as percentile scores, scaled scores, and percent correct scores.

### Reliability

The extent to which a test is dependable, stable, and consistent when administered to the same individuals on different occasions.

### Scaled Score/Scale Score

A mathematical transformation of a raw score into a score within an achievement continuum. Scaled scores can be useful when comparing test results over time. Most standardized achievement test batteries provide scaled scores so that comparisons can be made. (HBEM, 1998).

### Score

The result achieved by a student on a test or assessment. Scores are usually expressed as numbers with higher numbers representing higher achievement.

### Scatter Diagram/Scatter Plot

A type of graph that lets you look at the relationship between two variables. One variable is plotted on the horizontal (bottom) axis and the other is plotted on the vertical (side of graph) axis.

### Socioeconomic Status (SES)

An indicator determined by a variety of conditions including free/reduced price lunch counts, mother's level of education, occupational classifications, and realty classifications (Center for Effective Schools, 1991).

### Stacked Bar Graph

A type of bar graph that shows the percent of cases in a set of data so you can see how the percentages "stack up" within each of the bars.

## Standards

The content standard is the curriculum or what we want students to learn and be able to do. Content standards provide the big picture of what students are to learn and are also called the learning targets/goals. A standard can also be used to describe student achievement and accomplishment and is then called a performance standard. The performance standard is the level of achievement (e.g., the cut-off score for passing) a student is expected to attain, usually on a content standard.

## Standard Deviation

A commonly used measure of how "spread out" the data are. Many scoring systems are based on standard deviation units. Standard deviation is a measure of variability in a set of scores and the units represent how far away individual or group scores are from the mean. A small standard deviation means there is not much variance in the scores. A large standard deviation means there is variance in the scores. Sixty-eight percent of the scores are within one standard deviation of the mean in a normal distribution of scores.

## Standard Score

A scoring system designed to show student performance on an achievement test. A standard score is expressed as a deviation from a population mean. Standard scores may also be called growth scale values, developmental standard scores, and scaled scores. Each scoring system has its own units to represent the scores. Thus, a scaled score of 388 on one test may not be the same as a scaled score of 388 on another test. Standard scores have equal interval units of measurement, so you can use them to compute averages and gains (Rudner, 1989). Examples of standard score systems include T-scores, Z-scores, stanines, and Normal Curve Equivalents (NCEs). Standard scores can be used to compare a student's standing on two or more different tests.

## Standardized Tests

A standardized test is a test that is administered under the same testing conditions to different groups of examinees. Certain things are the same: the content, the number of questions, the amount of time to take the test, and the way the test is scored. Standardized tests may be norm-referenced (e.g., *Iowa Tests of Basic Skills*, *Stanford Achievement Tests*, *California Achievement Tests*). Standardized tests may also be criterion-referenced, as with many state tests of standards.

## Stanine

A standard score system that represents groupings of percentile ranks into a nine-unit scale. A stanine is one of the steps in this nine-point scale of standard scores.

## Statistics

A statistic is a number that provides a summary of some characteristic set of data. Examples of statistics include means, medians, modes, ranges, percent correct scores, percent passing scores, scaled scores, and percentile scores.

## Test Blueprint

These are also called assessment blueprints. Test blueprints are used to design tests, just like an architect uses a blueprint to design the specifications of a house. Blueprints outline such things as the content and number of test questions included
on a test. Test blueprints may also include other useful information including a description of the format of the test.

## Triangulation

Using three or more data sources or multiple measures to get a more complete picture of achievement for your classroom, school, or district.

## Validity

The extent to which a test measures what it was intended to measure.

# References and Resources

## Curriculum

Bloom, B.S., M.D. Englehart, E.J. Furst, W.H. Hill, and D.R. Krathwohl, (Eds.). (1956). *Taxonomy of Educational Objectives: The Classification of Educational Goals. Handbook I: Cognitive Domain.* New York: David McKay.

Brickell, H.M., and Paul, R.H. (1988). *Time for Curriculum: How School Board Members Should Think About Curriculum, What School Board Members Should Do About Curriculum.* Alexandria, VA: National School Boards Association and Chicago, IL: Teach 'em, Inc.

English, F.W. (1988). *Curriculum Auditing.* Lancaster, PA: Technomic Publishing Company, Inc.

English, F.W. (1992). *Deciding What to Teach and Test.* Newbury Park, CA: Corwin Press, Inc.

Jacobs, H., ed., (1989). *Interdisciplinary Curriculum: Design and Implementation.* Alexandria, VA: Association for Supervision and Curriculum Development.

Jacobs, H. (1997). *Mapping the Big Picture: Integrating Curriculum & Assessment K-12.* Alexandria, VA: Association for Supervision and Curriculum Development.

Logan, K. (1997). *Getting the Schools You Want: A Step-by-Step Guide to Conducting Your Own Curriculum Management Audit.* Thousand Oaks, CA: Corwin Press.

Mager, R.F. (1984). *Preparing Instructional Objectives.* Belmont, CA: Lake Publishing Company.

Marzano, R.J. and Kendall, J.S. (1996). *A Comprehensive Guide to Designing Standards-Based Districts, Schools, and Classrooms.* Aurora, CO: Mid-

Continent Regional Educational Laboratory and Alexandria, VA: Association for Supervision and Curriculum Development.

Ornstein, A.C. and Behar, L.S. (Eds.). (1995). *Contemporary Issues in Curriculum.* Needham Heights, MA: Allyn and Bacon.

Wiles, J. and Bondi, J. (1989/1984/1979). *Curriculum Development: A Guide to Practice.* New York, NY: Macmillan Publishing Company.

## Instruction

Bellanca, J. *Active Learning Handbook for the Multiple Intelligences Classroom.* (1997) Arlington Heights, IL: IRI/Skylight Training and Publishing, Inc.

Blosser, P.E. (1995). *How to Ask the Right Questions.* Arlington, VA: National Science Teachers Association.

Buzan, T. and Buzan, B. (1994). *The Mind Map Book.* New York, NY: Penguin Books USA Inc.

Canady, R.L., and Rettig, M.D., (Eds.). (1996). *Teaching in the Block: Strategies for Engaging Active Learners.* Princeton, NJ: Eye On Education.

Hanson, R.J., H.F. Silver, and R. W. Strong. (1986). *Teaching Styles and Strategies.* Moorestown, NJ: Prentice-Hall.

Hunter, M. (1982). *Mastery Teaching.* El Segundo, CA.: TIP Publications.

Jones, P. (1988). *Classroom Strategies to Improve Student Achievement.* Atlanta, GA: The Right Combination.

Joyce, B., and M. Weil. (1986). *Models of Teaching.* Englewood Cliffs, NJ: Prentice-Hall.

Marzano, R.J. (1992). *A Different Kind of Classroom: Teaching With Dimensions of Learning.* Alexandria, VA: Association for Supervision and Curriculum Development.

Marzano, R.J., and D.E. Arrendondo. (1986). *Tactics for Thinking.* Alexandria, VA: Association for Supervision and Curriculum Development.

McAuliffe, J. and Stoskin, L. (1993). *What Color is Saturday?* Tucson, AZ: Zephyr Press.

Morgan, R.F. and Richardson, J.S. (1997). *Reading to Learn in the Content Areas.* Belmont, CA: Wadsworth Publishing Company.

National Science Teachers Association (1988). *Science Fairs and Projects.* Washington, DC: National Science Teachers Association.

Pike, R.W. (1989 and 1994). *Creative Training Techniques Handbook: Tips, Tactics, and How-to's for Delivering Effective Training.* Minneapolis, MN: Lakewood Books.

Wahlstrom, D. (1998). *Practical Ideas for Teaching and Assessing the Virginia SOL.* Virginia Beach, VA: Successline Inc.

Wycoff, J. (1991). *Mindmapping: Your Personal Guide to Exploring Creativity and Problem-Solving.* New York, NY: The Berkley Publishing Group.

## Assessment

Bellanca, J., Chapman, C., and Swartz, E. (1994). *Multiple Assessments for Multiple Intelligences.* Palentine, IL: IRI/Skylight

Burke, K. (1993). *How to Assess Thoughtful Outcomes.* Palentine, IL: IRI/Skylight

Burke, K., Fogarty, R., and Belgrad, S. (1994). *The Portfolio Connection.* Palentine, IL: IRI/Skylight

Costa, A.L. and Kallick, B. (Eds.). (1995). *Assessment in the Learning Organization: Shifting the Paradigm.* Alexandria, VA: Association for Supervision and Curriculum Development.

Guskey, T.R. (Ed.). (1996). *ASCD Yearbook 1996.* Alexandria, VA: Association for Supervision and Curriculum Development.

Herman, J.L., Aschbacher, P.R., and Winters, L. (1992). *A Practical Guide to Alternative Assessment.* Alexandria, VA: Association for Supervision and Curriculum Development.

Hibbard, M., et. al. (1996). *Performance-Based Learning and Assessment.* Alexandria, VA: Association for Supervision and Curriculum and Development.

Hill, B., and Ruptic, C. (1994). *Practical Aspects of Authentic Assessment: Putting the Pieces Together.* Norwood, MA: Christopher-Gordon Publishers, Inc.

Jasmine, J. *Portfolios and Other Assessments*. Huntington Beach, CA: Teacher-Created Materials, Inc.

Johnson, B. (1996). *The Performance Assessment Handbook*. (Vols. 1-2). Princeton, NJ: Eye On Education.

Kulm, G. (1994). *Mathematics Assessment: What Works in the Classroom*. San Francisco, CA: Jossey-Bass Inc.

Marzano, R.J., D. Pickering, and J. McTighe (1993). *Assessing Student Outcomes: Performance Assessment Using the Dimensions of Learning Model*. Alexandria, VA: Association for Supervision and Curriculum Development.

McCullough, L., C. Merritt, and P. Buly (1992). *Defining Our Outcomes: A Handbook for Modelling and Assessing Science Thinking Skills and Habits of Mind*. Charlottesville, VA.

Northwest Regional Educational Laboratory. (1991). *Developing Assessments Based on Observation and Judgment*. Portland, OR.

Northwest Regional Educational Laboratory. (1991). *Paper-and-Pencil Test Development*. Portland, OR.

Northwest Regional Educational Laboratory. (1991). *Using Portfolios in Assessment and Instruction*. Portland, OR.

Perrone, V. (Ed.). (1991). *Expanding Student Assessment*. Alexandria, VA: Association for Supervision and Curriculum Development.

Rudner, L.M., Conoley, J.C., and Plake, B.S. (Eds.). (1989). *Understanding Achievement Tests: A Guide for School Administrators*. Washington, DC: The ERIC Clearinghouse on Tests, Measurement, and Evaluation.

Schmoker, M. (1996). *Results: The Key to Continuous Improvement*. Alexandria, VA: Association for Supervision and Curriculum Development.

Schurr, S.L. (1993). *The ABC's of Evaluation*. Columbus, OH: National Middle School Association.

Stenmark, J.K. (Ed.). (1991). *Mathematics Assessment: Myths, Models, Good Suggestions, and Practical Suggestions*. Reston, VA: National Council of Teachers of Mathematics, Inc.

Stiggins, R.J. (1994). *Student-Centered Classroom Assessment*. New York: Merrill.

Tierney, R.J., Carter, M.A., and Desai, L.E. (1991). *Portfolio Assessment in the Reading-Writing Classroom*. Norwood, MA: Christopher-Gordon Publishers, Inc.

Wiggins, G. (1991). *Toward One System of Education: Assessing to Improve, Not Merely Audit*. Education Commission of the States.

Wiggins, G. (1989). "A True Test: Toward Authentic and Equitible Forms of Assessment." *Phi Delta Kappan* 70, 9: 703-713.

Wiggins, G. (1991). "Standards, Not Standardization: Evoking Quality Student Work." *Educational Leadership* 48,5: 18-25.

Wiggins G. (1992). "Creating Tests Worth Taking." *Educational Leadership* 49, 8: 26-33.

Wiggins, G. (1993). *Assessing Student Performance: Exploring the Purpose and Limits of Testing*. San Francisco, CA: Jossey-Bass Publishers.

# Data Analysis

Bernhardt, V. (1998). *Data Analysis for Comprehensive School Improvement*. Larchmont, NY: Eye on Education.

Cawelti, G., (Ed.) (1995). *Handbook of Research on Improving Student Achievement*. Arlington, VA: Educational Research Service.

Fitz-Gibbon, C.T., and Morris, LL. (1987). *How to Analyze Data*. Newbury Park, CA: Sage Publications.

Harcourt Brace Educational Measurement. (1998). *Glossary of Measurement Terms*. Internet Document. San Antonio, TX.

Herman, J.L., and Winters, L. (1992). *Tracking Your School's Success: A Guide to Sensible Evaluation*. Newbury Park, CA: Corwin Press.

Holcomb, E.L. (1999). *Getting Excited About Data: How to Combine People, Passion, and Proof*. Thousand Oaks, CA: Corwin Press.

Hopkins, K.D., Hopkins, B.R., and Glass, G.V. (1996). *Basic Statistics for the Behavioral Sciences*. Boston, MA: Allyn and Bacon.

Lezotte, L. and Jacoby, B. (1990). *A Guide to the School Improvement Process*

*Based on Effective Schools Research.* Okemos, MI: Effective Schools Products, Ltd.

Lezotte, L. and Jacoby, B. (1992). *Sustainable School Reform: The District Context for School Improvement.* Okemos, MI: Effective Schools Products, Ltd.

Lezotte, L.W. and Levine, D.U. (1990). *Unusually Effective Schools: A Review of Analysis of Research and Practice.* Madison, WI: National Center for Effective Schools.

Lyman, H.B. (1998). *Test Scores and What They Mean.* Boston, MA: Allyn and Bacon.

Olson, M.W. and Miller, S.D. (1993). *Reading and Language Arts Programs: A Guide to Evaluation.* Newbury Park, CA: Corwin Press, Inc.

## Communications

Bagin, R., Ferguson, D., and Marx, G. (1985). *Public Relations for Administrators.* Arlington, VA: American Association of School Administrators.

Engel, P.H. (1996). *Business Presentations & Public Speaking.* Los Angeles, CA: McGraw-Hill Companies, Inc.

Meek, A. (1999). *Communicating With the Public: A Guide for School Leaders.* Alexandria, VA: Association for Supervision and Curriculum Development.

# Successline Inc.

930 Virginia Avenue • Virginia Beach, VA 23451
Phone 757-422-2802 • Facsimile 757-422-5421

# Order Form

| Title | Quantity | Unit Price | Total |
|-------|----------|------------|-------|
| Book: Using Data to Improve Student Achievement | | **$34.95** | |
| **Shipping and Handling**<br>**$01.00–$40.00 ($5.00)**<br>**$40.01–$60.00 ($6.00)**<br>**$70.01–$200.00 ($10.00)**<br>**$200.01–$300.00 ($15.00)**<br>**$300.01–$400.00 ($20.00)**<br>**$400.01–$500.00 ($25.00)** | **+ VA Resident Sales Tax (Total x 4.5%)** | | |
| | **+ Shipping and Handling** | | |
| | **= Grand Total** | | |

### Yes, I'd like to order!

❒    Check made payable to Successline Inc. (Payable in U.S. funds only.)
❒    Bill my institution. (Please include an official purchase order from your institution.)

## Ship to

Name _____

Street Address _____

City _____ State _____ ZIP _____

Daytime Phone _____ FAX _____


_____
**Tax Exempt Number**